PRAISE FOR *BOY ERASED*

"[A] powerful convergence of events that Conley portrays eloquently."

—*The Washington Post*

"The power of Conley's story resides not only in the vividly depicted grotesqueries of the therapy system, but in his lyrical writing about sexuality and love, and his reflections on the Southern family and culture that shaped him." —*Los Angeles Times*

"This brave and bracing memoir is an urgent reminder that America remains a place where queer people have to fight for their lives. It's also a generous portrait of a family in which the myths of prejudice give way before the reality of love. Equal parts sympathy and rage, *Boy Erased* is a necessary, beautiful book."

—GARTH GREENWELL, AUTHOR OF *What Belongs to You*

"An essential document of the early twenty-first century. Conley bears witness to something history will eventually condemn as too horrible to have happened, but he also takes the pain of 'ex-gay therapy' and makes of it not just a record but a wonder."

—ALEXANDER CHEE, AUTHOR OF *The Queen of the Night*

"Many readers of *Boy Erased* will be as enraged as Conley. But they will also see the story through the lens of his compassion for those who genuinely thought they were trying to help, particularly his mother, who's finally the one to say, 'We're stopping all of this now,' when Conley reaches the breaking point." —MEGHAN DAUM, *The New York Times Book Review*

"That he is more sinned against than sinning doesn't lessen the poignancy of this honest, often painful memoir; Conley avoids questions of blame and judgment in favor of celebrating his deepened relationship with his mother and reconciling (mostly) with his father." —*The Boston Globe*

"A brave, powerful meditation on identity and faith, *Boy Erased* is the story of one man's journey to accepting himself and overcoming shame and trauma in the midst of deep-rooted bigotry." —BUZZFEED

"A moving memoir about discovering your true self, *Boy Erased* is a must-read." —*Bustle*

"[A] gut-punch of a memoir, but the miracle of this book is the generosity with which Conley writes in an effort to understand the circumstances and motivations that led his family to seek the 'cure.' . . . His memoir is not simply a story of survival—in this book, a true writer comes of age. Conley writes vividly, with intelligence, wit, and genuine empathy. By embracing complexity and compassion, he reclaims his life and reminds us that a story rarely belongs to one person alone." —*Los Angeles Review of Books*

"*Boy Erased* is one of those books that'll make you think. And think, and think." —*San Diego LGBT Weekly*

"Well-written, compelling, disturbing, and ultimately quite bracing, this is an important, refreshingly unsentimental perspective on the dangers and abuses of ex-gay therapy ministries." —*The Bay Area Reporter*

"Wrenching and absorbing." —*Travel & Leisure*

"A compelling story of perseverance and humanity." —*OutSmart*

"In spite of the struggles he faced growing up gay he has emerged triumphant, which is why *Boy Erased* will have a strong and positive impact on readers tackling similar issues concerning faith, family and community."
—*Electric Literature*

"An unlikely triumph of hope: Conley reflects on execrable circumstances without self-pity—rather, with the humility of a man who survived but still doesn't know all the answers. He shows us how what was learned can be unlearned—and how what was nearly erased can be slowly, carefully, patiently redrawn." —*Pacific Standard*

"*Boy Erased* isn't a smug tale of liberal awakening: Conley is frank and articulate about the sense of loss that has come with denying his religion and, as a consequence, the family he still loves. . . . [Conley's] writerly eye often wanders outside nonfiction's usual constraints. Writing stories is the work he wants to do; this book is clearly the work he needed to do."

—*Toronto Star*

"Heartbreaking but beautifully written memoir." —*Winnipeg Free Press*

"A brave account of a young man coming to terms with his sexuality in an environment that reviles him for it. A triumphant, heartfelt story."

—JULIA SCHEERES, *New York Times*–BESTSELLING AUTHOR OF *Jesus Land*

"Garrard Conley has a hell of story to tell, but he tells it with complete intelligence and gravity and beauty. This is a book that matters on every level, from the most intimate to the most political, and it settles into the reader's memory perfectly and permanently. *Boy Erased* is the book for our times—an important book, and a true companion."

—REBECCA LEE, AUTHOR OF *Bobcat and Other Stories*

"Conley tells his story beautifully, with candor and courage and with compassion not only for the boy he was but for the parents who sent him to ex-gay therapy. Here at last is a story of evangelical homophobia from the inside, from a survivor and former believer, rather than from the incredulous outside. A vital book for young people still struggling with self-hatred inside the church and for anyone who's escaped it."

—MAUD NEWTON

"Garrard Conley's memoir about his time in the ex-gay movement is actually about surviving an attempt at soul-murder. This is a book that had to be written, and it deserves a wide audience."

—CHARLES BAXTER, AUTHOR OF *The Feast of Love*

"In 1982, Edmund White broke literary ground with his memoir *A Boy's Own Story*. Now it's Garrard Conley's turn to bring his own story to readers. As White was three decades ago for his generation, Conley is an important and necessary contemporary voice."

—Ann Hood, author of *The Knitting Circle* and *Comfort*

"Exceptionally well-written . . . This timely addition to the debate on conversion therapy will build sympathy for both children and parents who avail themselves of it while still showing how damaging it can be."

—*Publishers Weekly* (starred review)

"In a sharp and shocking debut memoir, Conley digs deep into the ex-gay therapy system. . . . An engaging memoir that will inevitably make readers long for a more equal future." —*Kirkus Reviews*

"Closely observed feelings are the fuel that drives this complex coming-of-age account. . . . Moving and thought-provoking." —*Booklist*

BOY
ERASED

a memoir of identity,

faith, and family

GARRARD CONLEY

RIVERHEAD BOOKS

New York

RIVERHEAD BOOKS
An imprint of Penguin Random House LLC
375 Hudson Street
New York, New York 10014

Copyright © 2016 by Garrard Conley
Penguin supports copyright. Copyright fuels creativity, encourages diverse voices,
promotes free speech, and creates a vibrant culture. Thank you for buying
an authorized edition of this book and for complying with copyright laws
by not reproducing, scanning, or distributing any part of it in any
form without permission. You are supporting writers and allowing
Penguin to continue to publish books for every reader.

The Library of Congress has catalogued the Riverhead hardcover edition as follows:

Conley, Garrard.
Boy erased : a memoir / Garrard Conley.
p.   cm.
ISBN 9781594633010
1. Conley, Garrard.   2. Gays—United States—Biography.   3. Sexual
reorientation programs—United States.   4. Ex-gay movement—United
States.   5. Gays—Identity.   6. Gay men—United States.   I. Title.
HQ75.8.C665A3   2016   2015024641
306.76'6092—dc23

First Riverhead hardcover edition: May 2016
First Riverhead trade paperback edition: February 2017
Riverhead trade paperback movie tie-in edition: August 2018
Riverhead trade paperback movie tie-in edition ISBN: 9780525538981

Printed in the United States of America
3   5   7   9   10   8   6   4

Book design by Meighan Cavanaugh

---

*Penguin is committed to publishing works of quality and integrity.
In that spirit, we are proud to offer this book to our readers;
however, the story, the experiences, and the words
are the author's alone.*

For my parents

AUTHOR'S NOTE

During my time at Love in Action (LIA), no journaling, photographing, or any other method of recording was allowed inside the facility. To that effect, all events, physical descriptions, and dialogue have been reconstructed to the best of my ability. My mother's and my memories, LIA's ex-gay handbook, newspaper articles, blog posts, and personal interviews have supplemented the empty spaces where trauma has made dark what was once painfully clear. As in most memoirs, the chronology is accurate, altered only in places where the narrative requires it. I have excluded details that seemed irrelevant to the nature of the story. The names and certain identifying characteristics of some key figures in my life, including Chloe, Brandon, David, Brad, Brother Stevens, and Brother Neilson have been changed.

I wish none of this had ever happened. Sometimes I thank God that it did.

Yet she could see by their shocked and altered faces that even their virtues were being burned away.

—FLANNERY O'CONNOR, "REVELATION"

If I'm looking at that wall and suddenly I say, "It's blue," and someone else comes along and says, "No, no. It's gold." But I *want to believe* that that wall is blue. It's blue, it's blue, it's blue. But then God comes along, and He says, "You're right, John, it *is* blue." That's the help I need. God can help me make that wall blue.

—EX-GAY LEADER JOHN SMID, IN AN INTERVIEW WITH THE *Memphis Flyer*

TIMELINE OF THE
EX-GAY MOVEMENT

1973 The American Psychological Association declassifies homosexuality as a mental illness.

    Love in Action (LIA), a nondenominational fundamentalist Christian organization, rejects APA's decision and opens its doors in San Rafael, California, promising to cure LGBT congregants of their "sexual addictions."

1976 The first ex-gay conference takes place in Anaheim, · California, where more than sixty-two attendees form what becomes Exodus International, the largest ex-gay umbrella organization in the world. LIA is its flagship program.

1977 Jack McIntyre, a four-year member of LIA, commits suicide, prompting one of the group's founding members, John Evans, to condemn the program. In a suicide note, McIntyre writes: "To continually go before God and ask for forgiveness and make promises you know you can't keep is more than I can take."

1982 Exodus Europe, an independent organization working in coalition with Exodus International, holds its first ex-gay conference in the Netherlands. Ministries now exist in Australia, Brazil, and Portugal.

1989   Exodus expands its mission to include the Philippines and Singapore. The organization, which at its peak supported more than two hundred ministries across the United States, has reached mainstream attention, with spots on national television and radio.

1990   John Smid takes over as director of LIA.

1993   John Evans, a cofounder of LIA, writes an article for the *Wall Street Journal* denouncing ex-gay therapy: "They're destroying people's lives. If you don't do their thing, you're not of God, you'll go to hell. They're living in a fantasy world."

1994   Under John Smid's direction, LIA moves its headquarters to Memphis, Tennessee, purchasing five acres of land to house its residential program.

1998   Ex-gay leader John Paulk, soon to be featured on the cover of *Newsweek* with his ex-lesbian wife, founds Love Won Out, a series of yearly ex-gay conferences.

2000   First Latin American Exodus Conference is held in Quito, Ecuador. Ministries are now in China, India, Indonesia, Malaysia, Mexico, Sri Lanka, and Taiwan.

2003   LIA opens its controversial Refuge program, bringing together teenagers and adults suffering from various sex-based "addictions."

2004   My ex-gay story begins.

I

John Smid stood tall, square shouldered, beaming behind thin wire-rimmed glasses and wearing the khaki slacks and striped button-down that have become standard fatigues for evangelical men across the country. The raised outlines of his undershirt stretched taut beneath his shirt, his graying blond hair tamed by the size-five hair clippers common in Sport Clips throughout the South. The rest of us sat in a semicircle facing him, all dressed according to the program dress code outlined in our 274-page handbooks.

Men: Shirts worn at all times, including periods of sleep. T-shirts without sleeves not permitted, whether worn as outer- or undergarments, including "muscle shirts" or other tank tops. Facial hair removed seven days weekly. Sideburns never below top of ear.

Women: Bras worn at all times, exceptions during sleep. Skirts must fall at the knee or below. Tank tops allowed only if worn with a blouse. Legs and underarms shaved at least twice weekly.

"The first thing you have to do is recognize how you've become dependent on sex, on things that are not from God," Smid said. We were learning Step One of Love in Action's Twelve Step program, a set of principles equating the sins of infidelity, bestiality, pedophilia, and homosexuality to addictive behavior such as alcoholism or gambling: a kind of Alcoholics Anonymous for what counselors referred to as our "sexual deviance."

Sitting alone with him just hours before in his office, I had witnessed a different man: a kinder, goofier Smid, a middle-aged class clown willing to resort to any antic to make me smile. He had treated me like a child, and I had relaxed into the role, being nineteen at the time. He told me I had come to the right place, that Love in Action would cure me, lift me out of my sin into the light of God's glory. His office seemed bright enough to substantiate his claim, the walls bare save for the occasional framed newspaper clipping or embroidered Bible verse. Outside his window was an empty plot of land, rare around this suburban subdivision, an untended grassy mess peppered with neon dandelions and their thousands of seed heads that would scatter across the highway by the end of the week.

"We try to blend several models of treatment," Smid had assured me, swiveling in his office chair to face the window. An orange sun was climbing its way up the back of the hazy white-washed buildings in the distance. I waited for the sunlight to spill over, but the longer I watched, the longer it seemed to take. I wondered if this was how time was going to work in this place: minutes as hours, hours as days, days as weeks.

"Once you enter the group, you'll be well on your way to recovery," Smid said. "The important thing to remember is to keep an open mind."

I was here by my own choice, despite my growing skepticism, despite my secret wish to run away from the shame I'd felt since my parents found out I was gay. I had too much invested in my current life to leave it behind: in my family and in the increasingly blurry God I'd known since I was a toddler.

God, I prayed, leaving the office and making my way down the narrow hallway to the main room, the fluorescents ticking in their metal grids, *I don't know who You are anymore, but please give me the wisdom to survive this.*

A FEW HOURS LATER, sitting in the middle of Smid's circle, I was waiting for God to join me.

"You're no better and no worse than any other sinner in this world," Smid said. He kept his arms crossed behind his back, his whole body tense, as if he were tied to an invisible plank. "God sees all sin in the same light."

I nodded along with the others. The ex-gay lingo had by now become familiar to me, though it had come as a shock when I'd first read it on the facility's website, when I'd first learned that the homosexuality I'd been trying to ignore for most of my life was likely "out of control," that I could end up messing around with someone's dog if I didn't cure myself. As absurd as the idea seems in hindsight, I had little else to go on. I was still young enough to have had only a few fleeting experiences with other men. Before college, I'd met only one openly gay man, my mother's hairdresser, a bearish type who spent most of his time filling out what I saw as a stereotype: complimenting my looks; gossiping about coworkers; discussing plans for his next fabulous Christmas party, his pristine white beard already sculpted for the role of Dirty Santa. The rest of my bigotry I learned from pantomime: limp wrists and exaggerated sashays from mocking church members; phrases that lifted out of natural speech into show-tune lilt—"Oh, you *shouldn't* have"; church petitions that had to be signed in order to keep our country safe from "perverts." The flash of neon spandex, the rustle of a feather boa, the tight ass shaking for the camera: What I did manage to see on TV just seemed further proof that being gay was freakish, unnatural.

eed to understand one very important fact," Smid

said, his voice so close I could feel it in my chest. "You're using sexual sin to fill a God-shaped void in your life."

I was here. No one could say I wasn't trying.

THE MAIN ROOM was small and halogen lit, with one sliding door opening onto a sun-sick concrete porch. Our group sat in padded folding chairs near the front. On the walls behind us hung the laminated Twelve Steps that promised a slow but steady cure. Aside from these posters, the walls were mostly empty. Here, there were no crucifixes, no stations of the cross. Here, such iconography was considered idolatry, along with astrology, Dungeons & Dragons, Eastern religions, Ouija boards, Satanism, and yoga.

LIA had taken a more extreme stance against the secular world than any of the churches I'd grown up in, though the counselors' way of thinking was not unfamiliar to me. Within the fundamentalist strain of Christianity that goes by the name Baptist, my family's denomination, Missionary Baptist, forbade anything that had the power to distract the soul from direct communication with God and the Bible. Many of the other hundred or so denominations that comprised the Baptist spectrum often quibbled about what could or could not be permitted within the flock, with some churches taking these issues more seriously than others, subjects like the ethics of dancing and the pitfalls of non-Biblical reading still up for discussion. "Harry Potter is nothing more than a seducer of children's souls," a visiting Baptist preacher once told our family's church. I had no doubt that my LIA counselors would also shun any mention of Harry Potter, that my time spent in Hogwarts would have to remain a private pleasure, and that I had entered into an even more serious pact with God by coming here, one that required me to abolish most of what had come before LIA. Before entering this room, I had been told to cast aside everything but my Bible and my handbook.

Since most of LIA's customers had grown up within this literal-minded Protestantism and were desperate for a cure, the counselors' strict rules were met with mild applause. The unadorned white walls of the facility seemed appropriate decor for a waiting room in which we would wait to receive God's forgiveness. Even classical music was forbidden—"Beethoven, Bach, etc. are not considered Christian"—a heavy silence blanketing the room during our morning Quiet Time, drifting into our daily activities and inspiring an atmosphere that seemed if not holy, then at least not secular.

The study area at the back of the room, home to a bookshelf filled with inspirational literature and a hefty stack of Bibles, contained dozens of testimonies from successful ex-gays.

"Slowly yet surely I began to recover," I'd read that morning, squeaking my finger down the glossy page. "I began to recover from not having a male friend unless it involved sex. I started learning who I really was, instead of the false personality I created to make myself acceptable."

. . .

I HAD SPENT the last several months trying to erase my "false personality." I'd walked out of my college dorm one winter day and jumped into the campus's half-frozen lake. Shivering, I walked back to the dorm in water-suctioned shoes, feeling rebaptized. In the hot shower that followed, I watched, dazed by the shock of icy heat on my numb skin, as a drop of water traced the edge of the showerhead. I prayed, *Lord, make me as pure as that.*

During my stay at Love in Action, I would repeat the prayer until it became a kind of mantra. *Lord, make me as pure as that.*

I REMEMBER little about the ride to the facility with my mother. I had tried to look away, to prevent my mind from recording what passed by outside the passenger's-side window, though a few details remained: the muddy caramel-colored Mississippi passing behind the steel girders of the Memphis-Arkansas Bridge, the scale of our American Nile feeling like the perfect stimulant for my uncaffeinated mind; the glass pyramid glittering at the edge of the city, spreading its hot light across our windshield. It was early June, and by midmorning almost every surface in the city would be too hot to touch for more than a few seconds, everything sweltering by noon. The only relief came in the morning, the sun resting at the edge of the horizon, still only a suggestion of light.

"Surely they could afford something better than this," my mother said, steering us into a parking space at the front of a rectangular strip mall. The location was more upscale than much of rest of the city, part of a wealthier suburb, though this strip mall was arguably the least attractive landmark for miles around, a place for lower-end retail stores and small clinics to find a temporary home. Whitewashed red brick and glass. Double doors that opened onto a white foyer with fake plants. A logo above the entrance: inverted red triangle with a heart-shaped hole cut out of the middle of it, a series of thin white lines spreading across the gap. We stepped out of the car and headed toward the doors, my mother always a few steps ahead.

Once we entered the foyer, a smiling receptionist asked me to sign my name in a ledger. The man looked to be in his mid-twenties. He wore a polo shirt that fell loosely from his chest, and his eyes were a bright honest cobalt. I'd been expecting some wan-faced wraith who'd already erased everything inter-esting about himself. Instead, here was someone who looked like he'd be willing to play a few rounds of *Halo* with me, then use video-game analogies to tell me a little about what God had done for him. *You have to fight against the enemies, the aliens trying to invade your soul.* I'd met plenty of hip youth pastors with a similar look and attitude.

I can no longer remember his name. I can no longer remem-ber if there were any signs in that foyer of what was to come, any paintings on the wall, any rules posted. The foyer exists for me now as a blindingly white waiting room, the kind you see in Hollywood depictions of heaven: a blank space.

"Can I see the place?" my mother asked. Something about the way her voice lifted into a polite question made me feel uneasy, as if she were asking to look at real estate.

"I'm sorry, ma'am," the receptionist said. "Only clients allowed in the back. Security reasons."

"Security?"

"Yes, ma'am. Many of our clients deal with repressed family issues. Seeing a parent, no matter whose parent, no matter if it's someone nice like you"—a winning, deep-dimpled smile—"can be a little unsettling. That's why we call this a safe zone." He stretched out both his arms at his sides, sweeping them wide—slowly and a little rigidly, I thought, as though his movements had once been much grander and he had since learned to rein them in. "Since you're only in the two-week program, you'll have access to your son at all hours except program time."

Program time would be from nine to five. Evenings, nights, and early mornings I would spend with my mother in a Hampton Inn & Suites nearby, leaving the room only for necessities. I was supposed to spend the majority of my free time in the room doing homework for the next day's session. The schedule sheet the receptionist handed me was fairly straightforward, with each hour accounted for in a black-bordered square, words like "quiet time" and "activity time" and "counseling" written in all caps.

The receptionist handed me a thick LIA handbook and a folder. I opened the handbook, its plastic spine crackling, and was greeted by a black-and-white welcome note with my name printed in large type. Beneath my name, a few Bible verses, Psalms 32:5–6, written in a casual modern English different from the formal King James Version I'd grown up with.

I finally admitted all my sins to you and stopped trying to hide them. I said to myself, I will confess them to the Lord; and you forgave me! All my guilt is gone.

I flipped through the pages at random as my mother peered over my shoulder. I wanted to close the book the minute I saw the obvious typos and clip-art graphics. I wanted my mother to think the best of the place before she left, not because I felt like defending the poorly designed handbook, but because I wanted the moment to pass as quickly as possible without any more of her overly polite interrogations. If she started asking questions about design and casual Bible language, she might start asking questions about qualifications, about why we were even here in the first place, and I knew this would only make things worse. Questions only prolonged the pain of these moments, and they almost always went unanswered. I was done with asking questions about how I had ended up in this situation, with searching for other answers, other re- alities, other families or bodies I could have been born into. Every time I realized that there weren't any other alternatives,

I felt worse for asking. I was ready to take things as they came now.

"Call me if you need anything." my mother said, squeezing my shoulder. She was all blond hair and heavy blue mascara, blue eyes and a perennial floral-print top: a spot of Technicolor in this drab place.

"I'm sorry, ma'am," the receptionist said, "but we have to keep his phone while he's here." *For security reasons.* "We'll inform you if anything important pops up."

"Do you think that's necessary?"

My mother and the receptionist finished their conversation—"It's the rules, ma'am. It's in his best interest"—and then my mother was saying good-bye, telling me she was headed off to check us into the hotel, that she would be back to pick me up at five o'clock sharp. She hugged me, and I watched her go, her head high, her shoulders square, the glass double doors swinging closed behind her with a sigh from their pneumatic hinges. I'd seen her like this once before, during the year both my grandparents died. She had carried me through that year, patted a space for me next to her on the sofa as visitors wove in and out of our living room carrying casseroles and baskets filled with glazed pastries. She had run her fingers through my hair and whispered that death was a process, that my grandparents had both lived happy lives. I wondered if this was how she felt now, if she thought that LIA was part of a necessary process— difficult, yes, but easier to accept once you knew it was part of God's plan.

"Let's get you checked in," the receptionist said.

I followed him to another room, also white walled and empty, where a blond-haired boy stood beside a table and asked me to remove everything in my pockets. The boy was barely older than I was, perhaps twenty, and he carried an air of authority that made me think he'd been here a while. He was handsome in a svelte, twinkish way, tall and angular, though he wasn't my type. Then again, I didn't really know what my type was.

On the nights when I'd allowed myself to look up images of men in underwear on line, I'd only been able get halfway down the page, the pixels threading strand by strand in a slow-motion striptease, before I felt the need to exit the browser and try to forget what I'd seen, the laptop growing too hot in my lap. There were flashes, of course, hints of attraction emerging in my occasional fantasies—a toned bicep here, the sharp V of a pelvis there, a collage of various dimples beneath a series of aquiline noses—but the picture was never complete.

The blond-haired boy waited, tapping his index finger on the folding table between us. I dug in my pockets and removed my cell phone, a black Motorola RAZR whose small screen suddenly lit up with an image of the lake, my college campus's obligatory slice of nature: a few maple trees clustered around a glassy surface. The blond-haired boy scrunched up his nose at the sight of it, as though there were something perverse lurking under the peaceful scene.

"I'm going to have to look through all your pictures," he said. "Messages, too."

"Standard procedure," the receptionist explained. "All pictures will be taken for the purpose of sobering reevaluation." He was quoting from the False Images (FI) section of the handbook, a section I would later be asked to memorize.

We want to encourage each client, male and female, by affirming your gender identity. We also want each client to pursue integrity in all his/her actions and appearances. Therefore, any belongings, appearances, clothing, actions, or humor that might connect you to an inappropriate past are excluded from the program. These hindrances are called *False Images (FI)*. FI behavior may include hyper-masculinity, seductive clothing, mannish/boyish attire (on women), excessive jewelry (on men), and "campy" or gay/lesbian behavior and talk.

I looked down at my white button-down, at the khaki pants my mother had pressed for me earlier that morning, starched pleats running down the center of each leg. Nothing in my wardrobe or phone could be considered an FI. I'd made sure of that before coming here, checking my reflection in the mirror for any wrinkles, deleting long strings of text messages between friends, waiting for the gray delete bar to finish eating up all of the hope and anxiety and fear I'd shared with the people I trusted. I felt newly minted, as if I'd stepped out of my old skin that morning, my "inappropriate past" still rumpled on the bedroom floor with the rest of my unwashed laundry.

"Your wallet, please."

I did as he said. My wallet looked so small sitting there, a tiny leather square containing so much of my identity: driver's license, Social Security card, bank card. The boy in the license photo looked like someone else, someone free from all problems: a smiling face in a vacuum. I couldn't remember how the DMV had gotten me to smile so goofily.

"Please empty the contents of your wallet and place them on the table."

My face grew hot. I removed each card. I removed a small wad of twenties, followed by a torn piece of wide-ruled paper with the telephone number of the college admissions office I'd written down at a time when I'd been nervous about my chances of college acceptance.

"What's the number for?" the boy asked.

"College admissions," I said.

"If I called this number, would I find out you're telling the truth?"

"Yes."

"You don't have any phone numbers or photos of ex-boyfriends anywhere on you?"

I hated the way he spoke so openly of past "boyfriends," a word I had so carefully avoided because I felt that just saying it might reveal my shameful desire to have one. "No, I don't have any inappropriate material." I counted to ten, breathing out through my nose, and looked up once again at the boy. I wasn't going to let this get to me, not this early on the first day.

"Do you have anything else in your pockets?"

His questions made me feel paranoid. Could I have unwittingly carried in some kind of inappropriate object? At the moment, it seemed as if everything about me was inappropriate, as if I might be banned from the premises simply because I was already too dirty. His tone suggested that I was desperately trying to hide an extensive sinful past, but the truth was that, although I did feel the weight of this expected sin, I had very little physical evidence, and even less physical experience, to account for it.

"Are you sure you don't have anything else?"

I did have one other thing, though I hoped I wouldn't have to give it up: my Moleskine journal, the one in which I wrote all of my short stories. Though I knew these stories were amateurish, that I was just playing around with serious writing, I looked forward to returning to them the minute the day's activities ended. I suspected that the long descriptive paragraphs on nature, innocuous as they had seemed when I wrote them, could be construed as too florid, too feminine, another sign of my moral weakness. One of my latest stories even featured a young female narrator, a choice I knew was hardly gender affirming.

"There's this," I said, holding the Moleskine in front of me, not willing to put it on the table with the other belongings. "It's just a notebook."

"No journaling allowed," the receptionist said, quoting from the handbook. "All else is distraction."

I watched as the blond-haired boy took the Moleskine in his

hands, as he laid it on the table and began flipping the pages back and forth with disinterest, frowning. I can no longer remember which story he found, but I can remember the way he ripped the pages out of my notebook, wadded them into a dense ball, and said, in a voice free of emotion, "False Image," as if that was all they were.

"Well, that should be it," the receptionist said. "Now I just have to do a quick pat down, and you'll be ready."

He patted my legs, ran his fingers beneath the cuffs of my khakis, worked his way to my arms, the cuffs of my shirt, and then, as if to comfort me, patted my shoulders—one-two-three—looking in my eyes the whole time.

"It'll be fine," he said, his too-blue eyes fixed on mine, hands still weighing down my shoulders. "We all have to go through this. It's a little strange at first, but you'll come to love it here. We're all one big family."

I watched as the blond-haired boy tossed my story in the trash. *Lord, make me pure.* If God was ever going to answer my prayer, He wouldn't do so unless I became as transparent as a drop of water. Crumple the first half of the story and toss it in the trash. All else is distraction.

"FOR THE WAGES of sin is death," Smid continued. Afternoon sunlight slanted through the sliding door behind him. Each time he walked past us, the shadow of the door's central rail passed over him like the sluggish pendulum of a metronome, marking the slow tempo of his pacing. Our therapy group sat quiet and still, our breathing calibrated to the slow pulse of his legs, the casserole from our lunch break sitting heavy in our stomachs. There were seventeen or eighteen of us in the group. Some had been here long enough to know to abstain politely from the meat and processed cheese, while others had brought their own lunches, opening neon Tupperware lids that sent off a whiff of tuna and mayo. Watching the older members eat their lunches, the ones who'd been at LIA for two or three years, I'd been able to see how the receptionist was at least partially right, that this was a family, however dysfunctional. Crustless bread and ultramarine Jell-O: This was a group that knew how to tolerate the idiosyncrasies of one another's food habits. People settled into their routines with little of the self-conscious buzz, of the surreptitious glancing that usually accompanies large groups who find themselves suddenly thrust into more intimate circumstances. I was the only one who seemed to be playing the outsider, scraping my fork through the Hamburger Helper as if I'd forgotten how to feed myself, hardly looking up from my plate.

To my left sat S, a teenage girl awkward in her mandatory skirt, who would later admit to having been caught smearing peanut butter on her vagina as a treat for her dog. "Pleased to meet you," she'd said that morning, before I had the chance to introduce myself. She seemed always poised for a curtsey, thumb and forefinger twitching beside the folds of her cotton skirt. She looked down at my feet after the introduction, her gaze locking on the tile behind my loafers, and for a moment I felt as though I must have tracked in some kind of sinful residue from the outside world. "You'll like it here."

To my right sat a boy of seventeen or eighteen, J, wearing Wrangler jeans, a cowboy smirk, and a frat-boy part in his hair that tossed his dangerously long bangs over warm hazel eyes. J continually bragged that he had memorized all eight of the Bible's "clobber passages," so named because of their power to doctrinally condemn homosexuality and champion traditional straight relationships.

"I read them every night," J had said, his voice serious but also a little playful. He gripped my hand in a practiced ironclad shake. There seemed to be a thousand handshakes behind this one, each of them gradually fortifying J's grip until he was strong enough to pass this basic test of manhood. "I've memorized whole chapters, too."

When our hands parted, I could feel his sweat cooling my palm in the downdraft. *No hugging or physical touch between clients*, I remembered from the handbook. Only the briefest of handshakes allowed.

"My favorite?" he said, smiling. "Thou shalt not lie with mankind, as with womankind: it is abomination."

Later he would go on to tell me more about his interpretation of this "clobber" verse. "Abomination," he would say, pushing back his bangs with the slow arc of his fingers, the white half-moons of his cuticles glowing large and bright. "Crazy word. In Hebrew, *to'e'va*. It can refer to shrimp as easily as it can to gay sex. All those little legs swimming through saltwater, it creeped the Israelites out, you know? They thought it was unnatural."

The other members of our group included unfaithful married men and women, former high school teachers or educators of some kind shamed by rumors of their sexuality, and teenagers kept here against their will as part of the Refuge program, a controversial branch that targeted parents who felt that sending their children to the facility was the only option.

Most of us were from the South, most of us from some part of the Bible Belt. Most of our stories sounded remarkably similar. We had all met with ultimatums that didn't exist for many other people, conditions often absent from the love between parents and children. At some point, a "change this or *else*" had come to each of us: Otherwise we would be homeless, penniless, excommunicated, exiled. We had all been too afraid to fall through the cracks; all of us had been told cautionary tales of drug addicts, of sex addicts, of people who ended up dying in the throes of AIDS in some urban West Coast gutter. The story always went this way. And we believed the story. For the most part, the media we consumed corroborated it. You could hardly find a movie in small-town theaters that spoke openly of homosexuality, and when you did, it almost always ended with someone dying of AIDS.

I was here as part of the Source, a two-week trial program meant to determine the length of therapy I would need. Most patients needed at least three months' residency, usually longer. In many cases, college students like me dropped out of school for at least a year in order to create distance from unhealthy influences. Many stayed even longer. In fact, most of the staff members were former patients who'd been with LIA at least two years, choosing to remain inside the facility rather than reintegrate into their old lives. To be allowed to work at the facility, former patients were expected to find preapproved jobs, support themselves financially, talk only to those whose character and status had been cleared by the staff, and keep clear of the Internet or any other "secular spaces"—including "malls of any kind" or any "non-Christian bookstores." Because patients weren't allowed to stray too far from LIA's offices, the support group became the central focus of patients' lives, the way and the truth and the light Jesus spoke of in the New Testament, the one true path to God's love.

Over the next two weeks, LIA staff, along with my parents, would determine what kind of hiatus was necessary in my case. As its name suggested, the Source was the fountainhead of a long and difficult journey.

"TELL THEM what you did, T," Smid said. We were in the Group Sharing portion of our afternoon session. "You need to admit what you did so it won't happen again."

T, an obese middle-aged man wearing several black cardigans, stood before our group to confess, stone-faced, that he had once again attempted suicide.

This was T's seventh suicide attempt since coming to the program. He'd tried pills, knives, whatever he could find.

"Typical," J whispered, leaning in, his warm cowboy breath tickling my neck. "The guy's an attention hog. Got too many daddy issues to name."

T seemed to shrink into his cardigans, the buried half of him stark black against his pale face. Whatever had first devastated him had left long ago, but LIA would try and dig it up.

"Who among us will cast the first stone?" Smid said, turning back to our group. "We have all sinned and come short of the glory of God."

It seemed earnestness was more than half the battle in the fight for an ex-gay lifestyle. You had to *want* to change, and until you wanted to change so badly that you'd rather die than not change, you would never make it past Step One—admitting you were wrong. The reason pre–ex-gays like T felt powerless to change, Smid said, was that deep-seated family issues kept them separate from God. "Suicide isn't the answer," he said. "The answer is God. Plain and simple."

"What I did was wrong," T said, pocketing his pink-scarred hands inside his topmost cardigan, his words scripted. "I know that with God's help I can learn to see the value in my life."

J coughed a laugh into the hollow of his fist. *Don't count on it.*

When T finally sat down, we all said, "I love you, T." It was a program requirement, rule number nine in the Group Norms section: *Once someone from your group stops talking, say "I love you, _____."*

All of God's children being equal, our names were interchangeable.

"I love you, T," Smid said.

ALTHOUGH I didn't know it at the time, Smid had given different advice before. He was still dealing with a decade-long backlash that had arisen from alleged advice he'd given to one of the first young men to attend his program. According to *Family & Friends*, a Memphis newspaper, Smid had told the man that it would be better for him to kill himself than to live as a homosexual.

Various bloggers have since approximated the number of suicides resulting from LIA's treatment as anywhere from twenty to thirty cases, though figures like these are impossible to pin down.

The controversy didn't end there. According to a *Daily Beast* interview with Peterson Toscano, a former patient of Smid's who attended LIA meetings in the late '90s, LIA had also been responsible for staging a mock funeral for a "would-be defector," a young man of nineteen or twenty who felt he might benefit from an openly gay lifestyle outside the facility. LIA members stood before the boy's reposing body and spoke about "how terrible it was that he didn't stick with God, and now look where he is, he's dead because he left." They read mock obituaries that described the boy's rapid descent into HIV, then AIDS, and cried over him. This went on until the boy was fully convinced that his sinful behavior would lead him to a death without any hope of resurrection. Though the boy did finally flee LIA, it was only years later and, according to a conversation I had with Toscano, only after years of psychological damage.

It was our fear of shame, followed by our fear of Hell, that truly prevented us from committing suicide.

SMID FINISHED his speech and waited in silence for our faces to register the importance of Step One. After several long seconds, he dismissed us for a break, cupping his palms together for a single clap. The sound was jarring. I stood and stretched, then walked through the sliding glass door and kept walking across the porch, feeling like I could walk for hours, days, weeks. The others followed, their shoes scratching the concrete.

I wanted to talk more with J, who seemed like a nice-enough guy, someone who hadn't been here long enough to forget what the first day was like. But J stayed seated inside, and I ended up standing at the far edge of the porch by myself. I could see S standing just on the other side of the glass, straightening her skirt and aiming the corner of a shy smile in my direction. T was still sitting at the end of our semicircle, his gaze fixed on a patch of concrete near my feet, where a few tawny birds pecked at crumbs left behind by one of the group members. He cupped his hands in front of him as though they were filled with birdseed, as though he might scatter a pecking trail from the door to his chair.

"Now," SMID SAID, walking over to a whiteboard on the opposite wall, "can anyone here tell me what a genogram is?" He clapped his hands together. "Anyone?" He picked up a black dry-erase marker from the silver tray at the bottom of the whiteboard.

S straightened her shoulders and raised one hand, the other hand tugging her skirt below the red knobs of her knees—what I would soon learn were rules two, four, and six of the Group Norms section of our handbooks: "(2) No slouching in chairs, sitting back on chairs' hind legs, sitting with arms crossed, rolling eyes, or making disgusting faces; (4) Raise hands to speak; (6) Clients are to sit in such a way as to not cause another to stumble." She'd obviously been here long enough to tame most of her False Images.

"Yes?" Smid said.

"A genogram is a family tree," she said, "only one that shows patterns of family history as well. Kind of like an illustrated genealogy." *Or a character list*, I thought, remembering the many hours I'd spent in my dorm room trying to chart the family history of *Wuthering Heights* in my Moleskine, annotations like "the meaner Cathy" written beside characters' names. I wondered if I'd get my notebook back.

"Good answer," Smid said, writing the words "Family Tree—Genealogy" in large cursive across the top of the board. He turned back to us. "Anything we can add to this?"

I shifted in the padded chair. I'd always felt this nervousness in classes, this need to put an end to the silence following a question no matter how inadequate my answer. I also wanted to impress my fellow group members. I wanted to show them how much I knew, let them see how much smarter I was, how I didn't make obvious typos, how I didn't belong here, not really, I was just passing through, I would find my way out of here in no time.

"That was a good guess, S," Smid said, retrieving a stack of posters from the blond-haired boy. He handed the stack to T, who took one sheet and passed it on. "A genogram shows hereditary patterns and sinful behaviors in our families. It doesn't trace our genealogy so much as the history behind our present sinful behavior."

Smid walked back to the board. He pulled off the marker cap with a flourish. First he wrote an *A* for alcoholism. Then he wrote *P* for promiscuous. He filled the board with the thick black letters we would use as a key for our genograms. *H* for homosexuality; *D* for drugs; *$* for gambling; *M* for mental illness; *Ab* for abortion; *G* for gang involvement; *Po* for pornography. I tried to ignore the lack of parallelism in Smid's list, a basic style rule I'd picked up in junior high English class. The medium, I told myself, didn't always have to be perfect. J took one of the poster sheets and passed the stack to me. I could feel his hand tremble as it passed between us. I placed my sheet on the beige Berber carpet at my feet.

Smid turned to face us, clicking the marker cap shut. "Trauma is often linked to generational sin," he said. "We have to understand where the sin came from in the first place. How it trickled down from father to son, mother to daughter." I recognized the sentiment from a Bible verse popular in our family's church—Exodus 20:5.

I the Lord thy God am a jealous God, visiting the iniquity of the fathers upon the children unto the third and forth generation of them that hate me.

The blond-haired boy handed each of us a stack of rubber band–wrapped colored pencils. The veteran members of our group slid from their chairs to begin the daily group project, bringing their posters with them. I quickly followed, my knees already accustomed to hours of kneeling at the tung-oiled altar of our family's church and asking God to change me. I had spent eighteen years of my life going to church three times a week, heeding the altar call along with my father and the other men, trying to believe in a literal interpretation of the Bible.

"The compulsive patterns of parents influencing children," Smid continued. "This is the most common root of sexual sin."

Our color-coded genograms would tell us where everything

had begun to go wrong. Trace our genealogy back far enough and we would find, if not the answer to our own sexual sins, then at least the sense of which dead and degenerate limb in our family tree had been responsible.

I scooted my poster over on the carpet so I could be closer to J. S slid her eyes at me as I passed, but I pretended not to notice.

J nudged my ribs with a red pencil, leaving a small check-mark on my white button-down. The weight of my gaze slid down his long ropy arm to where his purple-veined wrist was drawing a wavy red arrow of abuse from his father to his mother.

"I bet that's it," he said. His voice was so monotone, it was hard to tell if he was serious or simply regurgitating LIA lingo. I wondered if irony had been a greater part of his personality pre-LIA. I wondered if I would have liked him more outside of this place. "I bet some of that abuse turned me gay. Or it could have been Dad's *D*. Or maybe Mom had an *Ab* before I was born."

I wondered how anyone could know so much about his family. My clan was tight-lipped; when our past slipped through, it was only in accidental bursts or in code.

"I don't know where to start," I said, staring at the blank poster. It was a problem I experienced each time I sat down to write, but I had slowly started getting better at it. Relaxing my thoughts, I could enter my psyche through a side door, sit down cross-legged and examine the hieroglyphs.

"Start with the worst," J said, smiling, "unless *you're* the worst."

. . .

IT WAS HARD to conjure a family tree out of early childhood memories. My father's life had, from the moment of his calling to be a preacher, filled a vacuum within our family mythology. His importance in our town and community seemed to override everything we knew about ourselves. I was His Son. My mother was His Wife.

People had always seen my father as a devout believer, but at the age of fifty he had taken the next step, stumbling down our church aisle, shaking and crying, kneeling with the entire congregation until our preacher declared that God had called my father to the service. "I was aimless before I found my calling," my father repeated weekly, standing before pulpits across the state of Arkansas, until my mother and I started to believe him, to clap along with his audience. "I was nothing. But God healed me. He made me whole. Gave me purpose."

In less than a week, in the middle of the Source program, my mother and I planned to drive from the LIA facility to my father's ordination as a Missionary Baptist preacher, where we would be asked to stand with him on a brightly lit stage before a church audience of more than two hundred people. The trip was already preapproved by staff and considered integral to my development, a real opportunity to test my devotion to the cause. At the church, my mother and I would be expected to hold hands, smile, to burst into tears at the appropriate moment. Important Baptist Missionary Association of America mem-

bers would be traveling from every corner of Arkansas to publicly interview the man who many were hinting might be their
next Peter, their next Paul, the man whose moral compass
might set things to rights for the Baptists, usher in a stronger
belief in the Bible's inerrancy, distill many of the complex issues
that had recently begun to plague their association. Issues like
divorce, cohabitation, and—most pressing—homosexuality.

"Just think about who you are," J said, adding the finishing
touches to his poster. He was so accustomed to these exercises
he could have drawn the symbols with his eyes closed. "Then
trace it back to your family history."

I began by writing the names of my great-grandparents at
the top of the poster, followed by my grandparents, then my
parents. Next to my parents I added aunts and uncles and all
of my cousins. At the very bottom, in slightly smaller print,
I added my own name. I followed the genogram key as best I
could, placing only one or two sin symbols next to each rela-
tive's name. The grandfather with the alcohol problem: *A*. The
grandmother who divorced him because of the alcohol problem: a line with two diagonal slashes. The two grandparents
who'd died one after the other: twin *X*s. The aunt whose first
and second husbands both died in airplane crashes on the way
to Saigon, who'd later remarried and divorced: a line with two
diagonal slashes. The uncle with the drug and alcohol and
gambling problems: *D* and *A* and *$*, respectively.

As I diagrammed my family tree, coloring in the boxes and
arrows and textual symbols, the genogram started to make

sense. It provided a sense of security to blame others before me, to assign everyone his or her proper symbol and erase all other characteristics. I could place an *H* beside my own name, and everything else about me would cease to matter. If I wondered why I was sitting on this carpeted floor with a group of strangers, I could count up the list of familial sins, shrug, and move on to the next activity without asking further questions. All of this confusion about who I was and why my life had led me to this moment could be folded up with my finished genogram, slipped inside a folder, and tucked away in one of LIA's many filing cabinets.

"It looks like you've got a lot of *A* on both sides of the family," J said, admiring my poster, his voice a steady monotone. "That must've done a real number on your mom and dad. You know, they say sometimes the biggest sins skip a generation. You must be *really* gay."

"That sucks," I said, looking up to make sure no one had heard me. Even mild profanity was strictly prohibited. "I guess it'll take a long time to get cured."

Smid stepped between us, eyeing our posters. "Good work," he said, patting me on the back. Light and cool, the pads of his fingers barely registered. Later I would feel this touch again, on my elbow, as he corrected my flamboyant akimbo stance to something more straight appropriate, a flagging Cro-Magnon pose popular in small Southern towns like the one where I grew up.

"I don't want to hear that language again," he added, his

voice lower, a filed-down baritone worn by strain. "Only God's language is tolerated here."

I could hear S laughing quietly behind me.

"Newbie," she whispered.

"No shit," I said. The curse registered as a slap, but she quickly composed herself and laughed again, loud enough to draw Smid's attention back to us.

Looking back, I think she must have been glad, for once, not to be the object of the room's derision, to be rid of the attention of people who considered themselves lucky to know someone like her who hid an even more shameful secret. She must have been glad that people for one second had stopped picturing her lying on her back in the cramped living room of her trailer, the half-empty jar of peanut butter like a dark stain on the kitchen counter as her parents entered through the front door to find their daughter changed beyond recognition.

"Take your time," Smid said, circling back to me. "You'll want to get this right."

I slid the pencil behind my ear and surveyed the half-finished genogram, trying to recall the sins of my fathers. I sat like this until the activity time ended, afraid to write something I couldn't erase.

THE PLAIN DEALERS

The men gathered in the showroom, the soles of their leather saddle shoes squeaking against the tile. The previous night had brought several inches of rain that by now had gathered in the gaps of their rough concrete driveways, settled into the foam-rubber seals of their car doors, and spilled out of the hidden reservoirs of suspension beneath their floorboards. It was as if the weatherman with the practiced Midwestern accent had been wrong and there had been no rain. The roads dry as usual, and in the haze of only the second or third cup of coffee of the morning, these men might never have noticed anything different if it wasn't for the squeaking of their soles, a sound signifying that the night's activities had gone on without them.

"I tell you it's the End Times," Brother Nielson was saying. Two men helped him limp to a black leather couch in the corner of the showroom. As Brother Nielson passed his reflection in the red Mustang parked in the center of the room, he smiled briefly at his hulking form then looked away. "War in the Middle East. Over what? Why don't we just nuke them all?" Brother Nielson had earned his respect from twenty hardworking years as a deacon in our local Missionary Baptist church. As his health began to fail and his body slowly calcified, his stature as a pillar of the church and our small Arkansan town grew more pronounced. But in the end, his path to respectability had cost him his vanity. "I used to have all the girls a man could dream of," he was known to say. "Hundreds of them. Lined up. Every make and model imaginable."

Now, the hem of his khakis lagged behind his shoes, mopping up the hints of water that the other men had left behind. "I don't know why people have to make things so complicated. CNN wants us to think we shouldn't have gone over there in the first place. Don't they know Jesus will be back any day now?" He sank into the couch with a leathery squeak. "I can feel it in my bones."

Something my father and the other men liked to tell people about the Gospel: God has no time for anyone but a plain dealer. Speak your mind, and speak it clearly. "There is no neutral," my father liked to say. "No gray area. No in-betweens."

I watched them from the doorway of my father's office, holding a leather-bound King James Bible in one hand, gripping the wooden doorjamb with the other. In less than five minutes

I would be joining them on my knees in front of the couch, leading my father and his employees through the morning Bible study for the first time. Since my father moved to this town several years back to assume control of a new Ford dealership, he had held a Bible study every workday morning. Like most church members we knew, he was concerned with the lack of prayer in schools and businesses, and he believed that the country, though led by an evangelical president, was constantly trying to strip away all of Christ's original glory from its citizens' everyday lives, especially when it came to things like the Pledge of Allegiance and Christmas festivities, which were always rumored to be under attack. Like my mother, he had grown up in the church, and since there had been only one church where my parents had lived most of their lives, our family had always been Missionary Baptists, concerned with leading people to the Lord. *For where two or three are gathered together in my name, there am I in the midst of them.* My father took the verse literally, like all Missionary Baptists, and, like all evangelicals, he believed that the more souls you could gather in Christ's name, the more souls you would be saving from eternal hellfire. Two souls was the minimum, three was adequate, but nine or ten or more was best. "I want to lead at least a thousand souls to the Lord before I die," he would repeat to me almost daily.

Working for him as a car detailer each summer kept me at a respectable distance from the business of saving souls. At eighteen, I hadn't yet performed any actual ministering duties.

Though he never said it outright, each summer he required me to do the kind of manual labor that would help me turn out to be a normal red-blooded Southerner, the kind that would offset my more bookish, feminine qualities. My workday companions were spray bottles filled with sealants, polishes, body compounds, and tire glazes. Pink and purple and yellow liquids I hardly knew other than by the smell and feel of them baking into my sunburned skin, and then by the aggregations of foam that settled and eventually swirled into the shower drain at the end of each day. When my father would ask me how many customers I had witnessed to out on the lot, I was able to smile and say, "I don't think the pressure washer has a soul, even if it does make those crazy humming noises." And my father was able to say, "We need to get that thing fixed," and turn his head away from the sight of me.

But when it came to the morning Bible study, jokes wouldn't save me. I had to perform or else disappoint my father in front of the other men. Since I was seen as an extension of him— *Going to turn out just like your old man; can't wait to see what gift the Good Lord's given you*—great things were expected to pour from my lips. Wine from the jars of Cana: what was empty suddenly restored, the wedding feast continuing, the disciples believing in miracles.

When my mother would join us for our lunch breaks at the Timberline, one of the only restaurants in town, in a giant wood-paneled room whose walls were covered with splintering handsaws and rusty blades three times the size of my head, my father would look around at the people eating, and he would sigh, a wounded sound that left his voice hollow and quiet.

"How many souls in here do you think are headed straight to Hell?" he would say.

And before we could leave the restaurant, he would make a show of buying everyone's lunch. He would stand up from our table, pull a waitress from her autopiloted course through the sea of grease-stained faces, and whisper the order in her ear. As customers brushed past us, my mother and I would stand near the entrance, waiting for him to finish paying. Sometimes a customer would walk up to my father and protest his charity, and my father would say something like "The Lord has blessed me. He'll bless you, too, if you just let Him into your heart." Most often, the customers would sit at their tables absorbing the smell of fried chicken livers into their jeans, T-shirts, and follicles, oblivious until it came time to pay, when they would stare narrow eyed at the passing waitress, as if she might somehow be responsible for their embarrassment. No one in this small Southern town liked to feel beholden, and no one knew this better than my father.

I JIGGLED the wooden doorjamb of my father's office doorway until it almost came loose, listening as Brother Nielson and the others settled their speech into a steady rhythm. Many of the dealership employees regularly attended our church, some more devout than others, some perhaps exaggerating their piety for my father's sake, but all of them my Brothers, a name the Missionary Baptists applied to any follower of Christ. Brothers and Sisters all serving the same Father in the name of the Son. I couldn't make out their words, but I could feel their excited speech almost to the point of pain, each syllable a loud buzzing noise, a hurried wing beat.

"Another earthquake this morning," my father said. "Are you ready for the Rapture?"

I could hear him typing at his computer behind me, one key at a time, adding his own metronomic countermovement to the ticking of the polished chrome clock above his desk. He had recently swapped his dealership's 56k dial-up connection for high-speed DSL, and each morning he sped through Yahoo! headlines looking for Armageddon talking points. An earthquake killing hundreds somewhere in the Hindu Kush. A siege at the Church of the Nativity. The U.S. invading Afghanistan. All of this related to the predictions outlined by the dreams of St. John in the Book of Revelation. One simple logic guided these searches: If every word of the Bible was to be taken literally, then the plagues and fires of St. John's testimony were certainly the plagues and fires of today's news cycle. The only thing we could hope for in these End Times: the country announcing its allegiance to Jesus before the Rapture began, righting some of its wrongs, continuing to elect solid born-again Republicans into office.

"I'm ready," I said, turning to face him.

I pictured the coming earthquake, the miniature hot rods lining his office shelves crashing to the floor, their tiny doors groaning, hinges cracking open. For someone who had built fourteen street rods from scratch, for a man who could boast of winning a national street-rod competition in Evansville, Indiana, with his aquamarine 1934 Ford, my father was ready—eager, even—to watch all of his work burn to the ground the minute the trumpets sounded. He could do nothing halfway. When he decided to build cars, he built not one, but fourteen; when he decided to work full-time for God, he did it in the only way he knew how without jeopardizing his family's material well-being—by making his business God's business. His idol was Billy Graham, an evangelist who used the public sphere to such an advantage that he had been able to shape our country's political climate by whispering into the ears of no less than eleven presidents. Before my father came to be a pastor of his own church, his small-scale influence mirrored Graham's in its intensity. Members of our town's police force, who purchased their white square Crown Victorias from my father, never left the dealership without his admonishment to go out and bring order to our town—and, more important, to help spread the Gospel to unbelievers.

"We have to be vigilant," my father said over his computer monitor. "For there shall arise false Christs, and false prophets, and they shall shew great signs and wonders."

He clicked his mouse several times with his too-big hand, a

hand that could take apart a carburetor but whose rough edges and burned skin made it difficult for him to operate a personal computer.

SEVERAL YEARS before I was born, my father had stopped on the side of the highway that passed through our hometown to help a man whose car had broken down. As my father crawled beneath the engine to check for any abnormalities, the stranger turned the key to his ignition, igniting the gas that had been leaking from the carburetor, an ignition that spread third-degree burns across my father's face and hands. The burns left his nerves burned and dead so that now he could cup his hand over a candle flame for thirty seconds or more until my mother and I would scream for him to stop. When I was a colicky baby, he would comfort me by sitting in a wicker rocking chair with me and bringing a candle close to my face. He would press his palm flat against the open O of the glass holder until the fire almost fizzled out, repeating the act until I grew tired, my head falling against his chest while he quietly sang me to sleep with one of his many made-up lullabies.

He's a good old friend to me
As simple as can be
He's a good old pal
He's a good old friend
He's a good old pal to me

At certain moments in his life, my father must have asked himself why the stranger had turned the key. He must have asked himself why anyone would turn the key.

"Whatever you do," my father had said, stepping around the stranger's car to examine the motor, "don't turn the key."

There must have been some hiccup in communication, something in the stranger that said it was all right to start the engine at the exact moment the Good Samaritan crawled beneath the bumper of his car. Whatever his motivations, the stranger didn't hesitate.

My mother later told me that when my father showed up at the front door, his clothes covered in ash and his face half burned and his whole body shaking, her first reaction had been to ask him to stay outside. She was vacuuming the carpet. She assumed he was simply caked with dirt.

"Go away," she said. "Wait till I'm finished vacuuming."

Hours later, standing beside my father's hospital bed, waiting for his hand to heal so she could at least hold on to some part of him, what she felt in the place of love was pity and fear. Pity for a man who would risk his life for strangers without a second thought, and fear for a life lived with a once-handsome man, a twentysomething former quarterback with the cleft chin and deep dimples of a *Saturday Night Fever* John Travolta now transformed into—into what? No one could tell exactly. The bandages would have to be removed weeks later, and only then would doctors know if the grafted skin would resemble anything of his former face.

. . .

"Too many earthquakes to keep track of," my father said, tossing the mouse into a stack of papers beside him. He popped each of his knuckles. "But you don't need shelter when you're wearing the Armor of God." He pointed to the Bible in my hand.

"Sure don't," I said. I pictured armor-plated locusts swirling in corkscrews from the clouds. Scores of unbelievers with their bodies run through by silver-plated scabbards. And somewhere in my conscience, the beginning of an idea that had recently begun to plague me: that I might be one of them.

At eighteen, I was still very much in the closet, with a half-hearted commitment to my girlfriend, Chloe, whose predilection for French kissing ran a cold blade through the bottom of my stomach. A week earlier as we sat in my car outside her house, Chloe had reached for my leg. I had shifted away from her, and said, "It's so cold in here," flipping the lever for the heat, sliding back into the passenger's seat, wishing there was an eject button. I had experienced my own Armageddon fantasy in that moment: the depressed button of a radio controller, a hooded insurgent walking calmly away from our flying debris, pieces of my flannel shirt flying through the air on flame-tipped wings, a thick-necked policeman picking through the charred remains of the explosion for Chloe's purple hair scrunchie.

"Besides," I said, thinking that this moment might lead to more intimacy than we had ever allowed. "We should wait until marriage."

"Right," she said, removing her hand. Since we had already been together for a year and a half, the church congregation was expecting us to marry before too many years of college could change us. Earlier in the summer we had traveled to Florida with my mother and my aunt. As we were leaving for the trip, Chloe's mother leaned in through the driver's-side window to stage whisper into my mother's ear. "You know everything's going to change after this, right?" she said. "All of you in the same hotel room. E-ve-ry-*thing*."

But nothing had changed. Chloe and I sneaking out at night with my aunt's wine coolers to sit by the neon pool and watch its waves ripple across the plastic lining, an angry tide pulsing somewhere in the darkness ahead. I had started to think we didn't need anything other than friendship. Chloe had made me feel complete in a way no one else had. She made it fun to walk through the school hallways, to see the looks of approval on people's faces. I could see in her eyes a real love I might one day be capable of returning. When we'd first met in church, her smile had been so genuine that I'd decided to ask her out right after the service, and we'd quickly settled into a happy routine. Watching movies, listening to pop music, playing video games, helping each other finish homework. It seemed there hadn't been anything to confide until that intimate moment in the car, and suddenly there was this new pressure between us.

. . .

MY FATHER and I left his office to join the other men at the foot of the couch, each of us sinking to our knees on the cold tile. Above our heads hung a sign that read: NO CUSSING TOLERATED—THIS IS THE LORD'S BUSINESS.

The man to my left, Brother Hank, clamped his eyelids shut until faint white ripples appeared above his red cheeks. My father's number one car salesman, Brother Hank could tailor his speech for any occasion. "Dear Lord," he began, "give this boy the strength to deliver his message this morning." He wrapped his heavy arm around my shoulders and tucked me close to his ribs. I could smell the sharp scent of menthol and, beneath that, the earthy smell of his farm, a place I had seen only in passing during one of my long walks through the forest paths surrounding our house.

Brother Hank continued: "Bestow upon him Thy divine grace and mercy." He paused for a moment, allowing the distant ticking of my father's chrome clock to sober each man's mood. A few of the men groaned encouragement.

"Oh, yes, Lord," they said.

"Yes oh yes oh yes oh yes oh yes Lord," they said.

Brother Hank lifted his hand from my back and left it hovering above my hair, the way my father used to do before cracking an imaginary egg on my skull and causing the imaginary yolk to trickle down my cheeks. "Let him be a vessel for truth. Let no falsehood spill from Your blessed fountain. Amen."

"Amen!" the men shouted, rising to their feet, knees popping.

We settled into a circle of chairs around the couch, Brother Nielson and my father taking up the middle. Brother Hank removed a stack of Bibles from a nearby desk drawer and fanned them out like a deck of cards, each man choosing carefully, examining his book before flipping open the cover.

"Tell me something before we begin," Brother Nielson said, removing his own Bible from behind a couch cushion. His name glittered in gold on the front, along the bottom of the cracked leather cover. His cracked Bible said one thing to all of us: *Here is a man whose fingers have creased and uncreased each page for the past twenty years. Here is a man who has quietly sobbed into the open spine, allowed his tears to wet and wrinkle the red letters of our Savior.* "I've been talking with the men here," Brother Nielson continued, "and I want to know one thing, boy. What's your opinion on the Middle East problem? What do you think of our president's decision?"

I froze. The existence of Chloe had shielded me from too much direct questioning about my sexuality, but there were certain opinions that would make me a suspect no matter what. I was always nervous when I had to give an opinion on anything that could open me up to judgment. To be counted a sissy was one thing; to be counted a sissy *and* an Arab sympathizer was another. To be counted a sissy and an Arab sympathizer would pave the way for others to finally detect the attraction I felt to men. And when they discovered that secret, nothing would stop them from retroactively dismissing each detail of my personality, each opinion of mine, as mere symptoms of homo-sexuality. I could boast of detailing more cars than any of my father's other workers; I could point at a boy in high school and laugh at his tight jeans and coiffed hair; but once it was suspected that I felt certain *urges* or thought certain thoughts, I would cease to be a man in these men's eyes, in my father's eyes.

"Well, boy?" Brother Nielson said. He leaned forward and smiled a watery smile. It seemed to require all of his strength to lift his back from the leather couch. "Cat got your tongue?"

I had prepared a lesson on Job, the unluckiest of a luckless Old Testament cast. I thought that by sticking to the script I might avoid scrutiny, the feel of the showroom's glass walls narrowing their yellow microscope light on my flagging belief, my suspect mannerisms. Now I didn't know what to say or do.

I coughed into a closed fist and looked down at my Bible. I ignored Brother Nielson's stare. "The lesson of Job is that we can never know God's intentions regarding the world," I said. "Why do bad things happen? Why do bad things happen to good people?"

I turned to the passage, trying to will my hands to be steady. I could feel the heat of Brother Nielson's and my father's twin gazes, but I didn't look up. I flipped the pages back and forth, hoping my train of thought would return.

"Go on, boy," Brother Nielson said. "Let the Holy Spirit work through you."

I stared at the words until they became meaningless glyphs, until they swam across the pages. The simple declarative sentences I had prepared the night before refused to snap into place along the worn lines of reason the church had instilled in me three times every week since my first birthday.

"Job was a good man," I said. "He didn't deserve what he got. But his friends didn't listen. They didn't . . ."

What I was trying to say seemed impossible and too complicated for words. When everything went wrong in Job's life, when he lost his wife and two children and all of his livestock to a bet between God and Satan, his friends could only think to ask him what he did wrong, why he deserved God's punishment. To them, this seemed the only explanation: Bad things happened to bad people. But what happened when good things happened to bad people or vice versa?

I looked up at the showroom entrance in time to see Chloe drive up. She wore her long hair in a ponytail, her smile interrupted by a string of braces that I had used one too many times as an excuse to put an end to our French kissing. Though women didn't usually attend the men's Bible study, Chloe was a bit of a rebel when it came to the church's separation of men's and women's roles, believing that women had just as much of a right to be church leaders as men, though she told me this in secret. Most of the women in my church, my mother included, believed that the Bible had clearly appointed men as the leaders of the church, though there were a few members who were beginning to question this assumption. For now, though, Chloe stayed outside in her car, watching me for signs of what my father and these men hoped I might possess: the confidence of a future church leader. The patriarchal chain would travel directly from Brother Nielson to my father and finally to me.

I could feel my face glow red. I slapped the book shut and stared at my feet.

"I don't . . ."

The tile was dry now, and in the prints left behind by the men's rubber outsoles rested a skim of ultraviolet pollen. There were floors to be mopped. Outside, rows of cars would need spraying down with the pressure washer, last night's rain now dried water spots on my father's inventory.

"It's okay, son," my father said, not looking up from his Bible. "We can do this some other day."

My mouth was dry, my tongue a paperweight weighing down my syllables.

"I lost my train of thought," I said, looking away, catching sight of our group's reflection in the Mustang's rear window. Our figures stretched by the convex glass, we looked like one long thin band of a gold ring, broken only by the space between my right leg and the arm of the couch.

Brother Nielson opened his Bible to another passage and cleared his throat. "That's okay," he said. "Some of us aren't cut out for the reading of scripture." He began to speak of the glories of Heaven and everlasting life.

. . .

SITTING WITH my mother and father and Chloe hours later at the Timberline, I would fume about Brother Nielson's words. I would glare at the gigantic radial saw across from our table and imagine it lifting from the curved nail that pinned it to the wall. I would imagine it splitting our town in half. That night, I would dream of Brother Nielson standing at the edge of one half of a living room that had been split down the middle, drifting gradually away from the rest of our town, his sagging boxers flapping in the wind, unable to leap across the widening gap with his tired and broken body, lost in a continental drift.

The truth was, Job's friends *hadn't* understood. Not Eliphaz, Bildad, or Zophar. Job lost his livestock, his wife, his two beautiful daughters—everything. A toss of the coin, and everything was gone. Only a mediator like Elihu, the youngest of Job's friends, could hint at the complexity of Job's loss.

A good family, a good house, a good car. To these men, and to me at the time, these were the necessary elements in securing decades of good luck. No matter that we now traded in cars rather than in livestock; no matter that the machinery of war, of Humvees cutting desert paths, was something we would never come to see or understand. At the end of the story, God would provide Job with a different wife, a different set of children, new livestock. Whatever happened—no matter how much we might suffer—if we had faith, God would restore it all, graft the skin back in place, mold us new bodies from our bone-tired ones.

. . .

LIKE THE NIGHT BEFORE, a thunderhead was moving across the Ozarks. "A cold front that'll break up by morning," the weatherman had said, his Midwestern accent clipping his words before they could slide into a Southern drawl. "You'll hardly feel it," he said, smiling, hazel eyes sparkling in the studio lights.

I lay awake in my bed, rereading Job in the hopes of finding a simple explanation for the scripture. I tried to quiet the critical part of my brain, the one that had caused me to stutter and falter during that morning's Bible study.

Sometimes it was simply the act of looking at the open Bible that gave me a sense of belonging. Sometimes opening the Bible and pressing the pages flat with my palm, adding an extra crack in the spine, brought me closer to my father. I ran my thumb down the indented tabs, pressed into the sides of the book until the words took on a heft I might carry and lift up as proof of my devotion. I closed the Bible and placed it on my nightstand.

Chloe texted me a few minutes later, the phone's vibrations pulling me out of semiconsciousness: "What's up?"

"Nothing," I wrote, burying the clamshell phone under my pillow. I felt like smothering the vibrations until they stopped. From the moment she showed up at the dealership, Chloe had continually asked me how the Bible study had gone. I had evaded the question by mumbling a "fine" every now and then.

Because he wasn't snoring as usual, I could tell my father also lay awake. I was afraid that the storm wasn't what kept him from sleep. The reverberating claps that shook so many households awake that night, sending deer scurrying across roads to smash into the sides of cars, were less severe than those that must have accompanied my father's own fears for his son. I listened for his praying for several minutes, wondering if he was experiencing another moment when Jesus stood over his bed and bled onto the sheets. My father claimed he was often burdened with such visions.

When he finally fell asleep, his snoring was almost loud enough to shake the gilded picture frames lining the hallway just outside my bedroom. Years before, my mother had moved to an adjacent guest bedroom, saying she needed time away from the earthquake that was my sleeping father, from the whining bedsprings accompanying each inhalation. When I was very young, seven or eight years old, I would wake from scripture-inspired nightmares—blue cones of flame licking my feet, chasm after chasm opening up out of a blackness more felt than seen—and walk the hallway to my father's bedroom to stand at the edge of his bed and wish him awake. I thought he should have understood me without the need for words, that the current between us was so free-flowing and deep he would have no choice but to wake up that instant. I would stand beside the mirrored closet and see the reflected room limned by the blue light of the television he left going all night, shaking and furious, terrified that I would have to return to my nightmares. Hours later, I would cross the hallway to my mother's bedroom to perform the same absurd ritual. But after only a few minutes, my mother would feel me standing there and pull me beside her in the bed, moving over so I could have the warm spot.

"Love," she would say.

"Love," I would mumble, turning on my side, gliding my hand across the warm sheets until the scent of her lavender body lotion covered my skin.

The phone buzzed again under my pillow. The buzzing grew stronger, louder, until the blurred edges of my vision snapped into focus. I stared into the slats of the bunk bed I had kept even through high school because my mother would sometimes take the top bunk in the middle of the night, falling asleep with one thin arm dangling over the side. Now I pictured the wood cracking, the board coming down hard. Finally, after several rounds of buzzing, I reached under the pillow and snapped open the phone.

"Why are you ignoring me?" Chloe said.

"I'm just tired," I lied. I knew she was the one who could most comfort me, but I was afraid that by telling her about my failure at the dealership I'd have to reveal a truth I wasn't ready to admit to anyone. Not just that I might not be cut out for my father's line of work, but that I might not be cut out for any of the Lord's work, that just by having certain urges and entertaining certain thoughts I had already ended up on the wrong team.

"The storm." When she grew worried, her voice rose nearly an octave. I wanted to be the kind of boyfriend who felt like her natural protector, the one to shelter her, even if it now seemed I needed her much more than she needed me.

"It'll be okay," I said. When was the right time to tell her what was going on? What would I even say? And if I told her, if I just came out and said it, what would stop her from leaving me for someone more promising, someone with less baggage? I knew it was wrong to assume she'd just quit on me. Chloe wasn't the kind of person to give up on anyone; she was one of the most optimistic people I'd ever met. But I couldn't imagine a scenario in which she stayed, in which we both had to live with the knowledge of my brokenness. Telling her the truth would end whatever tenuous grasp I now had on a normal life. Whereas if I could just work through it on my own, if I just had enough time, I might be able to preserve our innocence. If it all worked out in the end, I might be able to live with my deception, and my past urges would come to seem like nothing more than lies Satan had tried to make me believe. I would have the satisfaction of knowing that I had never listened to those lies, never given them a proper expression, that I had chosen the true version of our life together. None of this felt like selfishness at the time.

We were now settling into the silent part of our conversation. The part where I felt anger and guilt until boredom finally conquered all. But underneath that boredom was the sense that God wanted us to be together. How could it be otherwise? How could our church be wrong? What feelings I couldn't muster for her must only be side effects of our immaturity. We would grow into it: into each other, into God. So we would wait like this for hours each evening, Chloe on the other end of the line reading a book or watching TV while I played video games, both of us silent and waiting for the next chunk of awkward conversation to arrive.

I sat up, threw the sheets off, and sat down cross-legged in the center of my bedroom, my sunburned knees flaring with pain, the phone tucked into my neck. I could still smell the false lemony scent of the dealership's chemicals on my skin. I turned on the TV in front of me, picked up the Sony PlayStation controller I'd left on the carpet, and pressed start. The pause menu split into thirds and disappeared to reveal the image of a tall male avatar with spiky black hair standing in the center of a vast forest. He wore a fur-lined leather jacket and a long chain that dangled from his thick black belt, and carried a sword that fascinated me not because it was part blade and part gun, but because of the gaudy silver embellishments running along its hilt. The details reminded me of my mother's collection of Brighton bracelets, the way they sparkled in any light and rested their outsize beauty on her thin wrists.

The goal of the game was to travel from town to town in search of special items and adventure. Traveling was treacherous: There were few cars in this world, most things were done by foot, and at any moment the screen could swirl into a vortex, the colors of the forest bleeding into one another, until I was firmly planted in front of an enemy, usually some chimera that could have easily been lifted from an eighteenth-century besti-ary, like horses with roaring lion heads, green slime globs with tree limbs for arms and canine fangs. A victorious battle would yield shiny new accoutrements, objects that, once itemized and collected neatly in the main menu, yielded a sense of accom-plishment.

Like order out of chaos. The face of God moving over the waters of the deep. In the book of Job, it is the Creator piercing the fleeing Leviathan.

There were times when I would stare for hours into the vir-tual rooms of a baroque palace, never moving from my spot on the carpet, while the avatar scratched his head and shifted into the kind of *contrapposto* pose the men of the dealership would have considered sexually suspect. I felt that to move would be to break the spell, cause me to reenter a world where I was too old to crawl into bed with my mother if the fear of Hell got to be too bad.

When I first hit puberty and started fantasizing about men more often, I had become so entranced with the world of video games that I would hardly ever move from the carpet for entire weekends. On the few occasions when I could no longer ignore my body, I would stand up to release angry streams of piss onto the carpet at the foot of my bed. I had no way of knowing if my mother ever entered my bedroom while I was at school, but I wanted her to; I wanted her to interpret the damp hiero-glyphs I had spelled out for her—sometimes my name; more often a figure eight or, depending on the angle, the symbol for infinity—even if I didn't understand them myself. Feeling guilt after I arrived home from school, I would sneak into the bathroom, steal some cleaning chemicals, and spray them into the carpet until the room no longer smelled like piss. Though I'd stopped all this by the time I turned sixteen, I still felt like violating our house in some way, and I would sometimes even fantasize about the whole place going up in flames, our little family huddled outside while the walls collapsed in slow motion. It wasn't that I thought violence would solve our problems. It was just that the need to tell my parents something—anything— was overpowering, and at the time I didn't have a proper language for it.

I moved my avatar deeper into the forest path, his footfalls like wooden shoes dropped from a great height. The trees folded around him, and in the distance appeared the mouth of a cave. I moved him toward the cave and hunched forward, forgetting the phone at my neck until I heard Chloe's sigh.

"We have to do something," she said. "I'm worried."

"The storm will be over soon," I said.

"No," she said. "About us. We have to do something drastic." We hadn't talked about how we would stay together once we went off to college at the end of the summer, how we would manage to pull off the miracle of a successful long-distance relationship. We'd been admitted into different colleges, would be heading in different directions, though we'd still be in the same state. It was another of the many topics I had pushed to the back of my mind. She was right. If we were going to hold this relationship together, we needed to do something drastic. But neither one of us knew what. Do *it*? Not do *it*? Get married? Break up? The questions themselves were driving us both crazy. We debated the question of virginity. Whose virginity? Mine? Hers? And if we did *it*, when?

"There's no such thing as time anyway. Time only exists on earth. In Heaven there won't be any time, so we're technically already married. We're technically already doing it."

"Then we've technically *always* been doing it. So what's the point?"

"Because we still have free will. I think God is telling us to act now in order to demonstrate our love for Him."

At the beginning of our relationship, Chloe would sit with me while I played video games, pointing excitedly as some new creature bounced across the screen. When we first met in church a few years back, I had felt something I rarely experienced outside of the virtual world: a leveling up, a sense of worthiness, of a whole group of people smiling in approval. During lunch breaks at school, I no longer had to crouch on the toilet seat to hide from overcrowded lunch tables. There had been an easiness between us as we explored the forest behind her backyard with her younger brother, Brandon, who still liked to pretend he was on a safari. We could drive around in one of my father's new cars, making up directions as we went, asking

Brandon in the backseat whether we should turn left or right or keep going straight. "Go to Memphis," he would say, confident as a distinguished playboy, faux-smoking a candy cigarette. "Let's see the glass pyramid, boys." With Brandon between us, it was less confusing; we had something to focus on other than ourselves.

The storm was growing louder, the thunder nearer. "Okay," I said, the phone hot against my ear. "We'll figure it out."

Another silence stretched out between us. I stood and walked to the bedroom window and lifted one of the aluminum blinds with my index finger. Yellow lamppost lights cradled low-hanging clouds. A line of pine trees shook in the wind, their needles spilling onto the driveway. Headlights flickered for a moment on a distant highway then disappeared beneath a heavy sheet of rain that passed almost as quickly as it came. I could hear no thunder.

Unlike Brother Nielson's and my father's bombastic dooms-day scenarios, I feared Armageddon would take the quiet form of radio static. White noise: after the thunder, the world suddenly muted by the sound of heavy rain. Even more terrifying than my nightmares was the thought of being left behind by my sleeping family, their bodies turned to husks. I might arrive home from school one day to find only a simmering pot on the stove, the radio droning on in my parents' absence. After my parents decided to move their old television into my bedroom, I used to stay awake to watch the midnight news so I could imagine there were other people still awake, other people doing things at that moment, and I would think about how God wouldn't leave so many people behind and I would feel safe for a few minutes. With Chloe, I had always felt safe, at least before she reached for me in the car. Until that moment I felt like God might grant me a free pass, since I was *trying* to be the man my father could recognize as a peer. Now, with Chloe's growing intimacy, I thought I would need to perform. Without hesitation, without stuttering, without alternate interpretations. Perhaps one sin would be a substitute for the even greater sin of homosexuality, and then we'd at least have a chance to live our godly lives together.

"Still there?" Chloe said.

"Yeah."

We arranged a date to watch a late-night movie at her house. There seemed to be something hidden in this arrangement, something we left unsaid but that we both must have known. When the time came for sleep, I figured Chloe could express interest in cooking a big breakfast with me the next morning and insist that I sleep in the basement, not far from Brandon's bed. Her mother might slide her eyes at us, but she would eventually give in; after all, we had already spent the night in the same hotel room in Florida. We would be quiet. Safe. I could buy a twenty-five-cent condom from a gas station vending machine in a distant town, telling my parents I needed to go on another long drive to clear my head, to talk to God. Then, if conditions seemed right, I would sneak up to her room and see what happened between us.

When thinking about sex, I had never before wondered

how long it would take. I had never wondered what postsex breakfast might taste like or what movie might be most appropriate before commencement. Most important, I had never wondered whether or not sex—not kissing or cuddling or grinding, but *sex*, jumping right into the very act itself and skipping all the other steps—might finally turn me, if not straight, at least into someone capable of performing straightness. I had never assumed I would want to go this far, that I would break one of the cardinal rules in our church. When I had fantasized about men, I'd always shut down the thoughts before I imagined myself entering the fantasy. It had always been one body, performing alone, performing only for me. What would it be like to do something with another person, a person you'd have to face for the rest of your life, both of you living with the knowledge of what you did in your most desperate moment? Would you ever be able to make it up to God? And what if it didn't work? What if the transgression led to failure, and you were left alone to rot in your sin?

"Is it raining there now?" Chloe said, yawning. "It's raining here."

"No," I lied, listening to the sound of raindrops pinging against the shingles. I wanted to keep our lives separate. Then I was afraid of what it would mean if I did. "I mean yes."

"How can it be both?" she said.

"I don't know. It just is."

I sat back down on the carpet and pressed the start button on the controller. "It's not both. I don't know why I said it was both." The cave was now directly in the avatar's path. There was no other way around it. Whatever was hidden inside was probably going to be worth it.

IT WAS my mother's treasures, her silver necklaces and gaudy rings, their shiny symbolism, the way many of them were handed down through the maternal line, the way these symbols could make up a home and present a family history with more than one plotline—it was their complexity I craved each time I urged my PlayStation avatar to open another treasure chest, to sink deeper into the cave with its quivering stalactites.

When I was nine, these treasures had taken on a literal quality that I could never quite shake from my mind. My family and I were on a soon-to-be-condemned pier. We were on vacation in Florida. The pier shook each time the tide slapped its splintering pillars. There was a groaning as the water made contact with its rusted metal joint bars. My father ruffled my hair. I threw a plastic Coke bottle into the water, and inside that bottle was a message.

Dear Pirate,

How are you? It's nice to meet you even if I don't know who you are. I'd like to know you, so please write back. Also, if you could, please send me treasure.

Your friend Garrard

We arrived back at our house, exhausted from a ten-hour car ride, to find a yellowed piece of notebook paper taped to the front door, a map of our yard with a giant X where the note claimed a pirate named Lonzo had buried his treasure. My mother feigned shock, pressing her fingertips to her cheeks and leaving ten red marks on her face after she dropped her arms. "This is wild," she said. "This is just so wild." My father helped me carry a shovel from the garage to the spot in the yard Lonzo had marked on his map. The X was spray-painted in silver on the grass. Together, we pressed our tennis shoes to each of the shovel's shoulders and dug into the hard-packed clay. Three feet deep, we found a box filled mostly with costume jewelry but also with real jewelry that I would later discover belonged to my grandmother, items for which she had no further use. She and my grandfather had arranged the whole thing on the night my mother called to tell them about the message in a bottle.

After we ran water from a garden hose over the box, I kept the jewelry in the bottom drawer of my desk. I would take the shiny gold pieces out of the box and place as many of them as I could on my neck and wrists and stand in front of the mirror. Twirling. I did this again and again until my father walked in on me one day and told me I needed to stop, that Lonzo would feel sad if he saw me mocking his treasure that way.

"I want to *live* with Lonzo," I said. "I want to be a pirate."

"You probably wouldn't like it," my father said. "You'd have to mop the deck all day. He'd turn you into one of his slaves. You'd get sick of the water."

THE COLD FRONT from the night before brought severe wind gusts that sent sheets of water from my pressure washer over the tops of other cars, leaving water spots on their windshields, the drops fizzling and evaporating on contact with the roasting metal. I stepped out of the service garage, shielded my eyes, and stared at the long line of car windows I would now have to Windex. Behind me, one of my father's employees was pressing the button to a hydraulic lift, and Chloe's car was being lifted to the height of the man's shoulders so he could begin replacing the oil. I was to drive her car back to her house later that afternoon, leave my car at the dealership overnight, and carry out the plan.

Earlier that morning during Bible study, Brother Nielson had lingered in the showroom for a little longer than usual, holding himself upright with one hand on the side of the Mustang.

"I keep wondering," he said, as I passed by carrying a handful of car keys, "if you're ever going to answer my question." I couldn't tell if he was trying to test me or if he seriously wanted to know what I thought about the Middle East, to know that the next generation was secure in its fight against terrorism.

"Leave the boy alone," Brother Hank said, sticking his head out of a nearby office.

"He's not old enough to care about politics. Girls are all he's got on the brain right now."

"Girls, huh," Brother Nielson said. "Nothing wrong with that." He straightened his back as much as he could, wincing. "Just don't forget there are bigger things in this world."

He stuck his hand out in front of my path, and I moved the keys to my other hand and clasped his in a firm handshake that grew firmer with each second until the grip was so severe I thought we might crack each other's knuckles. His eyes stared directly into mine, full of some secret knowledge. I felt almost as though he could detect the contamination I had passed into my palm earlier that morning before the sun rose, as though the condom I had purchased from the gas station carried a hidden scent or an oil undetectable except by the most righteous of men.

"We're living in the End Times," he said to me. "Stay sharp."

I SET the pressure washer down on the concrete, grabbed the Windex bottle and some paper towels, and walked onto the blacktop lot to tackle the line of water-spotted windshields. In the distance ahead I could see the pine trees on the hills begin to sway in the wind, and I was grateful for this, for the relief of the current as it swept past me, even though I knew it might increase the chances of sunburn, my SPF-40 lotion already washed away by the water, the tips of my fingers already pruned.

I was on my fifth or sixth windshield when the woman approached me.

"Excuse me?" she said, her smile blending into the glinting line of the windshield's sun glare. "Can you tell me something about this car? I'm looking to buy soon, and I really have no idea."

I turned to face her. Her makeup was smeared along her dull-lidded eyes; she fidgeted with the black string of a purse draped haphazardly over one shoulder. The car in question was a standard Taurus, one among a long line of them. There seemed to be no reason for singling this one out. There seemed to be no reason for singling *me* out. I thought of something my father would say during Bible study: how every now and then God presented a moment of perfect opportunity. It was our job as Christians to seize that moment and lead one of His lost souls to salvation.

The woman's dented, hail-beaten Camry idled behind her, the driver's-side door left open. I thought of saying, *Ma'am, you look lost.* I thought of saying, *Ma'am, there is no neutral.* I thought of how happy it would make my father if I was able to tell him I'd ministered to my first customer. But I couldn't do it. Her question had been so direct, so real, that to dodge it felt like a betrayal.

"There's nothing wrong with a good Taurus," I said. "Dependable. Fairly decent mileage. They hardly ever wear out on you if you take them in for tune-ups on time. But, you know, it's just a Taurus."

She placed her hand on my forearm and smiled again. "You're so kind," she said. "You didn't have to tell me the truth."

I wanted to fall against her chest and feel her arms wrap around my shoulders. I wanted to toss the paper towels and the Windex bottle on the asphalt, slide into her car, and disappear into the hills, then, whenever she wasn't looking, toss the condom package out of the cracked window.

"This is so weird," Chloe said. "Where did they get these creepy sound effects?"

We watched as Janet Leigh stepped into the shower, her pale calf tensing. We knew what would happen next, but we held our breath. Though she didn't need it, Chloe had applied extra foundation to her face, removing the shallow pockmarks where acne had once scarred her. She wore her hair down. We had both dressed for the occasion. I wore a black button-down and a light jacket that I had waited to remove until I was in the doorway. Chloe wore a dress I'd never seen before. If her mother thought there was anything strange about our outfits, she never said so.

We sat on the couch in her basement in front of the blue light of the television. Occasionally, Brandon would sneak down the stairs and hide behind the couch, jumping out to scare us.

"You're too old for that," Chloe said, after he had grabbed her arm just as the shower curtain parted. "Get a life."

"You're the one who needs to get a life," he said, tossing his head back in a remarkably accurate parody of his sister. "Watching scary movies on your big romantic date night."

Brandon was dressed in his Sunday-morning blazer. He wore a bright pink rose in his lapel, one he must have stolen from a neighbor's garden. He liked to dress up like his favorite video-game characters. When we asked who he was today, he said, "I'm James Bond from *GoldenEye*," and made a gun of his index finger and thumb. I was glad for his occasional interruptions, the way his sudden appearance caused Chloe to unconsciously scoot away from me.

Every movement on that couch was either a victory or a failure. Often both. I was on a different side of the war from one moment to the next.

Brandon removed a candy cigarette from his pocket and acted as though he were about to perch it delicately on the edge of his lips. Instead, he bit into it. "Don't forget you're rooming with me tonight," he said, making a stabbing motion at me with what remained of the cigarette. "*Psycho II*. Bates strikes again."

We watched the camera move in a gyre up from Leigh's gaping pupil, Hitchcock's shot held intentionally for one second too long, the fear excruciating in that second. Chloe scooted closer.

"It's still scary," she said. "Even with the stupid sound effects."

. . .

I FIRST LEARNED about sex when I was Brandon's age, on a stormless night when my father wasn't snoring and I could be certain he was awake. I felt the house relax and settle into its hidden joints, and so I could walk through the dark living room without fear, running my fingers across the cool glass of the living-room table, fingering the sharp plastic jonquils in their china vases. I sat in my father's leather recliner and switched on the television. Since the living room shared the same satellite connection as my father's bedroom—but not my mother's—I could see what he was seeing in those sleepless hours after he had already exhausted his prayer. I watched the snow-fizzled channels settle into hints of a bare thigh, an open mouth closing over something long and hard, bright red lipstick shining through static. I heard the woman's low moaning—so scripted, so different from my father's spiritual moaning. But the display didn't last for more than a minute or two, the amount of time I imagine it took for my father to feel the weight of his guilt. Still, I would tell my mother of his transgression the next day, knowing even then that by airing his secret I might better hide my own darker secret.

"I'm sure it was by mistake," she said, always the mediator. "Why would you spy on him like that?"

Then she forced a smile and said, "Let's make crème brûlée tonight. We'll get your grandmother's silver out and everything."

. . .

I HAD BEEN lying on a sleeping bag in the dark basement of Chloe's house for about an hour. I decided to sit up and listen for Brandon's steady breathing before I made my attempt up the stairs. I kept the condom package tucked into the elastic band of my pajama pants; the plastic scratched my skin, burning. I had no idea how I planned to do it. Sneak up to her room and announce my intentions? Stand in her doorway in the hopes that she made the first move?

"I'm *not* asleep, in case you're wondering," Brandon said. I heard him throw his sheets to the ground beside his bed. "Your movie kept me awake."

"Sorry," I said. "I thought it might be fun. Theft, murder, cars sinking into tar pits."

"You know?" he said, bare feet slapping the concrete floor as he came toward me. I made out the outline of his cowlicked hair, then his thin arms sticking out of his pajama top. "You're not like her other boyfriends. You're a lot nicer."

"Thanks, I guess."

He stood at the edge of my sleeping bag, his toes wiggling into the taffeta lining. "Can I ask you something?"

My eyes adjusting to the dark, I could see that his face was contorted, twin wrinkles running down the center of his forehead. I could hear footsteps coming from the spot on the ceiling directly below Chloe's bedroom floor.

"How do you get your character to level up to fifty?" He smiled an impish smile. Whatever he had planned to say was still unsaid.

He sat down on the edge of the sleeping bag. "Do you mind?" he said, holding the television remote close enough so I could see it. He switched on the television and crawled over to the PlayStation to press the power button. We settled into our gaming positions, hunching toward the screen. We were now standing in the chamber of a large Gothic castle lit by torchlight. Dark red carpet shot across the room from one door to the next, and guards in gold uniforms stood before every entryway.

Brandon's eyes glazed over. He licked his lips unconsciously. "This part is tricky. Those guards will come running if I move another inch."

"Check your inventory first."

The two of us riffled through potions and equipped stronger weapons. Brandon had obviously not kept track of his inventory. Using too many potions when he didn't have to. Tossing crossbows aside without first selling them in the market. Though I continued to think of Chloe in the bedroom above us, I tried to block her out. I had already crafted an alibi: How could I leave if her brother saw me?

After a few more hours of intense concentration, we both lay back on the sleeping bag.

Brandon propped himself up on his elbow, his palm cradling his chin. "You know what?" he said.

"I don't," I said.

"I think he's probably gay," he said, his voice suddenly breaking at the last syllable. He looked away. His breathing was shallow. It took several seconds for me to realize that he was talking about our avatar.

"Yeah?"

"Yeah, I really do," he said. "*So* much hair gel."

When he looked back at me, we both knew what we were.

We decided to keep playing until he reached the next level. By the time an orange sunrise worked its way through the blinds and shaped itself into slanted rectangles across the concrete, Chloe had already prepared breakfast by herself.

"Surprise," she said, standing on the bottom step, refusing to touch the basement floor. She didn't sound at all surprised. She hadn't bothered to change out of her cotton gown. I tried to shut out her pain, kept my eyes on the wadded sleeping bag at my feet. "Breakfast is served."

MY FATHER wrote a note to God, left it in my desk drawer, and told me never to open it. Never to touch it, but to leave it there. It was the formal promise he made to God after the car explosion that he had folded into a tiny square and tucked away behind the scores of mechanical pencils I would chew in frustration when I couldn't get my journal entries to come out right.

That last summer I spent at his dealership, old enough for my curiosity to outweigh my reverence, I read the note.

Heavenly Father,

*Thank you for saving me from literal hellfire. I have
made a promise to you that I intend to keep. From this
moment on, as for me and my house, we will serve You.
I promise to raise my son in the church. I promise to be a
God-fearing man and to bring others into Your divine
flock. Please, spare my son from all that I have suffered,
and from my mistakes. Spare him from the confusion
of the world. Out of the mouths of babes and sucklings
Thou hast perfected praise. Let him rest in the truth of
Your holy Word.*

Your Servant

"Why haven't you answered any of my calls?" Chloe asked.

A week of silence had passed since our failed night. I was
sitting on my bedroom floor, the PlayStation controller tucked
into the triangle between my crossed legs, the phone nestled
against my shoulder. "I don't know."

"How do you not know? You either answer or you don't."

After a minute of silence, she hung up.

Another week passed. Two. I opened the phone, thought
about pressing speed dial for Chloe's number, snapped it shut.

"I don't know," I said to the screen.

It wasn't relief I felt. More like fear: of the unknown, of myself. What kind of person was I becoming?

ANOTHER WEEK PASSED. My parents were concerned. They wanted to know why Chloe and I hadn't been hanging out. Her mother was calling, people from church were asking, and nobody could believe we would end things so suddenly without any real explanation. I pretended I was sick on Sundays so I wouldn't have to see her again at church.

Another week. When I could no longer fake being sick, I volunteered to work at the projector booth at the back of the sanctuary, far from the congregants' questioning gazes. Chloe was sometimes there, sometimes not, but we made sure we never ended up in the same part of the church together.

Another week. It was almost time to move to the small liberal arts college where I'd been accepted. My mother and I took occasional trips to Walmart to buy what I'd need for the dorm, coming home with heavy sacks full of plastic storage containers, with jumbo packages of T-shirts and socks and underwear. Then, late one night, my father received a phone call from Chloe's mother. She was hysterical. Brandon had been caught with another boy in his bed, a close friend. They had been experimenting. She couldn't think of anyone else to call. She wanted to know if my father could come talk some sense into the boys. I sat in our living room for most of the night, trying not to shake, waiting for him to return, my mother beside me on the couch.

"Why did you two really break up?" she asked. "You were so cute together." I couldn't answer. There were no words, no clear explanations that didn't involve some terrible admission. I knew my sudden silence was hurting my mother, was hurting all of us. But in only a few months I had already managed to ruin everything. I didn't want to say anything else that might make things worse.

My father came home around four o'clock in the morning, his eyes red, his hair a mess. He wouldn't tell us much of what happened, just stood in the kitchen shaking his head. The boys had made a mistake, he said. He had explained to Brandon and the other boy that continuing their sinful behavior would turn them against God, expel them from the Kingdom of Heaven. Brandon would grow out of it, my father said. His voice sounded unconvincing, and I could tell he was shaken by the visit, that perhaps he suspected something about me that he hadn't suspected before. I turned away, walked to my bedroom, and shut the door.

Another week. Video games every night. I hardly thought about the next phase of my life. I hardly thought about anything other than what I would need to equip for my avatar's journey through the wilderness. In the few moments when I wasn't playing a game, I tried to ignore the fact that not talking to Chloe also meant that I would have to stop talking to

Brandon. That the only person who seemed to know who I really was would never again be part of my life. That whatever either of us decided to do about our *urges*, we would be alone.

A month before I was to go to college, I finally put down the PlayStation controller. I walked into the living room, where my parents were sitting on opposite ends of the couch. I invited them to follow me to the bathroom to view the corpse of my gaming life.

"I want you to see something," I said. I hardly knew what I was doing. I wanted to tell them everything: about why I broke up with Chloe, about how I was just like Brandon. I wanted to tell them, but I didn't have the right words. I wanted to let them know that something was wrong, that I had been trying to ignore a part of me but that I wasn't going to ignore it any longer. I was going to fix it.

In the center of the bathtub sat my PlayStation, its two controllers curled up beside it like sleeping cats. My parents stood in the doorway, wearing what-is-this-all-about looks on their faces. My father ran a hand through his thick black hair. My mother crossed her arms over her chest and sighed.

I slid back the clear plastic shower curtain and turned the knob for the shower. My parents and I watched the water rush over the console and swirl into an oval before disappearing with a hollow gurgle down the drain. I imagined the water trickling through the motherboard, following tributaries formed by the microchips. I kept the water running for a few extra seconds than needed until I heard my parents shift uncomfortably behind me. I slid the curtain back in place.

"I'm done with games," I said.

Whatever I would face after this moment, I would face it directly.

WEDNESDAY, JUNE 9, 2004

It was seven o'clock in the morning, but the air-conditioning was already at full blast in the Hampton Inn lounge. According to my schedule, I had two hours to shower, dress, eat, and travel to the facility, but my mother and I were drawing out the minutes, dragging our forks lazily through the scattered mess of cold eggs on our plates, my hair dripping dry, the varnished wood of the table machine-pressed, its edges sharp against my forearms. The world that morning seemed harder, as if overnight someone had removed a thin translucent film from the atmosphere, a soft focus I had taken for granted when my mother and I used to come to Memphis for weekends of shopping and movie binging, the city alive and glowing then, pulsing beneath our shoes. Two full days at Love in Action, and the city had already lost its shine, the back-and-forth trips between the Hampton Inn & Suites and the facility revealing only a gray stretch of interstate, its traffic beaming hot in the sunlight, each of its oversize suburban houses yawning with their water-timed green tongues.

I had once heard someone call the city a trash dump, and I'd been offended at the time, but now I could see how they were right. It was the place where things came and went, home of the FedEx headquarters, the city with the most available overnight flights to other cities in the country, steel barges on the Mississippi floating right through the center of it—but the things that gathered and collected here, the things that stayed and took root, these were the things that gave the city its sense of abandonment. If you stayed long enough, you could see how it was perpetually reaching into its shallow past, hanging pictures of Elvis in its many diners, taping signed autographs to its walls, its many sex shops promising thrills that had once electrified the streets amid the buzz of jazz and blues.

"We'd better get going," my mother said, though she made no indication that she wished to move, her small hands still flush against the table.

I unrolled my sleeves, the air-conditioning already freezing, my wet hair an icy helmet. Summers in this city meant freezing and sweltering temperatures, sudden changes of atmosphere that shocked the system, sent goose bumps rippling across the skin.

"Okay," I said, not moving. We'd be late if we didn't leave soon. Though I'd intentionally left my watch in the room, hoping to lose track of time in the facility, I could see from the plastic clock above hotel reception that it was twenty to nine.

An odd mix of families and business types poured out of the elevator opposite our table: navy blue and black suits and tight pencil skirts, pajamas and hoodies and unsocked feet, a light slapping against the tile as children circled their groggy-eyed parents. It was strange to think of these people going about their daily routines, drinking their morning coffee, staring into the face of a day that must have seemed to them much like any other. CNN droned on in the corner of the room, a streaming canopy of monotonous words spreading across the dining area, seeming to connect the morning to all the ones before it, the syllables almost indistinguishable amid the clatter of plates and silverware—"any effort by Congress to regulate the interrogation of unlawful combatants would violate the Constitution's sole vesting of the commander-in-chief authority in the president"—people looking up from their tables every few seconds to anchor their gazes to the screen.

I felt lost in all of this, adrift, the daily patterns of life having come unstitched in only a matter of days, and so it seemed absurd to me, even at the time, that the "Guantánamo" written across the bottom of the screen even existed, all that senseless torture going on somewhere overseas while glittery-eyed newscasters debated its constitutionality. I felt crazy. *Wasn't it painfully obvious that we shouldn't be torturing people?* And yet, at the same time, I thought I could easily be wrong. Hadn't I been wrong before? Wasn't this questioning, liberal attitude what brought me to LIA in the first place? If I had managed to stay secure in the Lord's Word, unquestioning, I might have stayed with Chloe, well on my way to a normal life by now.

But I had allowed secular influences to shape me. The day before, one of the staff counselors, Danny Cosby, had asked us to take a long, hard look at our lives and draw a timeline that demonstrated our sinful progression into homosexuality, and I had realized, much to my horror, that most of my same-sex attractions had developed right alongside my love of literature. *Sideways Stories from Wayside School*: first gay crush; *To Kill a Mockingbird*: first gay porn search; *The Picture of Dorian Gray*: first gay kiss. *It's no wonder*, I'd thought. *No wonder they took away my Moleskine.*

Reading secular literature was discouraged at LIA—patients could "only read materials approved of by staff," our handbooks said, which usually amounted to only fundamentalist Christian authors—but even going a few days without reading had sent me into a nightly depression that made it difficult to sleep. During my high school years, I'd spent so much time and energy guarding myself against enjoying books too much, afraid that a compelling narrative might turn me into a heretic, send me rushing off on one of the sinful life paths I'd enjoyed seeing my favorite characters follow. My year of college had been so freeing, and reading so widely encouraged, that I'd almost forgotten what it felt like to suspect a book of literal demon possession, like I'd believed when first reading *A Clockwork Orange*. Burgess's electric language ran through my body so quickly my skin felt aflame, charged with what I could only then describe as demonic power. I wondered if I would ever get the chance to read so freely again or if I would have to stay here at LIA for as many years as the counselors had been here, learning to live with the side effects of my sin, keeping the rest of the world at bay.

Lord, make me pure, I prayed, looking through my water glass at the blurry newscasters, "Guantánamo" morphing to something like "Gargantuan." I wanted to join all these other people in their obliviousness, in their laughter, in the casual flip of the newspaper, digest the morning the way I had so many other mornings. But the LIA lingo had already taken up permanent residence in my thoughts, and I had no room for the habitual comforts that usually quieted my mind and made the world seem like a normal place. The night before, lying on the foldout bed in our suite, my mind buzzing with the LIA handbook's rules, I'd wanted more than anything to take up the plastic Nintendo 64 controller attached to the hotel television and play a few levels of *Mario* or whatever—anything to stop my mind from its infinite blame loop—but this was forbidden as well.

THE MORAL INVENTORY (MI), another piece of AA borrowed by LIA, took the place of my regular reading and writing schedule. Every night I was to focus exclusively on my sinfulness. Every night I was to find an example of sinful behavior in my past, write about it in great detail, share it with the therapy group, and put faith in God that I could be absolved of it.

MIs helped us recognize our FIs, the development of which we could now trace clearly in the *As* and *Pos* and *$s* and *Ms* of the genograms that were designed to chart our families' sinful histories. Though I'd barely revealed any of what I'd learned each day at LIA to my mother, the small amount of terminology I'd let slip through was already too much for her to keep track of—so much so that, speeding down the interstate as I tried to fill her in, she almost missed our exit, another set of numbers and symbols crowding her periphery, demanding her attention.

"Which step is the MI in?" she said, turning sharply toward the exit. A mall on our left, a shopping center on our right, morning light sifting through the leaves of an occasional tree.

"They use MIs for all twelve steps," I said, the handbook open in my lap, my homework on top. I was rereading the page quickly, scanning to see if I'd written anything too embarrassing to share in front of our group—but, really, all of it was embarrassing. The whole purpose of the exercise was to realize how shameful these memories were and refashion them to fit God's purpose. My therapy group would provide the necessary feedback to help the transition go smoothly. The whole thing reminded me of a poetry workshop I'd taken in my second semester of college: how I'd felt as I listened to my peers' contradictory opinions, that the whole point of writing seemed to be to fashion a product that offended no one, supported nothing but the officially accepted dogma.

Perhaps this was the entry fee for the Kingdom of Heaven:

cleanse yourself of all idiosyncrasies, sharp opinions, creeds—put no false gods before Him—become an easily moldable shell, a vessel for God. The Bible speaks plainly of what is required. Concerning God's commandments, The Book of Proverbs says, *Bind them about thy neck, write them upon the table of thine heart.* If I could have done it myself, I would have already done it: pried open my ribs and etched the Word onto my heart's beating chambers. But it seemed my ex-gay counselors were the only ones with enough skill and experience to wield the scalpel.

Perhaps part of the reason I couldn't sleep well at night was that I'd never, before this moment, truly emptied myself of all sin. Without my Moleskine or my books or video games, stripped down and without distraction, I was forced to confront the ugliest, most shameful parts of myself. In order to be filled with the Holy Spirit, I had to be emptied of the human one. Sitting in the car with my shameful past open in my lap, I had no idea if this was even possible.

"How often do you have to do an MI?" my mother said, hands gripped at ten and two on the wheel. I'd never seen them stray from this, not in all her years of driving. Trees passing at perfect intervals; high-line wires dipping and rising; signs along the side of the road all at the same regulation height and width; my mother's hands never moving.

"Every night." Despite how pointless I suspected many of LIA's activities were, I took pride in knowing them so well after just one day, in being the first of the newbies to memorize all the steps. It was a role that felt comfortable, being the good student. It must have been comforting for my mother as well, seeing me act the way I'd often acted in high school.

"What happens if you don't have anything else to write about?" The whine of her lotion-scented skin against leather. She wanted to know what I'd written but was too afraid to ask. "What happens if you run out of material for your MI?"

MIs were designed to bring about personal awareness of an instance when you had sinned against God. In our group's case, an MI always explored a moment of sexual impropriety, either a physical act or a temptation. What my mother didn't yet know about being gay in the South was that you never ran out of material, that being secretly gay your whole life, averting your eyes every time you saw a handsome man, praying on your knees every time a sexual thought entered your mind or every time you'd acted even remotely feminine—this gave you an embarrassment of sins for which you constantly felt the need to apologize, repent, beg forgiveness. I could never count the number of times I'd sinned against God. If I wanted, I could fill out a new MI every night for the rest of my life.

"WE ARE UNDER the control of a sovereign God who reigns over all aspects of our lives," Smid said, quoting the Moral Inventory Flow Chart in our handbooks, a page that featured two black-lined text boxes, one with the word "God" centered in it, the other below it with the words "World," "Flesh," and "Satan" equally spaced at full justification. The idea was that, as Christians, we were all under God's control, but as human beings, we were also subject to Satan's temptations, a fact that Smid pointed out a few seconds later: "We are affected by a sinful world system, our sinful flesh, and the manipulative attacks of Satan."

Smid continued reading the worksheet aloud. The MI was based on the following set of additional assumptions, ones I needed to swallow whole if I was to be cured.

1. We are constantly faced with various challenges in life.
2. We experience the consequences of our decisions as a result of the challenge.
3. We receive strength from God both to desire changes in our lives and to take action based on our goals to achieve these changes.
4. We can find a blessing and see God's goodness based on scripture for each aspect of our lives.

I was sitting on the far right of our group's semicircle, the kitchen at my back. I could hear someone washing dishes behind me, a steady stream of white noise followed by the occasional clatter of silverware, metal hitting metal, the rustling of a trash bag. J sat beside me. Every few minutes he would start chewing his pencil, white with a blue logo of his home church's name.

Something Something Something Calvary Baptist. Then he would stop midchomp through the church logo and hold the half-chewed pencil tightly in his grip, this wedge of cratered moon in his hand: a piece of the remote, floating world he'd broken off from all those late nights he told me about, hours spent in isolation and low gravity reading the clobber passages again and again. His hair, slicked back with wax, fell to one side of his face and covered one of his eyes. I was grateful for the shield between us. I kept my MI folded beneath my right thigh, dreading the moment when I would have to stand in front of this group and share my shame. I was especially worried about sharing this story with J, who seemed to have developed a great deal of respect for me in only a few days.

"I think you really get it," he'd said during one of our patio breaks, scraping his shoes against the blinding concrete. "You get how difficult it is here. You can't just believe in change. You have to actually work through it, you know? If you want the treatment to last, you really have to allow for the doubt."

"It feels like that's all I've been doing," I said. "Doubting."

"So many people, when they first get here, they don't really let themselves doubt," J said, his voice lowering to a whisper. Most of the other group members were still inside, so it felt safe to talk. Only T remained, hunched on a bench with a package of unopened peanut-butter crackers in his hands, the sleeves of his black cardigans still rolled down despite the heat of the afternoon. It didn't look like he was going to open the package anytime soon, much less engage in conversation. "Doubt isn't all that encouraged here. People here are too desperate for an answer. But you seem to be all about it."

I liked being analyzed this way, like a character in a book, like someone with a rich inner life. The only therapy I'd experienced was the ex-gay therapy I'd had during the few intro sessions I'd taken before coming to LIA, and most of those sessions had been conducted under the assumption that the therapist already knew what was wrong with me, a process that felt like the opposite of how I felt when reading a book. Regular therapy was discouraged in our family's church, our pastor believing that prayer was all you needed to dispel any mental and moral confusion. But J seemed to be a natural at this. He seemed to believe that people could also be understood by their complexities. I wanted to ask him what books he'd read to see if we shared the same loves, but it was against the rules to talk about non-LIA literature.

"I guess you're right about doubt," I said. "I don't want to take the wrong step. I've already taken too many bad ones."

"No," he said. "You don't look like you've ever done anything too bad. There's a look people have here when they've done something they don't want to share." Though we knew there were former pedophiles in therapy, no one talked openly about it, and it was only vaguely hinted at by our most dull-lidded members.

"I don't want to share any of this," I said. "It feels too personal." It wasn't that I was afraid of my role in the production of sin. It was that I was ashamed of the lack of experience I actually had, or at least the lack of agency I'd had in my experience. How could I let J know, in front of everyone, that my first and only time had already been taken from me against my will?

"You've got to share with people," he said, walking back to the sliding glass door and pulling it open, a gust of cold air hitting my arms. "It's the first step in the right direction."

"But what if none of this works? What if it only makes me more confused?"

"Good question," J said, turning for a second before heading back, as always, to our semicircle around Smid.

IT SEEMED CONFUSION was a key feature of Step One. Out of our confusion we would come to see that we were truly "out of control," that we needed to rely on God's and the counselors' authority. The day before, Smid had asked me to think back to a time when my father and I had played sports. Had I felt uncomfortable? Had I received enough masculine-affirming touch from my father? Had I sought out love from him that he didn't want to give? After only a few questions, I no longer remembered what I felt. It was true that I was never any good at sports. It was true that I never liked to toss the ball with my father in the front yard. Yes, I might have caught my father's initial pitch, but I'd eventually thrown down the baseball glove and let the ball roll out of its leather grip. But did that mean I hadn't enjoyed the way the grass felt beneath my toes? Did that mean I hadn't loved the feel of the hot sun on my face—hadn't felt my father's voice as a warm vibration passing through my chest? I could no longer be sure.

The Bible often spoke of sacrifice, of how the world wouldn't understand you once you took up the cross and followed Jesus. "You'll seem boring to a lot of people," my father had said on the day of my baptism. "They won't understand the deep joy in your heart. To them you'll seem crazy." But did that mean my father and I would no longer understand *each other*? Jesus spoke in Matthew: *For I am come to set a man at variance against his father.* And though I'd read those words dozens of times, I didn't know if I wanted to give up on experiencing in real life the beauty of the messy, complicated relationships I'd read about in my literature classes. *Lord*, I prayed in those first few days, *help me to know the difference between beauty and evil.*

LIA was clear on the difference. On almost every page of our 274-page handbooks lay some iteration of the following: In order to be pure, we had to become a tool, something God could use for the greater good. That meant there was no room for beauty as we had once known it. Any habitual behaviors that made us more than tools were considered addictions that developed out of the harmful messages we'd received in our childhoods. All of this was laid out clearly in the Addiction Workbook.

Addictions stem from a severely distorted belief system. Our minds were fallen from birth, naturally leaning away from truth. This problem is common to everyone. However, when we received confusing or hostile messages as kids, we became vulnerable to developing addictive patterns.

The Addiction Workbook went on to say that everything in our sinful, sexually deviant lives had been co-opted by the world, by Satan. In a section titled "You Are a Product of the World (and the Devil!)," we were told that "Satan is the god of this world," that he has free dominion over everything not directly issued from the church or the Bible, that "it is actually this world that is out of order and upside down, not God," and that we needed to be willing to test what we think and believe. But it wasn't enough simply to question our beliefs. We had to be willing to undergo extreme changes, leave people behind who were harmful to our development, who reminded us of the past. We had to be willing to give up any ideas about who we were before we came to LIA: "Also remember that now, as a Christian, you are NOT YOUR OWN, but you have been bought for a price (1 Cor. 6:19), you must see Jesus as Master." We had to give over our memories, our desires, our ideas of freedom, to Jesus our Master. We had to become His servants.

"IT'S UP TO US to ask God for help," Smid said. "It's up to us to beg for forgiveness."

When I looked at Smid from this angle, I couldn't help but notice his striking resemblance to Jeff Goldblum, the actor I'd most often seen in repeated viewings of *Jurassic Park*: narrow nose, wide smile, sharp eyes accentuated by sharp glasses. But when Smid cocked his head at another angle, his face grew flat, lost its Goldbluminess. One second it was there, and the next it wasn't. I wondered if Smid had practiced this effect, if he'd figured out the proportions: one Jeff Goldblum for every five boy-next-door, good-ol'-boy Smids.

I tried to keep from smiling. It was absurd, really, how much Smid could look like Goldblum. Afraid I'd start crying otherwise, I relaxed my face into an idiot smile. I wondered if J saw Smid's Goldbluminess, too, if his parents had even allowed him to watch *Jurassic Park* as a kid.

J seemed like someone who'd been homeschooled, his concentration too intense to maintain an active social life, and most of the homeschooled kids in the Bible Belt were heavily policed by their fundamentalist parents. Still, I wondered how similar our childhoods had been, though I never asked. No one in the program was allowed to talk much about the past for fear that it would unearth some sinful pleasure we'd once experienced. This was how I imagined it would feel to meet someone you once knew on earth in Heaven, all the things that had been so familiar completely absent, with only the essence, or the aura, remaining. *Death shall be no more*, the Bible says, *for the former things have passed away*. But J and I were still far from Heaven, the white-walled facility only a simulation, and I could still feel the weight of my sin in the bottom of my gut.

"We can find a blessing and see God's goodness based on scripture for each aspect of our lives," Smid repeated. He said it so quickly, his words came out as a string I had to unravel: "We-can-find-a-blessing-and-see-God's-goodness-based-on-scripture-for-each-aspect-of-our-lives." It reminded me of the prayers my parents taught me to recite every night as a kid, the words automatic, coming out in a sudden, desperate rush to make contact with an impatient God:

> Now I lay me down to sleep
> I pray the Lord my soul to keep
> If I should die before I wake
> I-pray-the-Lord-my-soul-to-take. Amen.

I no longer knew what time it was. I was staring at the strip of pale skin on my wrist where my watch had been. Smid's words continued running together, and before long the sunlight was slanting across the room, cutting the carpet into polygons. Smid circled our group, stepping around the light. I thought of a game my friends and I used to play after church as kids: one wrong step and you were dead, liquefied by lava; one wrong step and you had to sit it out on the sidelines and watch the other kids play. I angled my foot into the light, the plastic tips of my shoelaces glinting. If only it were that easy.

The handbook felt heavy against my knees, the MI ready to burn a hole through my thigh. Would I eventually learn, like many of the veteran members of our group had, to speak casually about a subject that terrified me? Perhaps it would be a change for the better, getting it all out in the open. I'd already read the sample MI included in our handbooks, and I'd been shocked at the language surrounding the writer's instance of sexual sin, at the near-constant therapeutic language that seemed to blanket each statement, render it almost unidentifiable in the physical world, all of the speaker's FIs removed until there seemed to be nothing left but pure godly repentance, a platonic form of recovery, all identifying features already erased.

It reminded me of how I'd felt after I finished my genogram the day before. Standing up from the poster, I'd thought, *There they are*, as though my family had gathered together in front of me for the singular purpose of revealing my place at LIA. Oddly, it was the first time I'd felt truly comfortable with all my relatives in one room. They were innocuous, staring up at me from their little patch of Berber carpet, surrounded by their labeled sins, stripped of their judgment. And though the grammar needed tidying up, the sample Moral Inventory I'd read promised the same: a life with God; a restoration to our purest presinful selves; the "spiritual awakening" Step Twelve promised we would all eventually experience if we stayed in the program long enough, the world growing dimmer and dimmer until it disappeared from sight. The sample MI felt like a dispatch from another world.

I sought an encounter and used and manipulated another person to medicate me from the pain of my life. I used fantasy as an escape, but when the fantasy was over, reality was even more painful. I believed that he would offer me hope and freedom, but all I found was more guilt, condemnation, and hopelessness. I lied to my friends and family about my struggle and attempted to hide from it. My struggle only intensified—my life became more out of control. I believed many lies that I was worthless, hopeless, and had no future. I rejected the people who could help me and embraced the things that were hurting me.

"Let's start here," Smid said, pointing to S, who was sitting on the far left of our group. "But first, let's remember a few ground rules." As he recited the rules, he ticked each one off with a finger until he opened his white palm to us: "Nothing illicit. Be respectful. No glamorizing, rationalizing, or mini-mizing what happened or how you felt."

The kitchen behind me was quiet now, the main room filled with the sound of hushed breathing, the sunlight so bright against the carpet that it seemed to give off an audible buzz.

S stood and made her way to the center of our circle. Today she wore a long denim skirt and no makeup, her hair pulled back in a frizzy ponytail. She looked like one of those Menno-nite women who sold brownies and various baked goods in small-town thrift shops all over Arkansas.

"It started with a kiss," she began. "I'm not going to go into the details, but that's how it started. I thought it was innocent, but I was wrong."

I looked at J out of the corner of my eye. He sent me half a smirk. *Get ready*, it seemed to say.

"I did . . . horrible things," she continued, reading from a wrinkled sheet of wide-ruled paper that trembled in her hands. "I felt so much shame. I knew God was disappointed—more than disappointed. I turned my back on God. I entered into a sinful relationship with another girl. It was disgusting. Now that I look back on it, I realize how disgusting it was." S looked down at her skirt. She closed her eyes.

"Don't be afraid," Smid said.

"That was why—that was why—" She kept her eyes closed. "I think that was why I ended up with the dog." The word "dog" sounded like a curse, something that had been boiling up inside of her for years.

She was in the Consequences section of her MI, well on her way to the Changes section—"I want to change myself. I'm tired of feeling empty inside"—the whole MI outline designed to lead her to redemption. The rest of her account was rather straightforward, with a string of stock phrases supplied for each section. Her voice, when reciting the phrases, swelled with a kind of pride that hadn't been there only a few minutes before.

Strengths: "I'm learning to rely more on God, to trust in His grace."

Goals: "I want to read the Bible more every day, really listen to God's voice."

Blessing: "I see now how much love I've been given, how many blessings God has bestowed upon my life. I see how truly ungrateful I'd been in the past."

Step Application: "I think this experience, and the memory of it, applies most directly to Step Three. I've made a decision to turn my life over to the care of Jesus Christ."

Scripture: "I took my scripture from John, Galatians, and Psalms. We can never trust ourselves. Every bit of our trust has to be turned over to God."

Three, four, five more people had gone, their stories fusing together into one long string of repentance. The room was freezing now. I rolled down my sleeves again, buttoned the cuffs.

"One of our new members is going to share for the first time," Smid said, walking toward me. I could feel J's eyes on me. I could tell he was trying to encourage me, but it only made me feel worse. I pulled out my MI from under my thighs, my hands shaking.

"Would you mind going?" Smid asked me. His voice was soft, polite, encouraging.

I stood up and made my way to the center of the group. I coughed. I wanted to tell everyone how cold I was, how I wasn't shaking from fear but only shivering.

"Take your time," Smid said.

I could make a run for it, I thought. I could push open the sliding glass door and run down the streets until I made my way to some public park where I could hide.

A clanging of metal on metal from the kitchen. I coughed again, and added my voice to the chorus.

OTHER BOYS

I stood in the dorm entrance with a cardboard box hugged to my chest, the white concrete blocks of the stairwell covered with a skein of cobweb and dust, breathing in the air of not-home: not flower-scented linen, not peroxided kitchen counters, not the pages of the family Bible crackling open to emit their decades-old scent of soft handling. Instead I got a whiff of partial decay, of apathy, and what I would soon recognize as the smell of other boys.

"Shit," I said, the box almost slipping from my hands. It felt good to say the curse aloud. It felt good to cut the quieting *shhhh* with a sharp consonant. Here in this small liberal-arts mecca with a sly Presbyterian bent that refused to take itself too seriously, there was no one to stop me from cursing. There was Thursday afternoon chapel to attend, if I wanted; if I didn't, no worries. I would belong to the majority of students if

I ignored the noncommittal bell chiming softly over the campus. I imagined hearing it as I walked back from class, smiling at the memory of so many mandatory church services receding behind the carpe diem mentality of certain humanities courses.

"Shit," I said again. My voice became an echo. A bathroom door opened in the adjacent hallway, and a slack-jawed, black-haired boy stuck his head out, gave me a bored once-over, and let the door slam shut. Here, no one seemed to care what I said or did.

I HAD WATCHED my parents drive away on the winding asphalt road down the slope of a pine-forested hill just thirty minutes earlier. I stood with my white sneakers on the edge of the curb, a first-day freshman, holding one last box full of empty picture frames that I would refuse to fill with photos of my family. A FAMILY IS WORTH A THOUSAND WORDS, the topmost frame read. A flash of sunlight from the rear window, and my parents were gone.

On the ride here, catching sight of the campus bell tower looming at the top of the hill, my father had whistled loudly from the driver's seat. I knew at once what he meant: He was impressed by any building that demanded ascendancy, anything that reached for an impossible elevation. Our home church had just installed a new white steeple, one with a narrow porthole window that captured the sun at sunrise and sunset before releasing it again to the sky. My father was making plans to build a similar church steeple, or perhaps a slightly bigger one, in anticipation of the day he would become an ordained pastor of his own successful church. Earlier that month, after years of private deliberation with God, he had decided to publicly surrender to the Lord's call to become a pastor. Now he was constantly talking about the kind of church he wanted to build, about the group of like-minded, God-fearing people he would one day call his flock.

"Shit," I repeated. The picture frames clacked together, threatening to spill. Only a few minutes earlier I had carried boxes two and three times this size just to prove that I was stronger than my father, had watched the moth-shaped sweat spread across the back of his cotton T-shirt as I followed him up these stairs, feeling sweat free and superior, my mother directing our ascent, begging us to watch our steps *for God's sake.*

Now that he was gone, my fingers relaxed their grip. One of the frames fell and clattered down the steps, a hairline crack forming a Z in the glass.

"Need help?" a voice asked. It came from somewhere below and leaped up to me. This was how I would later remember it: leaping. No, *pouncing,* I would think. *Tackling.*

I shifted the box to my right hip. Through the black metal railings below I could see two arms hugging a dense sphere of laundry, all whites, already wrinkled. The arms grew more defined as they drew closer: two thin bands remarkably similar to my own.

I had lost something like fifty pounds over the summer. It had come about gradually at first, just before cutting off all contact with Chloe, then so suddenly that several of my friends hadn't been able to recognize me whenever they saw me running along our town's potholed streets. I had refused to eat more than five hundred calories a day, punished myself further by running for at least two hours every afternoon. Partly a penance for my failure with Chloe, partly a defiance of what I felt people expected of my future in the church, my weight loss took an angry, masochistic turn that verged on anorexic and scared my parents into asking me what was wrong every other day, though they seemed to connect this behavior to my decision to become more active and renounce the sedentary gamer life I'd been living. I barely came out on the other side intact, but I was proud of what was left: this *other*, excavated me; the anonymity of the handsome and lean. I had what a Psychology 101 class would later inform me was the secret to human beauty: truly average proportions.

"Here, let me," the voice said, hand reaching for the box, a pair of white boxer briefs falling from his arms onto the mottled tile, our eyes meeting, and recognizing that we were both members of the Club of Truly Average Proportions.

"Are you sure?" I said.

"The Lord will provide," he said. One more shared membership, then. I wondered what others we had in common.

He had the empty zippered-up smile of a youth pastor. I will call him David. He was a freshman here, too.

"I saw you earlier," David said. He said he'd seen me on his way back from the laundry room and had waited until my parents left, that they looked nice but typically boring. As we talked, we found we had a lot in common. We spoke in the usual banalities: We both preferred waking up early in the morning, were both interested in running, both considered ourselves to be heavy studiers.

He took my box in one hand and piled his laundry on top with the other, taking the steps to the second floor—left, together, right, together; the careful baby steps of a formal procession—the backs of his brown loafers luminous in the dusty light, the heels of his unsocked feet peeking out with each step to lick the air in pale flashes.

The clashing of a big brass band echoed up the stairwell from the dorm entrance. Our college's marching band was making its rounds across the quad, marching in formation in full-dress uniform, instruments glinting in the sunlight.

"Do you like it here?" he said.

"It seems loud," I said. "But nice."

"Admin said they're always practicing."

"How can people concentrate on homework here?" I looked back at his boxers lying on the steps, wondering if he wanted me to pick them up for him.

"What? You don't like music?"

"Maybe I'm in the wrong place," I joked.

I looked away from the boxers. I don't know if he ever returned for them or if they were simply a dispensable prop. They would wait like a banana peel for the next unsuspecting freshman, part of a slapstick number for a very different play, a very different actor.

"One more question," David said, turning toward my half-open dorm room, one half of his smile still aimed in my direction. "To get to know each other better . . ."

I wanted to turn back and pick up the boxers, try them on, feel what it might be like to be near this other truly average body.

"Which superpower would you rather have?" he asked. "Flight or invisibility?"

The band marched off down the quad. A heavy gust of wind pulled open the door and slammed it shut.

Invisibility, I thought immediately. Free to do whatever I wanted, go wherever I wanted, undetected. I had felt anything but invisible in the weeks before coming here. After I'd cut things off with Chloe, I'd tried to continue ignoring her in church, but it seemed as though everyone there knew that I was the villain in the story, that I must have done something terrible to lose such a great girl. Chloe sliding her eyes at me from across the church sanctuary, clutching some other boy's thick football-throwing arm, drawing other congregants' glares in my direction, so that even my spoken, automatic prayers had induced a stutter. *Dear Lord*, I had begun, the hushed breathing around me growing louder, more expectant, *give me the strength to endure. Whatever comes*—the men at the dealership Bible study waiting for me to recover from my Job failure, their eyes searching mine for the answer to human suffering. No one watching or listening: It sounded like a dream to me.

"Invisibility," I said.

"That says a lot about you," he said. "That says you're an introvert." He kicked open the unlatched door to my room. "You're going to have some great times in here."

Later, after everything had happened, I would want so badly to change my answer. I would repeat this changed answer to myself again and again, wanting to forget everything that came after the moment I entered the dorm room with him.

Flight, I would think. *God, flight.*

"SINCE YOUR ROOMMATE isn't here yet, you get to choose. Which bunk do you want?" David said.

The room was small, cramped, and we stood in the entrance, facing our reflections in a black-splotched, wall-mounted mirror. I was the introvert to his extrovert. He smiled; I scowled. Where his hair seemed to reflect the gold light from the window, my dark brown hair seemed to absorb it, to steal it from every corner of the room.

"So?" he said. "Which one?"

"I don't know," I said.

The alder trees just outside the window shook their dried catkins. One of the flowers bounced with a thud against the glass and fell below the sill.

"Well," he said. "My arms are tired." He slid his hands around the front of the box for a better grip.

I walked to the front of the wooden bunks. The rest of my boxes lay in stacks behind me. I'd never thought about which bunk to take. At home, I'd always taken the bottom, left the top one open for my mother.

"Come on," David said. "I'm getting tired."

"I'll take the top," I said, thinking it would be easier to stay out of my roommate's way.

He set the box of picture frames on the empty mattress. The box bounced back, propelled by a loose spring that intended to cause me a great deal of pain.

"Where's your family now?" he said. "Already gone?"

"They left," I said. "They're gone." At the time, it felt good to say it.

I SPENT more than thirty minutes in the dorm bathroom that first night, afraid to change into my boxers, afraid the stretch marks where I'd lost all the weight would show as I climbed to the top bunk. I examined myself in the mirror, turning to view my legs from each angle. I remembered how Chloe would sometimes squeeze the sides of my thighs and lean in for a kiss, with me afraid that her hand would move farther up as our lips locked. I wondered if all of my running had finally managed to burn away that patch of contaminated skin.

The slack-jawed boy who'd eyed me that morning came in

through the bathroom door and entered a nearby stall. He released a heavy stream of piss that obliterated the memory of Chloe. Once I finally decided the marks wouldn't show, I made my way back to the room and climbed each wooden rung as quickly as possible, feeling my new roommate Sam's eyes move over my calves.

"Nice legs," he said. "You run every day, right?"

"Yeah," I said. "Pretty much."

Sam and I hadn't talked much when he'd first arrived earlier that evening. A few pleasantries, but nothing more. Like David, Sam was an early riser, a runner. He was studious. But, I realized, he wasn't nearly as charming.

I lay on the mattress with its freshly laundered sheets and hugged a pillow to my chest. I was clean, pure, in these cotton sheets with this new body. I thought of my father working in our family's old cotton gin, directing the cotton through its cleaning process, pressing this whiteness into bales that would then be used to make these sheets. To be the end product of all this labor felt comforting.

Sam stood and slapped off the light switch. For a few seconds I could still see the flash of his pale shirtless back hovering in the dark.

WE SETTLED INTO SILENCE. Each rustle of his bed sheets, each deeply drawn breath, each cough or loud swallow had the power to jolt me awake. I turned on my side. I still found it hard to sleep without television, without the steady sound of pre-recorded lives talking me out of my fear of Hell.

After we lay in silence for half an hour, Sam switched on the television. The room retraced its edges in blue, rediscovered its pockets of shadow.

"Does this bother you?" he said.

"Not at all," I said. "But there's nothing on right now."

"How do you know?"

"I'm kind of an insomniac. But I'm so hyped up right now that even TV won't help. I think I'll go for a walk."

I left the room and walked around the quad a few times. I was counting the number of cracks in the sidewalk when I ran into David, who also seemed to be an insomniac.

He walked toward me. "I can't sleep," he said.

"You're in a new place," I said. "Your body needs time to adjust."

I'd recently read an article that linked evolutionary traits to sleeping patterns. It was exhilarating to read something so overtly in favor of the science of evolution, so casually anti-Creationist, so different from what my church and school had taught me. "What kind of idiot do you have to be to think you came from a monkey?" our pastor would often say, a statement that earned him loud amens from the congregation. In my public high school, our biology teacher had skipped over the chapter about evolution, telling us we could read it at home if we liked. On the day we were supposed to be studying Darwin, she invited the cheerleaders in our class to perform their pep-rally routine.

For their finishing move, the girls were supposed to unfurl a Confederate flag and march in a circle so that all sides of the auditorium might see it. This was the part where our mascot, Rebel, a large-headed man dressed up like a plantation owner, was supposed to run out onto the football field and dance around the girls. At the time, my teacher's omission seemed relatively normal, though as I began to read more about biology on the Internet, I realized that my teacher had been ignoring what 97 percent of the scientific community now believed. Feeling both damned and excited, I had read several more articles on the subject. Though I still believed in God, I was uncomfortable with the idea of a God who would choose to ignore science.

"There's an evolutionary advantage to waking at almost any sound," I said.

"You believe that stuff?"

"I don't know," I said. "It's interesting to think that we might be the children of survivors. That maybe we're here because our great-great-great-grandparents were somehow stronger."

"I don't like that word," he said. He brushed something off his arm, as if he were peeling back my words from his skin.

"Grandparents?"

"No. Evolution."

"I didn't say 'evolution.' I said 'evolutionary.'"

"C'mon," he said. "Let's see what's on TV."

We walked back to his dorm and headed to the lounge, where we could watch TV. We settled into armchairs that lined one wall of the room, and David began flipping through the channels, landing on a popular infomercial about a revolutionary rotisserie grill. An orange-tanned man began to slide four raw chickens onto a rack. He wore a long green apron. Each time he stabbed another chicken onto the rack, his lips expanded into a wide smile. *I'll just walk over here*, he said, the camera zooming in on an oil-basted thigh. *I'll put these chickens in this new Promodel box, and then I'll*—the camera swirling in an arc to reveal a smiling audience composed of pale-skinned, middle-aged married couples—*what is it, audience?*

I could see David shift in his chair out of the corner of my eye. The light from the television cut the room into dark polygons.

What is it, audience? the orange-tanned man repeated.

"Set it," David and the man shouted in unison, "AND FORGET IT!"

Anyone who watched late-night television that year knew that catchphrase. The studio audience repeated the phrase every time the man put another set of chickens inside the box. The man encouraged the audience to shout it louder each time. *It's so easy*, he said. *So incredibly easy.* It would run like a shamanic mantra through the hallways of our dorm. Stressed-out students would repeat it as a solution to heavy academic workloads. Leave it behind and walk away.

"You really think your grandmother was a monkey or something?" David said.

"Yes," I said. "My grandmother could've been a monkey if she wanted. She could've been anything."

I told him about a game my grandmother and I used to play. I would dangle one of her long pocket watches in front of her face—*you're getting sleepy now, so, so sleepy*—until her blue-veined lids would begin to flutter then clamp tightly. I would then give her orders for the day. *You're going to act just like a ghost until I snap my fingers three times. You're going to feel like you're under water, a mermaid, until I yell, "Mimi, wake up!" You're going to do everything I tell you to do.* The watch would rest like a charm in my pocket for the rest of the day, my grandmother faithfully performing her roles. Once, she even entered her dining room on her hands and knees during one of her monthly ladies' bridge parties, barking like a dog, until I snapped my fingers again and again, embarrassed for her and more than a little terrified of the old ladies' exaggerated reactions, ones that I later realized were part of my grandmother's joke. One woman's cards spilled from her lap, red and black faces slipping into a zigzag formation behind her heels, and when she reached down to pick them up with her wrinkled, trembling hand, she nearly fell out of her chair. *Mimi, wake up!*

Hypnosis, self-induced or otherwise: It was a talent my grandmother and I had shared, believing we could trick ourselves into being something we weren't. Perhaps it was even genetic.

"So, according to this evolution crap," David said, "the longer you stay in a place, the more you begin to trust it?" He tapped the arm of my chair. I could feel the vibration through the armrest. "The easier it is to trust the people around you?"

"In a subconscious way, I guess."

The orange-tanned man turned toward the audience, teeth sparkling. *Once I close this Promodel box, it's going to be so easy*, he said. *How easy will it be, people?*

David switched off the television. The lounge snapped into darkness. I could still see his silhouette on the wall where I had been staring. The afterimage reminded me of one of those citizens of Pompeii, captured as they were before Mount Vesuvius trapped them in its ashen tombs.

Was this why people filled their frames with family photos? One sudden flash and the people you cared for would be preserved in their innocence, their happiness, before one could do harm to the other? The opposite seemed true for my father, who preached that the promise of a photograph was misleading, that our sinful states could only be transformed into goodness *after* the destruction, *after* the flash of the Rapture. He believed that our true bodies would be realized only once we ascended to heaven and stood face-to-face with God—no stretch marks, not an ounce of fat, no sinful urges—a white unwrinkled sheet draped between this life and the next. A tabula rasa glimpsed on this earth only once, if you were lucky, through the glittering baptismal waters, as your pastor guided the back of your head back to the surface, and you gasped for a new breath.

I felt safe. Invisible in the new dark.

"Set it," David shouted, "AND FORGET IT!"

. . .

NEED HELP? The choice to accept help from David would come to seem oddly menacing. Later, I would spend too much time thinking about the choices I made that year. Irrational as it was, I sometimes believed he might not have raped me just a few months later—lowered my face to the keyhole fly of his cotton briefs and forced me to go down on him until I gagged on a cocktail of my own vomit and his semen, the intimacy I'd thought I wanted from him only a few minutes before now forced on me in such excess—if I'd only chosen to carry my own boxes into the dorm.

"WHAT ABOUT CHURCH?" David said. We were almost two months into the semester, and we still barely knew each other. After our late-night chat about evolution, I thought it might be best to keep my distance, though we occasionally ran into each other in one of the dorms. We had gone running together. He was sitting on the edge of a chair in the lounge, his red gym shorts sagging nearly to the ground. An early morning runner, he would sit for hours after a run to watch talk shows, his sweat drying, his breathing growing slowly calmer. He took a sip of water from a bottle that bore our college's insignia, wiped his crusty mouth with the back of his hand.

"I go," I said, looking up from my copy of Dostoyevsky's

Notes from the Underground. "Sometimes." It was a lie. Two months into the semester, and I hadn't attended a single service. When my mother called, I would make up stories about how nice the people were at the local Baptist church, about the potlucks I would attend, the macaroni and cheese and green beans and roasted rotisserie chicken I would eat after Sunday services. I kept all of this a secret from David. Each night in my own room, I had stared into the constellations of my popcorn ceiling and imagined God might be looking down on me, that He might be deliberating on what to do about my sinful thoughts, the ones where I would think of sneaking down the ladder, out the door to David's dorm, to David's bed and curling up next to him, fitting my hardness into the groove of his ass, snapping something into place that couldn't be undone.

I licked my finger and flipped the page, shifted in my chair beside the window. Like Dostoyevsky's Underground Man, I hardly left my room or David's lounge unless absolutely necessary. I walked to class and back, barely making eye contact with my classmates, imagining each tiny exchange was portentous of something sinister. Girls, who had barely noticed me before I lost the weight, now whispered as I passed, their eyes shifting. Although I knew they were probably just trying to get my attention, I couldn't help but feel that they were whispering about my secret, that they could somehow detect the hidden part of me. For a fuck-off uniform, I wore a Radiohead *Kid A*–era jumble of jagged black-and-white lines resembling the sharp peaks of a nightmarish Kilimanjaro, and I made sure that my eyes almost never widened in pleasure or surprise beneath the dark shelf of my brow. If I didn't say too much, if people didn't notice me, then I might also escape God's roving Sauron eye.

The only time I felt safe outside the dorm was in literature class discussing hypothetical lives, hypothetical sets of events that constructed hypothetical systems of morality. I found it ironic, secure in my Underground Man superiority, that the same professors who looked down on many of their students' love of video games never seemed to realize that they shared the same love of the virtual, of the vicariously lived life.

Without realizing it, I had leaped from the body of one avatar to the next. No longer able to trust in a post-Rapture mentality, I found comfort only in books. To convince myself that I wasn't sinning *too badly*, I focused on Doubting Thomas, who after seeing proof of Christ's resurrected body finally believed in God, or on Peter, who denied Christ three times but still went on to spread Christianity across a hedonistic Europe. *I can turn it around at any moment*, I told myself, given the right impetus. At the time, I had no idea what would inspire such a change, what form it would take.

"I'll make you a bet," David said, squirting some of the water from the bottle's pull cap onto the front of his shirt. It spread like a dark breastplate across his chest. Sitting there in the beauty of his youth and averageness, he seemed invincible. "If I beat you in a race, you come to my church. I've even got a handicap. I've already run today."

"Isn't it a sin to bet?" I said.

"Not when someone's soul is on the line."

EVEN IF you know the person—especially if you know the person—rape, and the memory of it, becomes a blinding flash. A brush against something bigger than yourself. Sometimes the experience takes the form of a divine visitation, such is our need to displace the reality of it. Like Lot's daughters at Sodom, those beautiful virgins offered up in the place of angels for lascivious Sodomites—*Behold now*, Lot entreats, *I have two daughters which have not known man; let me, I pray you, bring them out unto you, and do ye to them as is good in your eyes*. Perhaps later they remembered the smell of the city market in the early morning; the feel of the sun as they turned their faces from one stall to the next; the shock of cool, stream-washed lentils passing through their fingers as they helped their mother prepare an evening meal. Like these daughters, I might remember, in ultraexposed detail, the swirl of wood grain at the base of David's bunk, the sound of the hallway doors closing one after another outside his room as my fellow freshmen returned from their nights of heavy drinking. But I would not remember the act itself.

I would never get close enough to the memory to see what was really there. For the longest time, I wouldn't allow myself to admit that it was rape at all. Like many victims, I was embarrassed. How could I have let this happen? What kind of man let another man do this to him? David was hardly stronger than I was, so how could I have been so weak, so helpless? I had only really heard of rape happening to women, though I knew the Bible talked about male-on-male rape in the Sodom and Gomorrah story, that one of the reasons God had punished those citizens was that they had wanted to rape the male angels. Added to all of this shame was the knowledge that I had secretly pined for the opportunity to be this close to another man, and it was extremely difficult after my experience with David to consider gay sex as anything other than rape. Was this what my church had been warning me about the whole time? And if this was the punishment I had received on earth, how much worse was it going to be in the afterlife?

Small details, flashes: These would be all I could remember. Look directly at the burning light, and you become nothing but a pillar of salt, as Lot's wife learned. Just another object lesson on passive obedience. But still, I reach for a language. I walk right up to the edge of an unknown border, line up the tips of my white sneakers, and try to remember the details.

The feel of the midmorning air on my face the day before the rape, as David and I raced up the college hillside. The intermittent blaring of the marching band through the alders. The white sneakers I'd laced up so tightly because I wanted to win the bet so badly. The way I stared into the passing forest, counting the waltz of the ascending trees on either side of the road—one two three, one two three—watching the high-line wires dip and sway through the branches. The way I tried to outstrip him until I ended up clutching my knees and doubling over, vomiting into the pebble-studded grass.

"Church it is," David said, overtaking me. "I win."

"You'll love it here," he said. It was the day after our run, a Wednesday evening, and I was true to my word.

David and I sat in padded folding chairs in an old post office, waiting for the Pentecostal service to begin. Old buildings like this one had lain dormant in this town for decades, their red brick walls crumbling, their wooden eaves sinking to steep angles from years of rain and rot. To cover up the decay, the church had draped a large banner over the brick front. THE POST YOUTH GROUP, it read. On my way in, a heavyset man with bright eyes told me more or less the same thing. He said he was a youth pastor.

"We just want you to feel comfortable," he said, patting me on the back. "We might be more *relaxed* here than you're used to."

I had heard my father preach against Pentecostal churches, against this "relaxed" attitude. "We don't do any of that hand flailing around here," he would say. "God doesn't want to see us crawling up and down the aisles, acting like fools."

One of the things that bothered me most about my father's

early sermons was his inclination to create a straw man, to set up an enemy and knock him down easily. Pentecostal churches were such enemies: speaking in tongues, convulsing on the floor, crying out for *Je*-sus and waving hands. To us Missionary Baptists, the only path to God was through a literal interpretation of the Bible, through baptism, through hard work, missionary work, dedication, and rededication. God's love never came as easy for the Baptists as it did for the Pentecostals, though it was a difficult path for both denominations. The only difference seemed to be that the Pentecostals relied a bit more on spiritual showmanship, while the Baptists relied more on righteous deeds and tended to be skeptical of any personal revelations that had not first been stated in the Bible.

We took a seat in the middle of the congregation. David tapped his sneaker on the concrete floor. One-two-three. "When people start crying really loudly," he whispered, "don't get freaked out, okay?"

"Okay," I said. I looked behind me at the smiling faces of the congregants. I recognized many of my fellow classmates, ones who had mostly ignored me, secure in the iridescent Pentecostal bubble that seemed to envelop them. Now they were inviting me inside their smiles, asking me to join. I let my gaze drift to the steel struts above their heads. I followed a line of flaking rust along the ceiling that led to a series of dirt-caked crescent windows above the pulpit. The sunset behind them had begun to fade, and THE POST's pale fluorescents flickered to life.

"You're not doing anything wrong," David said. "Being here."

"I know," I said.

"I don't think you do yet."

I picked up the red hymnal beneath my seat and thumbed the pages. The songs were different from Baptist ones. They were newer, more inspirational, less than a hundred years old. They repeated "Sweet Jesus" and "Oh Jesus" in long, seemingly endless refrains that could go on for as long as people felt necessary or for as long as the Holy Spirit held sway over the room.

"You won't be needing that," the youth pastor said, leaning in from the aisle. "We've got a new projection screen up by the band." He motioned toward the stage, where a guitar player was adjusting his tuning pegs. As if on cue, the guitarist waved at me with his free hand. Everyone here seemed eager to make visitors feel comfortable, special; it reminded me of the way my father would walk up to a customer in his showroom and offer to give a tour of the dealership, the way he would bring a customer around to the wash bay, point in my direction, and say, "This boy can outwork any other man here. He'll make sure whatever car you buy from that lot is cleaner than when it first came off the rack."

"Isn't this great?" David said.

The music began, a simple four-chord worship song, something about the blood of Jesus washing us clean. The congregation stood. One of the girls to my right turned to me, smiling.

"Sweet Jesus," David sang. "Oh Jesus."

He rocked back and forth on his heels, rubbing his hands together and blowing on them, as if he were starting a fire in midair. The other congregants' hands reached toward the ceiling, their fingers wriggling. The smiling girl beside me began to shake, her body convulsing.

I mumbled the words under my breath, hoping it looked like I was singing. I had never felt comfortable singing in front of people, even in my own church, though I fantasized that once I finally did, my voice would sound amazing. One day my mouth would burst open with a deep baritone the likes of which no one had ever heard. I waited for the inspiration to come.

I COME BY this desire for inspiration naturally, perhaps genetically. I'd heard stories all my life of my maternal great-aunt Ellen, about her crazy search for inspiration, my parents' tone whenever they spoke of her one of awe rather than concern. Nobody knew what had driven this beautiful woman to insanity, but the fact was that she lived alone for most of her adult life in her deceased mother's two-story plantation house, waiting for divine inspiration to reveal itself from inside the crumbling walls. Like many mystics and highly devout religious persons before her, Aunt Ellen believed that God had a special purpose for her. Yet rather than searching the sky for answers, she searched the limited world around her. To keep other people from discovering this mystery before she did, she nailed all of her bed sheets over her windows. She wore decades-old newspapers on her feet in lieu of slippers and covered her face in bright orange mercurochrome, moving from one room of her house to the next, in search of something she couldn't name. She would inhabit one room long enough to soil it, leave it no longer habitable, with food-encrusted plates, warped and moldy microwavable trays, open jars of pickled okra—whatever her concerned neighbors would send her—scattered all over her shag carpet. She seemed to believe she would never run out of rooms to soil, or at least that she would find the answer to her life's mystery before she reached the final room.

It was no wonder, then, that at the age of sixteen my mother hadn't been to Aunt Ellen's house in years, that her mother forbade her from seeing the woman who resembled a ghost more than an aunt. On the night of my parents' fourth or fifth date, my father drove along the highway that led to Aunt Ellen's, my mother with her head on his shoulder. My mother began to feel something like panic rise from the bottom of her stomach. *Surely*, she thought, *he couldn't be driving all the way out to Aunt Ellen's.*

"There's this haunted house you've got to see," my father said.

"I don't know," my mother said, serious now. "I don't think this is a good idea."

The cotton fields stretched out left and right from the road, their rows flicking by in the half dark, the sky settling down like the ceramic lid of one of my grandmother's quart-sized pots. The minute my father would marry my mother, in less than a year, he would inherit all of this, though he didn't realize it then. My grandfather would step back from the family business and hand the reins of the Caudill Brothers Gin over to my father. A soft bed of cotton would buoy him up from a childhood spent working as a mechanic for my alcoholic and abusive paternal grandfather to a life of good work, of progress matched by his skilled hands. Finally, after nineteen years of living as a nobody, he would be recognized as a person of importance. He would hold on to this feeling throughout the course of his three disparate careers—twenty-five years' hard work as the manager of the family cotton gin before it gave way to a corporate competitor; six years as one of the most popular Ford dealers in the tristate area; and finally, this latest calling of his to be a preacher and a soon-to-be pastor. He would refuse to let this feeling go, even when God bucked him off a direct path to the pastorate by sending him a gay son. Even then he would hold on to this sense of importance.

"It'll be fun," my father said, hugging my mother closer. "I'll protect you."

"No," she said. "I have to go home. Right. Now."

It was then that the white sheet visited them, drifted lazily over the windows of the Mustang and settled as an opaque, wrinkleless fog. It covered them in white light, the glare of the Mustang's headlights reversing its course, turning back to blind them.

"Like drifting into a cloud," my mother would later say. "Scary but not scary at the same time."

My father tried to keep his hands steady, pulling his arm from behind my mother's shoulder and gripping the wheel with both hands, but he could no longer remember where the next curve came. Only after the blinding sheet had passed did they begin to grow frightened.

My father overcorrected by slamming on the brakes.

"What was that?" my mother asked. Somehow the sheet had disappeared.

They stumbled out of the car. Nothing white for miles around. Only the steady chirping of crickets and the occasional flare of a firefly. Only my mother cracking her heels in the muddy ditch as she searched for the source of their vision.

"What *was* that?"

They never made it to Aunt Ellen's that night. My mother wouldn't tell my father the truth about her crazy aunt until several years into their marriage. By that time, the white sheet had taken on a new, sinister meaning. Lying in a bed in the Memphis Baptist Memorial Hospital as the doctor told her that she had somehow lost the baby that had been growing inside her, all she could think to do was grip the bed sheets in her fist, ball them up, stop the bed from slipping out from under her. She would remember the white sheet and see it as an evil omen, some sign of horrible things to come.

Years later, when she decided she would give birth to me despite the doctor's warnings about her weak heart, despite the very high chance that she might die, and after I'd been born and the doctor had cleaned me off and allowed her to hold me, she would see the white as a sign that everything would soon be washed clean, that we would all be given a second chance. She would learn to take the top bunk in my bedroom and pull the sheets in close and listen to her living son's steady breathing coming from below.

Though Aunt Ellen never discovered the mystery behind her walls, my parents certainly brushed against mystery that night. The mystery would haunt them, as it would later come to haunt me; this idea that at any moment some divine force—whether you were looking for it like Aunt Ellen was or driving away from it like my father did—could eventually overtake you. Sometimes this could be a good thing, but often it could be a terrifying visitation.

"Don't ask God to give you a sign," my father would sometimes tell congregants during his revivals, rubbing the side of a face that had nearly been burned to nothing. "You might not like what you get."

I WAS WAITING for a sign from God as David tapped his feet beside me in the church. I tapped back. One-two-three. We let our feet dance around each other.

The youth pastor positioned himself behind the pulpit. "As Christians," he said, "we must put on the armor of God."

His words came at the end of a euphoric song worship. A

few of the congregants' final notes carried over into his sermon, spiraling through the reading of scripture—"Finally, my brethren, be strong in the Lord, and in the power of His might. Put on the whole armor of God, that ye may be able to stand against the wiles of the devil"—and the girl beside me moaned and spoke in tongues, her hands pressed up against something invisible in the air before her, her voice filled with unfamiliar syllables, an ululation.

The youth pastor paused for a moment, his eyes flashing over each member of the congregation. "Stand therefore, having your loins girt about with truth, and having on the breastplate of righteousness."

Arming oneself, for the Pentecostals, seemed as simple as raising your hands in the air to receive the fruits of God's armory. The Holy Spirit would then fasten on you the breastplate of righteousness, place the shield of truth in your fist like some medieval page. Sitting beside me, David seemed as if he might already be wearing his invisible armor. He mumbled the syllables of a secret language to himself, one that his enemies would never be able to interpret. *No need for evolution*, this language seemed to say, *our God will keep you safe from your enemies, help you sleep at night.*

On this issue the Baptists and the Pentecostals agreed. Christians had to arm themselves against Satan's offensive against our country. I had recently heard Baptist pastors like Jerry Falwell condemning in militaristic terms our country's effeminacy, blaming terrorism against America on homosexuality, on the permissiveness of our culture. Brother Nielson and his nuke-'em-all philosophy had proclaimed more or less the same. Foreigners would have no WMDs, the logic went, if we hadn't gone so *soft*. I had heard it in our own church, when a bald, red-faced man burst into my Sunday school class carrying a church petition that asked us to stand against the LGBT pride parade taking place just hours from our town. "Sign it," the man had said, "or else how can you call yourself a soldier in the Christian army?" The paper passed from person to person until it came to me, until I felt everyone staring at me while I held the pen before the paper, afraid to sign, as though I would be drafted into some real-life army the minute I added my name—until I finally formed the letters of my name, hating its ability to fit so clearly and easily within the petition's dotted lines.

But now the youth pastor was telling me that I could be strong just by accepting God's gifts. I could enter into David's secret language, feel the weight of those syllables rolling off my own tongue, our separate bodies unified through the one body of Christ. In one blinding flash, the promise of such intimacy became everything for me. I might find my real inspiration there.

DURING THE second year of their marriage, when my mother and father still shared a bedroom, a singular encounter tested their faith in God's divine protection. My mother was sleeping beside my father—the television off, the room dark, the house quiet—when one of the cotton gin employees crept into the bedroom, knife in hand, and crawled onto the cool sheets. Like the man who turned the key and burned my father's face and hands, this man's motivations would never be clear to any of us. He moved close to my mother and grasped one of her legs, ran his hands up her thighs, and with his knife-wielding hand held the blade to her neck, kept her hostage, stopped her from crying out. The man had assumed my father was gone. My father's pickup truck wasn't parked out front, but this was only because he had, for reasons he could never explain, decided to park around the back of the house. The employee had not been thorough, his desire too strong to allow a slow approach. As the man slid up the bed toward my mother, my father was retrieving his shotgun from under the bed, preparing to shoot him.

"I couldn't really see him in the dark," my mother would later say. "But I could hear the click of the gun safety. *That* was very clear."

My mother sat up as the man's cold, rough hand fell against her skin. How did he not feel my father lying there next to her? This detail, like so many others, would remain a mystery. My father found the shotgun and, in the darkness, before he could adjust his eyes, he aimed the twin barrels at the space where he thought he could make out the man's silhouette, mistaking the back of my mother's head for this man's. My mother was directly in the line of fire. Once the man heard the click of the safety, he leaped from the bed, and my father chased him through the house until the man was able to escape out the back door and disappear somewhere in the cotton fields.

Though my father had been able to identify the intruder, he was never able to offer up any clear proof to the authorities, and my parents' only option was to fire the man immediately and place a restraining order against him. The one other time my father met his former employee in town, my father said, "Come anywhere near my wife again, and I won't just kill you. I'll torture you the way you intended to torture her."

My mother found it impossible to sleep after this incident. Blaming her insomnia on my father's snoring, she left the television going all night. She would take my top bunk when she couldn't sleep. I would hear her breathing slow within minutes of entering the sheets. When the two of us slept in the same room, the world outside seemed to recede, our fears along with it. We felt safe.

"My bunkmate," she would say.

"Love," I would say back.

My father never seemed to forgive himself for accidentally placing the twin barrels of the shotgun to the back of my mother's head. Raised to see himself as the protector of the family, the head of the household, he felt that he had failed to do his job. He had already failed with the first baby, had been unable to cure whatever complications had lain dormant in my mother's body. If he ever had a chance at another child, he promised himself he would never again let harm come to his family. But he could never predict what would come to all of us once I left his house.

A FEW HOURS after the church service, I was in David's room, and he was dipping his index and middle fingers into a can of motor oil. "We have to protect ourselves from sin," he said. He walked to the dorm window, stood on a chair, and smeared the oil in a line above the metal casing. "We have to cleanse this room of demonic forces."

He began to speak in tongues, what sounded like a faux African dialect mixed with long English vowels. He was wearing the outfit I had grown so fond of in the past few months when I'd seen him in the dorm.

"That's enough," I said, laughing. I sat on the topmost rung of the bunk ladder. "Stop it."

I loved him in that moment. I loved the way his leg hair snaked in a lowercase *j* that stretched from the back of his knee to the elastic band at the bottom of his briefs.

"Maybe it's not the best," he said, stepping down from the chair, "but it works."

The youth pastor had run out of anointing oil at the church. "You'll just have to use this," he'd said, leading David and me out of the old post office to the back of his car, popping his trunk, and removing a one-quart yellow Pennzoil bottle. He invited several of the congregants to pray over this bottle, to bless it with God's anointing power. "Thank you so much," David had said. "This is a life saver."

David dipped his fingers into the bottle again. He skipped around the room, playfully cocking his head at various angles, trying to decide what to anoint next.

"*Hmmmm*," he said. "I don't know."

"You're ridiculous," I said. "You don't expect me to believe this, do you?"

He walked over to me, looping his free arm through the rung where my bare feet were resting. He reached up with his other hand and placed his oil-covered fingers in front of my leaning forehead.

"Don't you dare," I said.

"Out, demon!" he shouted, half serious now, flinging back his hand. A drop of motor oil landed on the frozen avalanche of bed sheets that fell from the top bunk where I had flung them earlier.

He pressed the oil to my forehead, used his thumb to blend it into my skin.

A FEW HOURS PASSED, and then it happened. At first, it was like baptism. I felt my body go under, but someone else's hands urged me below the surface. Like my baptism, I had worried what it would feel like, what I would be asked to do, the exact logistics of the act. *Would I feel differently? Would I be changed forever, as people said I would?*

I worried about how my body would look. I worried about the stretch marks. Even as he forced my head down, I worried that I might not do it right. Even as I gagged and struggled, pulled at the hairs on his calves, trying to do anything that would make him stop, I worried about upsetting him. *This was not what I wanted it to be,* I thought.

I had thought this before. At the age of twelve, standing inside the baptistery of our family church, I had clutched at the gown that clung to the fat rolls along my waistline as the congregation looked on and clapped. I was a new man standing on new territory. Born again in Christ's image. Members of my church family shouted, "Amen!" I looked out at their faces, feeling as though I had stripped off all my clothes and revealed the most vulnerable part of myself. I was no longer invisible.

EVERYTHING ELSE that led to my enrollment in Love in Action felt like a deserved punishment. David confessed, the same night that he raped me, that he had also recently raped a fourteen-year-old boy in his youth group, that he didn't know why he did it, couldn't explain it. I'd been unable to move from the bed where he had placed me afterward—I believed that God was punishing me physically for my mental transgressions. Somehow the demons had entered this room despite our charms against them.

"I wanted to be a youth pastor," he said, sobbing so loudly the neighbors pounded on the other side of his concrete-block wall. "How can I be a youth pastor now? After what I've done?"

I didn't yet recognize it, but the logic of ex-gay therapy, the idea that my sinful urges were somehow equal to David's, began to invade my thoughts. Of course I was sitting on the same bed as a pedophile; according to scripture, I was no better than a pedophile, or an idol worshiper, or a murderer.

When I told the Presbyterian pastor at our college what David had done to the fourteen-year-old boy, she told me to stay quiet. That I had no real evidence, that it was a bad thing, yes, but there was nothing to be done. I believed my silence was due punishment. I didn't tell her about what he had done to me, in part because I suspected that rape and shame was what gay sex was all about, but mostly because I was too embarrassed to admit that I hadn't been strong enough to fend him off, and I was worried that she would interpret this weakness as a submission to homosexuality.

"Okay," I said, reading the leather-bound spines that circled her office shelves, wondering if these theologians, too, had found a way to dodge such difficult issues. If life was ever going to make sense again, I would have to search harder for clear answers.

David called my mother a few weeks later, out of his own desperate guilt, and told her that her only son was a *homosexual*, a *gay*.

"He's disgusting," he said to her. "A monster."

I found out from a mutual friend that my mother was on her way to the college to take me back home, and I sat in my friend's dorm room quietly sobbing into a plush pillow while she patted my back. According to a friend who'd heard it from David, my mother had said over the phone that my father wasn't going to continue paying for my education if I was going to be openly gay. I turned off my cell phone, hoping I could block out what was coming to me.

My mother drove to the college that night and asked me to come home to talk to my father. She brought another woman from church with her because she was afraid to face me alone. The other woman waited in the car, her eyes avoiding mine, as my mother and I sat on a bench just outside the quad. My mother asked me, in a voice quieter than I'd ever heard her speak, if what she had heard was true.

"No," I said at first. "David's a liar."

A minute of silence passed. Then, feeling I could no longer keep it inside, I burst into tears and told her it was true, that I was gay. Saying the word aloud made me feel sick inside, and I wondered if what David had forced me to swallow had somehow grown inside of me, rendered me permanently gay.

Embarrassed, my mother led me to the car. The other woman didn't say a word. As I lay in the backseat quietly sobbing, watching the high-line wires move among the stars, I thought, *What else could have come from this?* The moment I'd stepped away from the shower, the PlayStation soaking in the tub behind me, I'd taken on an independent life. I'd taken on too much at once, and I'd gagged on the freedom of it.

Later that night, when my father said, "You'll never step foot in this house again if you act on your feelings. You'll never finish your education," I thought, *Fair enough.*

I looked up at the gilded picture frames covering our living-room wall, at all the smiling faces of our family members looking down at me from happier vantage points, at Aunt Ellen when she was beautiful and oblivious, and I thought, *Anything. I'll do anything to erase this part of me.*

Wake up. Shower. Eat breakfast. Travel. Arrive at office.

By the third Moral Inventory, by the fifth day of therapy, I had already revealed to my LIA group what I felt were all of my carnal sins, though I never actually told them what David had done to me, too afraid God would punish me further if I revealed the secret. I felt hollowed out. Certainly not cured, but no longer filled with the sins I'd kept secret for so long. Yet rather than feeling relieved, I felt—what, exactly? My guilt and fear had all but disappeared in only a matter of days, replaced by what I could only describe as Nothing. It was Nothing that led me through the facility's white hallways. It was Nothing that brought the fork to my mouth during lunch breaks. Nothing steadied my voice as I read aloud my list of sins before the group. And it was Nothing that sent me to the bathroom to stare into the mirror at the gaunt, hollow-eyed face of a boy who, only a week before, I would have considered on the verge of some vague, awful business. It was the face of a newly minted addict, a stranger you might see on the city sidewalk carrying his childhood stereo to the pawn shop, rainbow Lisa Frank stickers still curling around the edges—but rather than the soiled T-shirt that usually accompanied such a face, here was a white button-down, a perfectly pleated pair of khakis, and the smile this face mustered was, despite the lack of emotion behind it, as real as any waiting outside the plywood door. In the brief moments when Nothing left me, I felt, just above an eddy of unsourced pain, a kind of pride. *I can do thi*s, I thought. *I can do this better than anyone else here.*

In my saner moments, I wondered why I'd ever indulged such hubris. Here was J, devoted to God as a slave to his master, as a "bond servant" to his owner, as our Addiction Workbooks instructed us it should be. Here he was, telling me he'd managed an almost perfect score on his ACT, an all but free ride to any university of his choice, and what did he make of it? "I know God can use this brain," he'd said one day. "I just have to fix the weak parts, study more."

And here was S, struggling with her sexuality for so many years and then suddenly discovered because of one act in the midst of a lonely afternoon in her trailer, an experiment you might hear about in any pocket of high school gossip—"Did you hear about that freak girl and her dog?"—now trying to twist her soul around so it could fit the image of corruption her parents saw in her.

And T, the man whose struggle was most evident; who took on all of our scars, Christlike, and suffered the almost daily stigma/stigmata of it while standing before our group—how could I compete? They had all been in the facility longer, knew on a day-to-day basis what the struggle was really like. They had gone through Nothing and come out on the other side with Something, even if that Something was the urge to keep struggling, keep fighting, keep denying the sin. But I wasn't so sure I would make it out of my doubt. One year of college had done exactly what my father and the church had warned me against: turned me into a skeptic, a heretic, someone who second-guessed everything he felt or saw.

"The more confused you feel, the closer you get to the source of childhood trauma," Smid had said earlier that morning. The Source: Unlike my program's name implied, I was being carried out by an undertow into shoreless waters, lost in this constant questioning of my past. The night before, while filling out my Addiction Workbook, I'd gotten so confused by the questions that I'd sneaked out of the hotel room sometime after midnight to jog a few laps around the suburban neighborhood, yellow pools of streetlamp light drawing me deeper into the cul-de-sacs, my sneakers squeaking, endorphins kicking in midjog so that I could concentrate long enough on my confusion to question it. *Describe fully knowing others and them fully knowing you.* Had I ever fully known anyone? Had anyone ever fully known me? What did that even mean?

I felt like running all the way down to the ink-black Mississippi and daring myself to jump in, to surrender myself to the pull. Though I wasn't suicidal like T was, I liked flirting with death. The glamour of Ending It All, and so suddenly, wasn't much of a leap up from the End Times sensationalism of our family's church. There was also pleasure to be had in knowing that the end could come at any time without warning. You might be going about your daily life, thinking everything is fine, when suddenly—*boom!*—the levees break, the waters rise, and every hateful object you know becomes treasure now belonging to a Lost Kingdom: artifacts for future, more enlightened excavators to ponder. Life taking on greater meaning in the aftermath. All this senseless pain somehow making sense in the end.

But suicide being one of the unpardonable sins, I kept to the suburban circuit, wrapped in amber-colored vapor light. I tried praying, *Lord, make me pure*, but all I felt was an echo in my head. For the time being, it seemed like God had abandoned me. Like the Underground Man, I was trapped in stasis, in Nothing.

THE FEELING reminded me of a story I'd heard when my family vacationed near Lake Norfork at the edge of the Ozarks. A local resident told us that an entire town had been buried deep beneath the water. Depression-era farmers and their families had been required to relocate once the Norfork Dam began construction. Schoolhouses and churches and post offices, all abandoned. Bodies in old graves exhumed and relocated to higher ground. Apocryphal tales soon followed: a motorcycle buoyed up by the water—the weight of objects no longer a factor in this underwater world, everything released from its station in life—now resting atop a steel bridge. Old town names like Henderson, Jordan, Herron, Hand. All nearly gone, eroded by water, every trace erased in the name of progress.

"Don't let it worry you," my mother said, catching sight of the fear in my eyes as I waded through the water beside our rented pontoon boat. I imagined steeples grazing my ankles. A literal hand from Hand pulling me under. "The towns are really, really deep." My mother spraying Banana Boat suntan oil onto her freckled arms, spreading it up to her red shoulders: a creature, it seemed to me in the moment, of the land, resisting the inevitable pull of the water that would one day bury us all. This was a source of both comfort and anxiety. None of this really mattered, yet *none of this really mattered*, an equally terrifying idea. Except, of course, when I considered what the Bible had to say about our brief lives on earth, and then *all of this really mattered*.

Pillars of flame and sand, locusts devouring cities whole: The stories of Christianity were swift demolitions leading, ultimately, to fulfillment. Sodom. Gomorrah. But what happened when the fulfillment never came? What happened when you never adjusted to the loss of what had once been so familiar? You can only walk on water, like Peter, if you don't question it. *People once lifted their heads in prayer to the very spot where the balls of my feet now tread*, you might think. *People once*

believed, and struggled, and lived—and now that's forgotten.
Once you begin to question it, you sink quickly to the bottom
unless someone like Jesus pulls you back up and chastises you
for your lack of faith, your lack of vision.

But where was Jesus in all my time at the facility? Where
was His steady nail-scarred hand? The prayers I continued to recite each night became even more desperate and meaningless.
Please help me to be pure. Please-help-me-to-be-pure. Please-
helpmetobepure.

Nowhere. Nowhere was the answer.

I'D STILL been able to return to the hotel room an hour after
my midnight run. I'd still been able to sit down at the desk
without fidgeting too much and write out the answers to the
Addiction Workbook's questions to the best of my ability: "I've
never fully known anyone. I only thought I knew who I was.
And then the thing with David happened, and I suddenly realized that I'd been faking it the whole time. Because I didn't
know myself, because I'd been faking it, I didn't know David.
This was one of the reasons why I was unable to protect myself
from him. I had allowed Satan to convince me that I was a
strong warrior for Christ when, in fact, I was living a sinful life.
I need God's strength to become stronger, to be filled up with
knowledge of who I am and who others around me truly are."

I no longer knew if any of this was true, if there were any
answers for what had happened, or if God even cared any-

more. But even if I lacked my peers' conviction, I might still prove to be the best at public confession.

Lunch. Moral Inventory. Short break.

All morning I stared at the pale patch of skin on my left wrist, willing time to jump forward, waiting for the moment when my mother would come again to pick me up. *One day is with the Lord as a thousand years, and a thousand years as one day.* My father had often quoted this verse in a popular sermon of his, "One-Tenth of a Day," asking congregants to consider the brevity of their lives. "Work out the math for yourselves," he'd preached, "and you'll see that our lives are much too short." It was to this idea that I returned as Nothing led me through each block of my schedule, as I prayed to Nothing when the counselors asked us to bow our heads before thick slabs of casserole and thank God for the Hamburger Helper. If I could just think of these two weeks as a few milliseconds. Once this was over, once my head felt less crowded, I might even find God waiting for me on the other side, ready to listen once again to my prayers.

"It's important to recognize the deficiencies in your life," Danny Cosby, one of the main staff counselors, was saying now, standing in the middle of our group, his salt-and-pepper hair backlit by the glare from the sliding glass door. Smid wasn't scheduled to lead any workshops this afternoon, so Cosby was taking his place. Cosby was giving a talk, once again, on the necessity of sports. Cosby was telling us that a lack of sports in childhood could lead to effeminate behavior. He told us he was just the man for the job. A recovering alcoholic who came by sports naturally, he was as straight as any man I'd ever met. He told us he used a work ethic he'd learned from being a team player to pull himself out of his alcoholism—all with the help of God, of course—his life containing all the necessary raw materials to form a full recovery. He had never experienced same-sex attraction (SSA), as LIA labeled it. He'd never been through LIA's program himself, since his only major impediment in life had been alcoholism, and LIA had hired him as a counselor because they believed his extensive AA experience was the only prerequisite for curing any and all forms of addiction. He couldn't seem to understand why none of us had come by the same straight impulses naturally, but he was prepared to talk us into it. He was as good, if not better, than any car salesman my father had ever employed, though I was skeptical of his qualifications. How could a man who never knew what it was like to live with our sin possibly know what was required to pull us out of it?

"Men, I'm talking to you," he said. The girls from our group had been dismissed for a separate talk on femininity. "Some of you haven't had the opportunity to bond with other men your own age." The shadow of the sliding glass door's rail fell over him like a dark sash. "Some of you have idolized other men's bodies because you didn't have enough physical contact when you were younger. Maybe you thought you were bad at sports. Maybe you thought you were different."

J was sitting across from me today. I tried to keep from looking at him each time Cosby repeated "physical contact." He
looked up only once, and his gaze was so cold it made me wonder if I'd only imagined that we'd shared a connection earlier.
Even so, looking into his eyes felt intimate, the coldness he shot
in my direction an indication of something acknowledged and
quickly hidden.

"The problem here is the powerful influence of labeling,"
Cosby continued. "You've labeled yourself the type of person
who doesn't play sports. Sadly, we grow into our labels. But we
can grow out of them, too."

I was scared of Cosby. He was a man who'd dealt with drug
addicts and alcoholics for most of his adult life, a man who
didn't see the difference between being gay and being addicted
to heroin. He'd done LSD, huffed gasoline. He'd robbed a con-
venience store. He'd completed all twelve steps of AA. He'd
written all about it in his testimony, included a picture of himself smiling on a Harley, the words "A Life Transformed" written in script beside him. I had no idea how to talk to him. For
all of my shame and guilt, I still couldn't see myself as equal to
a drug addict, a bank robber. My father always said you could
tell the character of a man by how he treated "low" people,
how a man who refused to talk to someone lower than himself
wasn't worth a cent. But I still thought I was better than all of
that, and I worried that Cosby would instantly see through to
my hypocrisy. I thought he might already be able to tell that I'd
stopped really praying to God.

"It's important to get in touch with this part of yourself," Cosby said. "This masculine part that's been missing for so long."

The blond-haired greeter entered the room from the back, wheeling in a television on a portable stand. I'd grown to hate this boy's self-satisfied smile, the same smile I saw every morning as he rummaged through my belongings in search of FIs. It was a smile that seemed to say, *I've lived through this, and what you're experiencing is only a small fraction of what I've experienced*. His smile said, *It only gets worse*, but without any of the pity I saw in Smid's face. The boy was too recent a graduate, his ex-gay status only recently conferred, and he seemed to have singled me out, to have detected in me some stubbornness he'd already put behind himself, some dogged rationalism that didn't belong in a place like LIA. "I hope you're here for the right reasons," he'd said earlier that morning, his finger slipping into the folds of my wallet. "Because if not . . ."

It was strange. As I watched him wheel the television to the spot beside Cosby, I felt a sudden pang of disappointment and I realized with a start that I missed Smid. At least Smid had been patient with me. At least Smid hadn't looked disgusted at the sight of me. Cosby and the blond-haired boy shared an expression between them that reminded me of all the judgmental looks I'd gotten from friends and acquaintances the minute they found out through David's gossip that I was gay. It was the *Stay away from my child* look, the *You're a pervert, you're a monster, you've got the wrong plumbing* look. "All those perverts," my next-door neighbor said one weekend just after my parents had found out, this little white-haired lady smacking her lips in a way that made me think she'd somehow heard about me. She'd been watching a debate on Fox News about gay marriage, had caught me as I was walking next to her yard. "They need to get their heads checked. Putting things in places where they don't belong. Plumbing the wrong pipes, if you know what I mean." I half expected Cosby to start in on the metaphors. Bad wiring? Wrong gears? Loose screws?

"We'll be watching a documentary this afternoon," Cosby said, pressing the power button at the bottom of the television. A high-pitched electronic wheeze spread across the room then faded into the background, joining the buzzing of the fluorescents.

I no longer remember exactly what the movie was about, aside from sports. What I do remember is the look of satisfaction on Cosby's face as he stood to the side of our group with his hands crossed over his chest. I almost envied him for his drug habit, for the masculine nature of his affliction. He had rough-housed with men in bars, gotten in fights. He didn't need this documentary to be straight. He just *was*. His straightness buzzed off him, inhabited the room. He was like an exotic animal in the midst of us, an instinctual being, with none of the self-consciousness the rest of us felt. When he didn't look disgusted with us, he looked amused, as though he couldn't possibly imagine what it must have been like to be in such a painfully distorted mind.

I had been wondering what it felt like to be in a straight mind *my whole life*, or at least ever since I discovered I was gay, when, in third grade, I'd first realized that my interest in our teacher, Mr. Smith, was much greater than that of my other male peers'. Though over the years I'd done my best to pretend otherwise, I'd had a string of male crushes that wouldn't go away, a constant guilty ache that ran through my body for so long that I came to believe the feeling was just a part of what it meant to be alive. The only moments when the ache became a sharp pain were when I allowed myself to imagine a happy life with these crushes, a rarity to be sure. As Cosby spoke, I wondered what it felt like to see yourself reflected in every movie, to have friends and family constantly dropping fun little hints about your love life, to have the world open up to you in all its magnificence. What did it feel like to not have to think about your every move, to not be scrutinized for everything you did, to not have to lie every day? In my most stubborn moments—the moments that must have accumulated to such a degree that the blond-haired boy distrusted me—I told myself that it must have felt really dull to be straight. When I was my most stubborn self, I thought, *This affliction is what makes me smarter. This disadvantage is what gives me my ambition. This is what first inspired me to write.*

But the handbook was clear on this subject, on the attitude of superiority that all gay people expressed, what basically amounted to an intricate ruse designed to hide their true inferiority: "When their manipulation fails, they become deeply depressed and their self-worth plummets. Often their value is connected to their ability to control others." *True enough*, I'd thought after reading this. It was clear to anyone around me that I was completely lost, that I wasn't in control, and that my self-worth was at an all-time low. After all, it was hard not to think that I was destroying my family, that its legacy would end with me, a dead end. Worse, it was hard not to think about all the money my parents were spending, the $1,500 they had to pay for only two weeks of therapy. Hardest of all was the thought of standing beside my father the next day during the ordination ceremony and lying to the two-hundred-plus people who would gather to celebrate his calling, beaming my fake smile to the crowd.

But was it wrong to think that I could be better than this blond-haired boy? Was it wrong to think that God would return to me, listen to my prayers once again, if only I worked harder? And even as I watched the documentary, smiling each time I caught the flash of pale flesh, the sudden motion of a player piling on top of his opposing mate's ass and taking the man down with the sloppy precision of the defensive tackle—was it wrong to think that I could play the game better than all of them?

THE LIVING WORD Lutheran Church was a conspicuous cluster of three A-frames surging out of this small suburban neighborhood with a string of narrow windows pinched at origami angles at each side, a sharp lotus flower of glass and concrete that seemed at least partially inspired by the 1960s Brutalism of old public libraries and post offices. As we approached, our small group of Source teens packed together in LIA's van, all of us turned to face its façade.

"The church inside is *gorgeous*," a boy behind me said, the adjective slipping into his sentence without pretense. Did certain words constitute FIs? "We *have* to see the sanctuary." Certain intonations? During the last break, an ex-lesbian had come up to me and tsk-tsked at my akimbo stance. I had been standing near the doorway with one hand on the wall and the other on my hip. "I'm not going to report you," she said, as if I was supposed to be grateful, to thank her in some way, "but you really need to change that FI before someone else sees you."

We pulled into the asphalt lot, yellow lines whooshing by, slowing. Cosby slid open the side door and ushered us outside. Steep triangles overhead, the glare of windows: complicated geometry I hardly understood. Less than a year later, this building would become LIA's new headquarters: a cleaner, loftier space, where the long line of windows would bathe patients in a holier light. For now, however, LIA merely rented out a few rooms from the church for occasional afternoon activities, the strip-mall facility too small to accommodate both older and younger patients at once. It was important to keep afternoon activities separate, primarily because patients attended LIA for very different reasons. The Source and Refuge programs, both youth groups, most of us under the age of twenty, shared our afternoon classes together, and since most of us were dealing

with homosexuality, it made sense that we'd have similar stories to share during our activities.

"You can have a short break," Cosby said, leading us inside.
"A quick look around if you want, and then we'll meet up in the
hallway."

Several of us entered the sanctuary. It was quiet inside, the
carpet absorbing the sound of our steps. Sun-drenched wooden
aisles, all with little crocheted tissue boxes nestled on the ends,
about thirty rows, three sections facing the pulpit. I could feel
something dark looming somewhere behind me, and I turned
sharply to face a low balcony, impressive to me because I had
never attended a church with a balcony. I imagined having to
walk down the aisle in such a place, all of those eyes looking
down on you from above. During my baptism, all the staring
had come from one direction, and I'd been able to look above
the congregants' heads to the blank white space at the back of
the church, devote myself to God as much as I could in such a
public moment. But in here it seemed like you'd never be alone
with God. Here it seemed like you would always be under the
spell of someone's watchful gaze.

I walked up the aisle, my feet treading softly on the carpet.
How many times had I seen my father do the same? How many
times had I seen his face wet with tears, shaking all the way to
the altar? It was strange to think of the picture I made now:
walking ahead of the group, my face placid, free of emotion.
The walking dead, I thought, squaring my shoulders. I didn't
feel. I wouldn't feel. I wouldn't let them see me feel. I wouldn't

be weak like my father. I wouldn't give that ex-lesbian another chance to "correct" me. By the end of my stay here, I would be the one correcting her. I was stronger than all of this, and I would prove it no matter the consequences, no matter how much feeling I had to sacrifice in the process.

The windows ahead were impressively unstained, as if the architect had made the bold decision to leave the beauty of the sanctuary up to nature, to God. No stains, no fragmented depictions of biblical scenes, no sharp colored light. Sometimes it was what you left unsaid or undone that drew you into a state of wonder. And as Nothing drew me closer to the altar, as I mounted the stage and looked out at all the empty aisles, imagining the crowd I'd have to face during my father's ceremony the next day, I wondered if this was what God was doing. I wondered if God was letting me go for a short time, cutting the connection, so that I could grow stronger and straighter by myself. Though I worried that God might choose to stop visiting me altogether, that I might have damaged our relationship beyond repair, I also knew that there was no going back. I was committed to becoming stronger, though I had no idea what that really meant. Could I even become entirely straight? And even if I could, would that mean that my relationship with God would be the same? Or did the process of becoming stronger entail losing my previous way of life? Whatever form that strength was going to take, I would have to accept it. I would face tomorrow's crowd with the stone-cold glare I'd seen in J's eyes today—the glare of a martyr—even if that was the furthest thing from what I truly felt myself to be.

"FOCUS ON YOUR FEELINGS," Cosby said. "I really want you to focus."

We were in one of the church's classrooms, the light different here, darker, with only one window looking out onto the parking lot. Cosby was at the front of the classroom, looking like a high school coach who also doubled as a math teacher, brow furrowed as if thinking of something else: the next day's game, the next equation.

"I'd like you to turn to the General Tools section of your handbook."

The fluttering of paper. Licked fingers. I found the page: five columns and six rows of cartoon faces, each face with a label beneath it. CONTENTED, DEPRESSED, FRAZZLED, FRIGHTENED, HAPPY. THOUGHTLESS, STARRY-EYED, DISGUSTED, SHOCKED, ENRAGED. All of the faces a simplistic rendering of each emotion.

"I want you to think about how you feel right now," Cosby said. "It can be a combination of several faces. Choose carefully."

On the table at the front of the classroom were several white posters. Next to them were colored markers and pencils. There were also feathers, beads, and multicolored string: various crafts a middle schooler might keep in a caboodle. Cosby explained that we were to craft masks symbolizing the two halves of our personality: the one we show the outside world, and the one we show only to ourselves—one mask on one side, the other on the back.

I slid my finger down the page, trying to find a word for what I felt. *Dead inside, but weirdly determined.* "Apprehensive" came the closest. Or perhaps "out of sorts." I followed the others to the table at the front of the room, picked up a poster and some markers and a few cotton balls. When I sat back down to work on my project, J sat next to me. We both got on our knees. I smoothed my poster out on the seat cushion.

"Could you pass me the red?" J said, coldness in his voice. *Red*, I thought. *The color of passion.* I would soon watch that passion turn into drops of blood on his poster—Jesus's blood. Not passion, but sacrifice.

I looked around for ideas. S began gluing cotton to her poster, making some kind of pale smiley face. I watched her for a long time before turning away to work on my own poster. She was creating clouds painted dark blue—rain clouds—a bright orange sliver of sun barely visible, with no signs of fur or peanut butter. I was happy for her.

"Looking good so far," Cosby said, walking past me, head bent, reverential. He sounded like he meant it. He sounded like the kind of person who had done this activity many times, learned how to forge only one face from his divided selves.

I uncapped a blue marker and scribbled a series of lines, then turned those lines into the outlines of waves, connected them with the cotton balls so that the tops of the waves looked as though they were cresting. A violent whirlpool. A great swirling mess with no direction. On the other side: the long-forgotten eroded city beneath.

PRISONER'S CINEMA

My father and I barely talked on our ride to the jail. It had been a month since my parents discovered I was gay, and now it was almost Thanksgiving break, the week I would spend mostly at home, feeling there was very little to be thankful for. I sat beside my father in the passenger's seat of his red F-150 Lariat, watching the trees advance and retreat along the edge of the snaking road, the mountains folding around us, leading us into the center of what a state governor had declared would one day become the "Mecca of the Ozarks."

I closed my eyes, but the afterimage remained: pine-studded peaks, browning pine needles, the morning sun hanging like a heat lamp over it all.

My family made the pilgrimage to this town in 1999 just after we lost our cotton gin to a corporate competitor, long after the town had already transformed itself into a place for retired Chicagoans and Southern fundamentalists to buy cheap property where it was safe to keep and bear arms and brag about it. In the five years since we'd moved, my parents had learned how to fit in with some of the Northerners, talk with a slight nasal accent, smile less. People came here to change their lives for the better, to live at a different pace, though later I'd learn that a change of scenery would never change someone like me, that no amount of camouflage could hide the same-sex fantasies I'd been having since seventh grade.

"Are you ready?" my father said, his eyes flicking from the road to the nervous hands I kept wringing in my lap.

"I'm ready," I said, my fingers freezing into a steeple. I remembered a rhyme my teachers taught me in vacation Bible school: *Here is the church. Here is the steeple. Open the doors and see all the people.*

"It'll be a different kind of education than you're used to," my father said. "Your college professors won't teach you this."

Much of my father's work now involved educating people outside of the church's doors. His increased ambition had led him to witness to an ever-increasing number of customers at his dealership, to walk the neighborhood streets behind our house to knock on doors in search of lost souls, and now, his greatest mission, to witness to the forgotten, the downtrodden, the inmates of the local county jail. This was my first time shadowing him on one of his early Saturday morning visits; I had never before visited the jail though he had come many times before, and I was still half-asleep, unaccustomed to the new schedule my parents had proposed after David outed me, which required me to drive back from college Friday afternoons and wake up early Saturday mornings to spend more time with my family.

After several minutes of silence, my father pressed the button for the radio. His Creedence Clearwater Revival CD replaced our silence with the nostalgic and happy light notes of a Louisiana bayou none of the band members had ever truly experienced. To anyone passing us on the road, we must have looked happy, off to see some roadside attraction.

I closed my eyes again, pressed the heels of my palms against my eyelids until the afterimages grew fractious and broke apart: an ice shelf descending into black arctic water.

THE IMAGES of what had happened the night of my rape stayed with me also, working their way into nearly every minute of my waking life: the blurry image of the younger boy David told me he'd raped; the sight of David towering over me, forcing my head down. One second I felt calm; the next I would recall some forgotten pocket of memory, and an uncontrollable rage would grip me, a rage directed toward me and everyone around me, a desire to destroy everything I saw.

After David called and outed me to my parents, my mother had driven me home from college, speeding through yellow lights to arrive at our house in record time. As she vomited in an adjacent bathroom, my father led me into his bedroom, the door clicking shut behind him, and explained that what I was feeling was wrong, that I was simply confused.

"You don't know what it feels like to be with a woman," he'd said. "There's nothing else in the world like the pleasure between a man and his wife."

I didn't know what to say. I traced the pattern of the comforter with my index finger, followed its stitching along the yellow-brown bulb of a jonquil. If I could just keep moving my hands. My religious studies professor had noticed my restless hands one day in class, inviting me into his office to teach me some of his meditation techniques. *Left hand, palm down. Turn left palm up. Do not say to yourself, "Turn the left hand." Awareness is all.* Though I'd experienced little success with these techniques, having something to do with my hands seemed better than giving in to the trembling.

"It's so warm, so natural," my father said, "being with a woman." I felt the sudden urge to join my mother in front of the toilet, our disgust perhaps uniting us for a moment, though for different reasons. None of us had wanted to know about each other's sex lives, yet here we were.

When my mother returned to the room, wiping her mouth with the back of her hand, my parents sat me down on the edge of the bed and explained that they would find a way to cure me. They would talk to our preacher, see what options were available. There were ways, they said. They'd once heard a visiting preacher give a speech about counseling options. In the meantime, I would spend my weekends at home, two hours away from the sinful college-educated influences that had led me to this point.

Sitting there with my sneakers hovering above the carpet like a little kid, tracing my fingers along the comforter while watching my mother continue to smear pink lipstick on the back of her hand, I couldn't find the nerve to tell them what my friend had done. David had trumped me: The knowledge of my homosexuality would seem more shocking than the knowledge of my rape; or, worse, it would seem as though one act had inevitably followed the other, as though I'd had it coming to me. Either way, our family's shame would remain the same.

"You'll never step foot in this house again if you act on your feelings," my father said. "You'll never get an education."

That night, I made the quiet decision to agree to whatever they had in mind, the shame and rage settling in my chest, filling up spaces I had previously reserved for love, spreading beneath my skin like invisible bruises. Unlike my mother, I had no way of purging myself, no way of staring into my watery reflection and obliterating my features with sick. Instead, I could only cup my hands in prayer and make a promise to God that I would try harder, the carpet burning its twin pointillist patterns into my kneecaps. I could only stand before my bathroom mirror and rub the sharp edge of a pair of scissors against my Adam's apple, back and forth, until the blade began to leave faint marks that would prove difficult to explain. I could only be like the sinful Narcissus I'd read about in Edith Hamilton's *Mythology*, which was nestled in my backpack, too in love with the image of myself reflected in other men's bodies, too haunted by what I saw to turn away. To prevent myself from drowning, I agreed to my parents' plan. As the weeks passed and the next steps solidified, we would decide if I was to stay in college or if more drastic steps needed be taken.

Each night, the images arrived fully formed, as if by clockwork: David and the boy; David towering over me; my father's lips moving as though independent of the sounds he was making; the look of fear that split the skin of my parents' faces into fractals with increasingly smaller worry lines.

I had chosen to accompany my father to his jail ministry as a way of ending these images, as an alternative to the suicide I contemplated almost nightly, to the scissors I began to feel for in the middle of the night, running my restless hands along the lip between my mattress and box spring until reaching those twin metal tongues.

Perhaps, had I known how close I truly was to suicide, I would have kept away from the jail and its dank cells, its display of lives broken by bad choices and bad luck, of people who had been unable to change themselves when it most counted—yet it's also possible that what I truly craved was the knowledge of how my father accomplished the impossible, how he reformed these men, gave them hope, brought them back to their best selves before God. "No sin is too great to be forgiven," my father would often say, paraphrasing Exodus. Maybe that could apply to me, too.

. . .

I WATCHED the gaps in the trees slice by the window, my father accelerating through the curves in the road, and for a moment I imagined popping open the door and tumbling out of the truck the way I had seen cowboys do it in the Westerns my father watched every night. But where would I go? Where would I find a new self? I had walked down many of these forest paths in my free afternoons after high school, some of them opening onto bone-white granite cliffs, some rushing down to the dam of a man-made lake, all of them circling back to the town center with labyrinthine flourishes that never failed to take my breath away. In *Mythology*, I'd read about Ariadne, how she used red string to guide Theseus free of the Minotaur's furry grasp. Yet in this town it seemed every path led back to the same dilapidated strip mall. In this town, it seemed the Minotaur would always find you.

I'D ALREADY learned that there were no simple, straight roads out of town. The night I'd been outed, after my father gave me his ultimatum, I ran a few Internet searches in my bedroom, straining the whole time to listen for my parents' footsteps in the hallway outside. I ran an online credit check and found that I had almost no credit to my name. I queried message boards on how to file for independence, but all of the answers seemed much too complicated; there were too many forms to fill out, too many signatures, too much thought required. As it stood, my parents were paying for more than half of my education, and if I couldn't change who I was, they were going to take this away from me.

Yet the thought of abandoning my parents, of joining a community of gay-friendly people and somehow continuing life without them—this seemed even worse than suicide. Cutting away my roots and the people I loved would transform me into a shell of the person I once was, an automaton stripped of all its gears. I somehow knew that leaving my family behind would destroy whatever love I hadn't already thrown aside to make room for shame.

During the past month at college, literature professors who had sensed something of my family situation took pains to invite me to their dinner parties, ushering me into their discussions of critical theory, of Foucault and third-wave feminism, of the Neo-Cons who were busy robbing the country blind. Around this time, President Bush felt inspired by God to find WMDs in Iraq, and it seemed every dinner I attended featured a heavy dose of fundamentalist bashing.

My new friends, Charles and Dominique, two of the few black students at our college, were constantly teasing me about how the Baptists had all been slave owners, how my family tree was full of white supremacists. "Your family used the Bible to keep our folks down," Charles said. "They probably beat us with all those Bibles they had lying around," Dominique added.

The thought of what King Cotton had done to Charles and Dominique's ancestors made me suddenly shameful of my family. One moment I was terrified that my ancestors were all sitting up in Heaven and judging my same-sex attractions, and the next I would judge them for what I assumed they'd done to black bodies. Less than a year later at LIA, I would wonder why our genogram keys didn't feature the sins of slavery or racism, why it seemed so much of history had been left out.

Sitting there in the midst of my professors' intelligent conversations, I had felt like both an impostor and a traitor. I smiled at the appropriate moments, made droll comments about my upbringing, mocked the politics of almost everyone in my hometown. Yet it was also true that coming home often made me feel, if not proud of my heritage, then at least grateful for its familiarity. At home I was able to say an elegant prayer, offer a bit of wisdom about God's grace, recite scripture at the appropriate moment, offer my best smile. At home, it was a relief to slip back into a world that was known, to deal in platitudes, quiet my mind. With each pilgrimage to and from home, the boundaries between the two territories grew weaker, and I grew more terrified of what would happen once I finally lost my footing.

Both sides seemed to suggest the same efficient solution: cut ties. Either abandon what you've known your entire life and your family, or abandon what you're learning about life and new ideas. I began to see strong evidence in favor of the latter, though I didn't think it would be easy to forget the sense of wonder I'd experienced in my Western Lit class while learning about what the church referred to as a sinful pagan past. There had been a moment in the middle of our class discussion of the *Odyssey*, Odysseus stopping up his ears to muffle the siren call, when I sat up in my desk, unplugged my own ears, raised my hand, and asked to be untied from the mast.

"It never gets old, does it?" my father said. The truck had slipped beneath a canopy of yellowing trees. "God's creation?"

"No," I said, pressing my hand to the glass, watching the pale leaves slide through the gaps between my fingers.

"We'll get through this," he said. "I've talked with Brother Stevens. He has some ideas."

Brother Stevens was the pastor of our church. After my father decided to become a preacher, the two of them grew very close, spending most of their free hours together on the paisley-patterned chairs in Brother Stevens's church office. Though my father had yet to be ordained as an official preacher, he often substituted for Brother Stevens when the man was sick.

I hadn't seen much of Brother Stevens since moving to college, and I was happier for it. There was something about his small close-set eyes that made me nervous. In high school, when I ran the church projector for him on Sunday mornings, I had felt as though he were directing every word of his condemnation against me, as though I were the Satan he warned us about, sitting up in my mounted booth above the rest of the congregation, mocking God with my fantasies of the straight-backed Brewer twins who sat in the front row. During sermons, he would sometimes speak of the prodigal daughter who continually made his life more complicated: her drug overdoses, her live-in boyfriends, her casual use of the Lord's name in vain, her frequent incarceration. She was the typical preacher's kid gone wild. As a result, Brother Stevens had developed a policy of tough love. He had left his daughter to fend for herself numerous times, though he'd often agreed to help foot the bill for rehab.

I knew that whatever advice he had to offer my father would be harsh. I had a hunch that inviting me to the jail ministry had been his idea, part of a scared-straight routine that the church employed when, for example, it invited ex–drug addicts to recount their horror stories in long-winded testimonies that took up the majority of the service, most of our congregants leaving teary eyed and feeling lucky to be alive in their own skin as they walked out the front door. Despite my hunch, I still believed Brother Stevens might be right. A strict, dark, new perspective might be exactly what I needed.

WE ROLLED to a stop in front of the main highway, and my father switched on his blinker. "It's the difference between what's natural and what's not natural," he said, the brakes hissing beneath us. "You've always been a good Christian, but you've somehow gotten the two mixed up. We'll get you to the right counselor."

I hadn't felt truly natural since junior high, when I first saw my handsome neighbor walking his dog down the street: a moment that had me begging secretly for a leash. "I don't want to talk about it," I said.

"Your friend what's-his-name didn't have a problem talking about it." *Friend.* The word sounded cavalier, without a trace of irony, landing smugly between the blinker's ticking like a hard fact. It made me want to jerk the wheel in the wrong direction, slam the gas pedal to the plastic floorboard, drive us into the side of the nearest building.

"He's probably told half the town by now," my father continued.

I had been avoiding public places for this very reason. David didn't live too far from our town, and odds were he'd already told several mutual friends I was gay in an effort to save face. I'd found out from one such mutual friend that he was on academic probation, that no one had seen him on campus for a month, that it was likely he'd moved back in with his parents. He'd probably exaggerated facts, made it sound like *I* was the pedophile. He'd probably told people I had tried to sleep with him. (My roommate, Sam, had already decided to move out of our room; I was now rooming with my friend Charles, and I suspected that the reason for Sam's sudden departure was that he'd heard these rumors.) There was nothing to do now but hide, wait for the current to calm, and try to find a cure.

"I don't care what he tells people," I said. "He's not a Christian."

"I thought he went to church," my father said, pulling onto the highway. "I thought you said he was a good kid."

"Yeah, a Pentecostal church," I said, remembering the old post office with its rusted metal beams and its brightly lit stage, its motor oil. "It's not the same."

The words came out of my mouth without my permission. Blaming, self-righteous in nature, they felt natural, marching into place somewhere between a truth and a lie, powered almost exclusively by rage. They leant themselves to a sense of conviction, of purpose. They snapped everything around us into focus: the double yellow lines, the strip malls along the sides of the road, the faces looking out from smudged windows. They carried with them the tone and lazy dinner-party logic of some of my professors, but with very little of the same content.

Months later, when first meeting the LIA staff, I would instantly recognize these hybrid words as my own, though I wouldn't know the full extent of their power until they were used against me.

"They speak in tongues and use anointing oil," I said. "It's disgusting."

"Judge not," my father said, the blinker snapping back into place as he turned the wheel, "lest ye be judged."

"Thou shalt not bear false witness," I said. More than a decade of Sunday school lessons, and I could recite scripture almost as well as my father, use it just as easily to justify my means.

"Honor thy father and mother," my father said, using the trump card that always put an end to our disagreements.

I crossed my arms. *That's what I'm doing*, I thought. *That's why I'm here.* But I couldn't really be sure. I was here, at least in part, because there seemed to be no other option.

My father steered us onto a back road lined with maple trees on either side. The dying leaves brushed the roof of the truck, a dry rustling followed by the light thump of a tree branch. *Right palm facing upward. Rotate. Repeat. Left palm facing upward. Rotate.* I focused my gaze on a distant tree trunk and held on until we swept past it, until the pattern of its bark grew indistinguishable, something easily forgotten in the forest.

WHEN I WAS in junior high, my father took me into the beating heart of the forest to go hunting. I had pushed aside its pine branches in the quiet haze of the morning, my breath fogging beside his, our twin clouds joining for a moment in front of us, blinding us as they caught the sun. As my father tapped my shoulder to draw my attention, I raised my rifle and aimed its scope at the space beneath the shoulder of a large doe. One eye to the scope, the other winking, I watched this doe for what seemed like several minutes, though it couldn't have been for more than a few seconds.

The doe appeared to me as an image of the forest itself, its wild grace effortless and unstudied, part of a natural world that didn't feel the need to question itself. It didn't seem to care if it lived or died. It simply *was*. Its awareness was all. The bullet I eventually fired landed somewhere in the path in front of us, missing the doe by several feet. My father spent the rest of the morning convincing me that I had hit this doe—that we were here to track its trail of blood, its thin red thread, through the forest—though I knew better. I knew he was trying to comfort me.

I wondered if this was how it was going to be. I would aim for something in the county jail, some truth just out of reach, perhaps behind a wall of thick black bars, and my father would spend the rest of his life trying to convince me that I'd hit the target. The deeper we descended into this labyrinth, the more lost we would become, to ourselves and to each other. Tracing everything back to where it had all begun would become impossible, our origins the raw materials of myths.

"HAVE YOU MADE many *good* friends at college?" my father said, speeding through a yellow light.

I thought of Charles and Dominique, the twin music majors who sang spirituals in the dorm lounge and asked me to watch *Imitation of Life*, what they described as a "white-friendly intro" into the black experience. "If you don't cry after watching this movie, you've got something wrong with you," Charles had said. "White people always cry with that one." Charles, Dominique, and I were quickly becoming close friends, but I was afraid of what my father would say if I described them. Though he claimed to have "no problem with black people," I didn't want to bring up race when I mentioned them, didn't want to parade them around as my token black friends, didn't want to dig too deeply into my ancestors' cotton-ginning history for fear I would inherit an even greater sense of shame than I already had. There was also the fact that my college life and my home life were becoming increasingly separate entities, and after David's call to my parents, I was afraid of what other secrets might come to light if I started talking about my other life.

"Most people aren't that good," I said, tapping the glass with my index finger. "You have to be discerning." Original sin was a concept my father and I knew well.

I thought of my professors, and of my Western Lit class, how exhilarated I'd felt being able to discuss ideas and opinions as though they were nothing more than dirt or tiny pebbles we could sift through our fingers. I recalled how ideas that had once seemed so otherworldly and unapproachable came unglued before my eyes, lost their many associations with the angry and loving God I'd been taught so long to believe in, how they had assembled themselves into grist for other religions, other philosophies, other ways of daily living.

After a few more minutes of silence, my father turned up

Creedence until the music blasted my eardrums, shook the windows with its bass.

I see earthquakes and lightning, Creedence sang. *I see bad times today.*

I slouched in my seat, propped my feet on the dash. The seatbelt locked, pinning me to the leather. I didn't talk the rest of the way. I was in my father's territory now, the Bible Belt more real to me than the one hugging my chest.

AT COLLEGE, Dostoyevsky's Underground Man still took over from time to time, inviting me to recede into the background, blend in with the furniture, observe. The only difference, post-David, was a deeper need to hide that sometimes overtook my days, kept me in my dorm room for so long that I would piss in discarded water bottles, tuck them under my bed, forget about them. When I later found them during one of my more sociable states, I would greet them as I would a stranger, shocked by their sudden appearance, looking back at my former self as an ugly impostor. *Who would do this?* I'd think. *Who would be so desperate?*

When I learned about Freudian theory during my first semester, I grew even more concerned. *This must be some unresolved childhood issue*, I thought, remembering my bedroom carpet hieroglyphs. *This must be another sign of my brokenness.* No, suddenly switching to an Old Testament perspective, *my sinfulness.*

There seemed to be no branch of psychology, philosophy, or literature I read that couldn't be bent to prove my guilt. By that same token, there seemed to be no idea I'd encountered that didn't complicate my understanding of Christianity, that didn't call into question my parents' God-given right to dictate my beliefs. I decided that this was what it was like to be truly insane, that only insane people clung to both sides so doggedly, refused to let them part ways, let them battle inside the mind.

THE TREES gave way to flat grazing fields studded with cows then to the rectangular buildings that served as the administrative center of the town, each one tethered together by the dark cracked asphalt whose deep potholes my father's truck easily absorbed. Through the cracked window, I could smell the strong scent of manure heated by the warm morning sun, and something else—some mixture of gasoline and rusted metal found only in farming communities where the methods of corporate farming have advanced so ruthlessly, so rapidly, that it is necessary to devote large plots of land to junkyards and fill them with old machines stripped of valuable parts.

The county jail sat on the outskirts of town, hidden behind a cluster of white-roofed buildings and a red Conoco gas station that also served as a tire and lube shop. Beside the jail stood the county courthouse, an identical building with only a few windows facing the road, last-minute additions that only temporarily relieved the uniform brick façade.

I sat up to get a better look, the warm leather leaving the back of my sweaty shirt with a quiet hiss. I had been expecting barbed wire, watchtowers, rotating guards in blue uniform. I had been expecting a series of security checkpoints, each more severe than the last. Some expensive Hollywood set. Instead, drawing closer to these squat buildings, I had a sense that what the town wanted most of all to hide might also receive the most traffic since there were so many cars darting freely in and out of the parking lot.

My father parked near the back, slamming the lever between us into park with the open palm of his hand.

"What do you think?" he said, turning to me, the leather squeaking beneath him.

I fear rivers overflowing, Creedence sang. *I hear the voice of rage and ruin.*

My father cut the engine, muffling Creedence midnote.

"It's different than I expected," I said, looking up at the white metal roof that caught the sun at a bad angle, sent it shining directly into my eyes. It made sense, seeing it now, that people in town wouldn't want to spend all of their money on a state-of-the-art jail. They could use their taxes for keeping the beautiful things beautiful, let the ugly things remain ugly, allow the facility's dark brick to recede beneath the mountain-studded mecca surrounding it.

I had learned by now that there was a cumulative effect to beauty. If people already saw something as beautiful, the object of their affection would continue to receive all possible praise and attention. *Rose is a rose is a rose is a rose*, Gertrude Stein, my new favorite poet, quipped. Naming something beautiful made it so. I'd seen this in the way the church spoke of marriage as a sacred institution and in the ONE MAN + ONE WOMAN bumper stickers people sported on their vehicles, the same ones my father would hand to any customer passing through his dealership's service department.

Naming something ugly had a similar effect. The sound of my mother's vomiting the night she drove me home had taught me this lesson better than anything else ever had. I was gay, had been named as such, a fact that, once ingested, had to be immediately expelled.

My father and I sat in silence for a few more seconds.

"We're not going to talk about your situation anymore," he said. "Not until we know something else."

I wondered if my parents had already arranged a therapy session, if they were just waiting to tell me after the jail. As irrational as it seemed to me even at the time, I thought of my visit here as a test. A test of my conviction, of my courage, of the love I felt for my family.

Without missing a beat, my father opened the console between us and pulled out a jumbo bag of peanut M&M's. It seemed magical, this gesture. One second before there had been only brown leather and the dark plastic of the dashboard and the dark colors of our clothes, and now here there was this bright yellow bag of hard candy reflecting the morning light in my father's hands.

"Catch," he said, tossing the bag in my direction.

My hands fumbled, botching the catch, the bag landing in my lap to the sound of a hundred tiny marbles clacking at once.

"What is this?" I said.

"M&M's."

I juggled the bright yellow bag between my hands. "I'm just wondering why you have them."

"Here's what you'll do," my father said, opening the driver's-side door, a gust of unseasonably warm air filling our cabin. "You'll give a handful of M&M's to any inmate who can recite at least two Bible verses."

"That's the plan?" I asked. "Candy?"

"A few pieces of candy might seem like nothing to you, but these inmates don't have much. They love it when I visit."

Church congregants often said my father's plans were inspired, and for good reason: They almost always came out of left field, caught you unawares, were just close enough to the point of absurdity to provide a little thrill in the pit of the stomach, made you question what could possibly happen next. Though I felt I'd outgrown them by now, I had to admit that my father's tactics often spawned from his own peculiar brand of genius. He understood what people wanted most of all, and he learned how to build his mission work around it.

Even though I hadn't asked him, I could already guess my father's logic. Give the inmates something they craved, something to work toward all week, and then lead them into a deeper understanding of scripture, their bodies giving way to their souls. It was a variation on what Jesus had performed near Bethsaida, transforming seven loaves of bread and a few fish into enough food to feed five thousand men. My father's miracle would be, like Jesus's, one of magnification: A few peanut M&M's planted like a seed in these men's bellies, and they would feel satisfied by the shock of the nearly forgotten taste. Then—only then—would they be prepared to receive the body of Christ.

This was a reward system that had worked for me when I was younger. At vacation Bible school, I would recite the books of the Bible in order—Deuteronomy, Joshua, Judges—the names strange and weighty on my tongue, conjuring up images of dusty scrolls and old bearded men sitting on gilded thrones; I had learned as many names as I could, knowing that our pastor would later reward me with candy. *Suffer little children*, the Bible says. I had heard my father explain once that the inmates were in many ways like little children caught with their hands in various candy jars—and that we were *all* like little children, lost until we found Jesus. Now we would teach the inmates that the rewards of candy, and eventually of heaven, came only after due diligence. "We have to appeal to their lower natures," my father said, "before we can appeal to their higher ones."

This past year my father had learned not to give the inmates anything that wasn't mass produced. He later told me that he had once filled a water cooler with grapes and ice, and passed out dripping bunches through the bars, only to find out later that the men had tried to make hooch, filling Ziploc bags with juice from his grapes and putting pieces of stale bread into them, tucking the bags under their bunks to ferment.

Lying in bed at night, I would imagine these men gathered around the little bags, whispering gently and caressing the cool plastic with their calloused fingers. I would imagine all of them with tattooed arms wrapped around one another's shoulders, acting soft and sweet when no one was looking. I would imagine joining them behind the bars, slipping into one of the bunks, gripping the plastic underbelly, and sipping their warm wine. Then, the moment the guilt began to flood my chest and my breathing grew shallow, I would erase the thought, close my eyes so tightly that orange spots began to crowd my vision. The images would then dim, fade behind a wall of swirling dots, no longer beautiful to me.

BEFORE AGREEING to come to the jail, I hadn't asked my father anything about what went on inside. I only knew that I needed to follow him, give him and God my best shot, do the things that might make me worthy in both of their eyes.

At the age of nine, while watching the Disney version of *Peter Pan*, I had sat transfixed before the living-room television as Peter shook his shadow out to dry—and it was to this sense of awe that I needed to return at the age of eighteen, to become a shadow, stitch myself to the soles of my father's feet until there was no longer any danger of being lost or trodden upon. I had already grown so much in that first semester of college, I

had already been through so much, that the thought of returning to eternal youth, of becoming a child once again in God's
eyes, seemed an impossible act. I had flown to a new territory,
but unlike what happened to Peter, this territory had altered me
completely, rendered me somewhat of a stranger in my own
home.

I imagined this was how David's boy had felt just after the
rape, a stranger to himself and others around him, and I wondered if—and hoped that—he had found someone to lead him
out of the maze where David had ravaged and left him. In my
unconscious, this unnamed boy had somehow become Brandon. I had nightmares about it, moments of transfiguration in
which the boy would stand up from a pile of soiled sheets and
walk across Chloe's basement floor to the edge of my sleeping
bag. The slapping of feet on cold concrete. And in the blue light
of the television his features would become Brandon's, and he
would ask me if I truly wanted to be gay, and when I didn't
answer, he would ask me if I truly wanted to kill myself, and
when I didn't answer again, he would lie beside me on the
sleeping bag, stare white eyed into my eyes like Janet Leigh in
Psycho until the dream ended.

Despite this dream, I hadn't called Brandon to check up on
him, too terrified of hearing something I didn't want to hear,
too unprepared for whatever Chloe might say if she answered
the phone. I still hadn't spoken to Chloe since cutting off communication, and I didn't want to face her judgment once she
found out what I was going through. How could I begin to

explain to her a situation that, for all intents and purposes, didn't exist?

On the ride to the jail, I had braced myself for David's sudden appearance each time our truck hugged a curve in the road. I knew it was irrational, that there was no reason for David to be on these roads, but just the mention of his name had the power to conjure him. I had examined each vehicle we passed for traces of his pale face, darting my eyes quickly from one passenger to the next so I wouldn't have to endure prolonged eye contact. Considering my current situation, however, the county jail seemed like the safest place to avoid him. I had already learned that no one was going to punish him for what he did. Our Presbyterian college's pastor had counseled me to keep my head down, avoid scandal, since it would only be my word against his.

Keeping my head down was something David taught me best of all, but it was the others—the ones whom I later told—who insisted on a permanent spinal readjustment. What David had done to this boy and me was invisible, something people around me simply didn't want to discuss. In taking on the power of invisibility, I had also given up my voice.

"Don't be scared," my father said, eyeing me. "These men are just like everyone else. They just got caught."

We both stepped out of the truck. I held the bag of M&M's in a tight grip.

"I'm not scared," I said, my syllables cracking open. *Ska-aired*.

My father clicked the remote on his keys and the truck honked beside me, flashing its useless headlights. He had dressed down for the occasion, standing in pale jeans and white tennis shoes and an untucked dark blue button-down, his graying black hair tousled by the occasional breeze that slipped between the mountains behind us. Since many of the inmates inside were poor and down on their luck, he didn't want to wear anything too expensive and give them the wrong impression. He wasn't Jim Bakker. He didn't want their money. He wanted their souls safe and secure in Heaven.

I stood beside him in a black *Legend of Zelda* T-shirt, frayed denim jeans, and flip-flops. I'd rediscovered the T-shirt the night before in the bottom of my old dresser, after the two-hour drive home from college. Though I hadn't touched a video game in over a year, *Zelda* seemed an appropriate choice. Link, the game's silent protagonist, was an expert at entering dungeons and solving puzzles. I needed him now more than ever.

I followed my father across the black asphalt. We stepped into the partial shade of the jail, and he rotated his silver watch until its glass face glinted up at him, burned a white half-moon onto his cheek.

"Wild Thing should be here by now," he said, the half-moon sliding between the cleft of his chin.

Wild Thing was my father's nickname for Jeff, a man who washed cars for him full-time and one of the members of my

father's prayer circle. I had worked alongside him every summer since my father took over the dealership, had learned how
to detail cars from him. He taught me to notice the smallest
blemishes in used cars: the dusty space between the speedome-
ter's face and its glass cover, the crumb-filled margins between
the front seats and the console, the gooey inner linings of backseat storage pockets. He taught me that details were what mattered most. People wanted to believe that someone was paying
attention, that someone cared enough to dig deep.

When my father first met him, Wild Thing's hair had been
long and greasy, slicked back like a rodent's, and his words had
run together in one long slur. After my father led Wild Thing
to the Lord, kneeling with him in his office, the name had stuck
as a sort of ironic misnomer. Wild Thing was hardly wild anymore.

We had made a good team. When we worked together, he
took to the chemicals while I took to the pressure washer. When
we encountered an impossible stain, both of us took turns
scrubbing it with a rag, picking up where the other left off.
Unlike me, however, Wild Thing had been able to give *himself*
a detailing, used his skills to tame whatever past he'd had. He'd
found a way out of the darkness—gotten a haircut, covered up
his tattoos with long sleeves, learned how to enunciate his
syllables—and it led him to teach these inmates to follow the
same path.

He showed up a few minutes later, his short hair slicked to
one side with a generous amount of product.

"Sorry I'm late," he said, his breathing shallow, his face sweaty. "Had to go back for my Bible." He held up a black King James Bible, fanned it back and forth in front of his face. He never went anywhere without it, a new Christian "hungry for the Word of God," as my father put it. As far as I could tell, he knew nothing of my situation. My father seemed to confirm this with a look that said, *You might be here because of your sin, but you don't need to acknowledge it, you don't need to let anyone else know our shame.*

"God didn't waste any time this morning," Wild Thing said, craning his neck to look at the sky, his Adam's apple bobbing. "Turned out to be a beautiful day."

I followed his gaze. A raft of cirrus clouds was breaking apart above the mountain peaks, tumbling lazily through the troposphere. It was one of those days when the blackness of space seems to press harder against the atmosphere, lending the sky a richer saturation, unnoticed until the eye chooses to reveal its depth.

"That's the sight of God resting," my father said. "'And He rested on the seventh day.'"

"We don't get to rest," Wild Thing said, gesturing to the jail entrance. "God made this world, and now we've got to make sure we don't ruin it with our sin."

The three of us walked up to the jail's metal door. My father pressed a small red button in the center of a metal box and announced himself. He turned back to us, clearing his throat.

"Ready to save some souls?" he said.

"Been waiting all morning," Wild Thing said.

From somewhere above our heads came the sound of a mounted camera revolving to face us. The three of us looked up, watched its lens zoom. From that high angle, our faces must have formed a triangle, with mine as the rear vertex.

The door hummed to life, the sound of a game show buzzer. My father pushed open the door. I followed him and Wild Thing inside the anteroom, the shock of air-conditioning on my skin, and waited for the other door to buzz open. We stood in a cramped metal box, as though in an elevator, with a small window looking out into an empty reception area.

"Just so we're all on the same page," my father said, his voice a sudden echo. "What's the only verse the inmates can't get any candy for?"

I squared my shoulders. This time I didn't hesitate to guess. "John 11:35." It was a verse every devout Missionary Baptist kid had tried "memorizing" at least once, usually when first asked to recite something in vacation Bible school, and usually because it was so short. My father didn't want the inmates to slack on reading their Bibles by studying such a simple verse; he wanted as many of God's words to enter their heads as possible. *Jesus wept*: two simple words that had haunted me. I hadn't cried since the night my mother drove me back from campus—since I had watched the high-line wires dip between the pale stars, thinking only of what my father would say once he found out, the wires stringing together constellations I couldn't name. I didn't plan to cry again anytime soon. When I saw a man crying in church, it seemed as though he were about to rip the skin from his face, peel it back for everyone to see his second, secret self. In the weeks following my rape, any time I thought about crying, I pinched myself hard enough to focus on the pain instead. I wasn't about to give anyone another opportunity to see my weakness.

My father turned to me, his hazel eyes flashing green in the fluorescents. The door buzzed open in front of us, but he didn't move.

"That's right," he said, raising his hand to clap me on the back. I flinched involuntarily, and his hand froze.

"Right," he repeated, opening the door.

Wild Thing and I walked with him up to the front desk. A police officer with a half-chewed cigar sticking out of one corner of his mouth nodded at us and buzzed us into the next door. This was a small jail in a small Ozark town, so the jailers knew my father well. No need to present ID, no need for a frisking.

"Make sure to stay at least five feet away from the cells," my father said. "And don't listen if some of them cuss at you."

He motioned for me to enter first. I nodded. I wanted to prove that I was as brave as he. I wanted to prove that I could change. *Open the doors and see all the people.*

THE HALLWAY inside was dark. It was dark, but this could have been simply because we had just stepped out of the sun.

Neon spots swirled in an arc across my path, popped along the edges of the dim cells. *Phosphenes*, my high school biology teacher called them when I fell asleep in her class. *Did you enjoy your visit with the phosphenes?* The night David forced me to his bed, I had seen hundreds of them, pink and yellow and orange swirls gliding like figure skaters beneath my eyelids. *Sometimes this is referred to as Prisoner's Cinema*, the biology teacher continued. A phenomenon that was associated with staring at blank walls for hours—in my case, staring at my blank bedroom wall with a pair of scissors in hand, hoping a solution would present itself, that God would write the answer with His disembodied hand, as He had for King Belshazzar in the Old Testament.

I kept to the wall, my shoulder dipping in and out of the gaps between its white concrete blocks. Occasionally I could make out the pale flash of a smiling face striped with dark metal bars. None of the inmates seemed to stir. None of them said a word except for the occasional "Hello" or "Nice to see you." I kept my candy-filled hands away from them, afraid they might lunge through the bars, though they all seemed overly polite.

I could hear my father's footsteps echoing behind me, but I didn't turn back, afraid he would detect fear in my eyes. The previous weekend, when I'd visited him at the dealership, my father had raised his fist to strike me, a moment when our mutual fear of my sexuality first met. I'd made some kind of joke in the showroom while everyone was watching, something about him not wanting to seem weak in front of his customers, something I hadn't been able to recall the minute he brought me into his office and threatened me with his fist. In the next moment, his face had filled with terror at the recognition of what he was doing, what his father had once done to him, and he relaxed his fist, apologizing, looking down at the carpet the whole time. *Do it*, I thought. *Do it, and I'll have a free pass. Do it, and I don't have to love you anymore.* But he hadn't done anything. A tear formed in the corner of his eye, ran down his cheek to the spot between the cleft of his chin, and that was it. Whether the tear was for his gay son or for himself, I couldn't say. I was mostly thankful he hadn't begun to weep. "We'll figure something out," he'd said, his voice trembling. "We'll get you to a specialist."

I reminded myself that he wouldn't knowingly lead me into danger—that despite everything he had chosen to relax his fist—and I relaxed a little in that dark hallway. My father was the one person in a crowd you could rely on to respond immediately if an emergency popped up. When I was younger, he would survey every carnival ride at the county fair before I was allowed to ride any of them. As I swung by him on the rotating swing, my legs kicking up, the summer air tickling the backs of my knees, I would see his serious face as a fixed point in the turning world, his eyes fastened to the bolt above my head. He seemed always to be right behind me, watching over me. College had made me stray from him, from his and the church's teachings, and I had been severely punished. The bolt had come unfastened, and I had plummeted to the spot where David could easily pin me down.

"Excuse me," the cigar-chewing policeman said, moving past me. He spat clumps of tobacco into a Styrofoam cup in his hand. Catapulting from his lips, they looked like tiny dark pieces of confetti. In his other hand he carried a large brass key ring filled with what looked like hundreds of keys. His fingers sped through several keys until he found the right one and plugged it into the door at the end of the hallway, jerking open the lock.

"Wait here," my father said, moving past me, heading inside with the policeman to an area where a large group of inmates awaited us in one large cell. The officer and my father were going ahead of Wild Thing and me to ensure that everything was in order for the service. Each time my father visited the inmates, he had to spend at least ten minutes calming them first, asking them to turn down the mounted television in the corner of the cell, to stop cussing at one another.

Through the open door, I could also make out the women's cell block at the other end of the large room, the figures of several older women moving away from the bars as my father passed, embarrassed grimaces overtaking their faces, strands of long hair falling limply over their shoulders.

"Your old man used to preach to those women, too," Wild Thing said, leaning against the wall.

The door groaned shut in front of us, followed by the sound of its latch sliding into the faceplate.

"What happened?" I said. "Why'd he stop?"

"They started getting too nasty," he said. "They offered him favors, if you know what I mean."

You don't know what it feels like to be with a woman.

"What did he do about it?" I said.

"You know how your dad can be," Wild Thing said, eyeing the cell across from us. The man inside didn't seem to be listening; he was lying on his back, his features concealed by the forearm he'd draped across his face. As I later discovered, this hallway was reserved for some of the more extreme cases.

"He tried even harder after that," Wild Thing continued. "Preached better than I'd ever heard him preach."

"Did he change them?"

Wild Thing shook his head. "The things those women said to him after that," he said. "I can't repeat it in good conscience."

I wondered when my father had told this to Wild Thing. Had they exchanged looks of momentary bliss, stories of the women they'd been with, of near misses that had almost resulted in a fall from grace? The one time my father took me to Hooters, around the time I hit puberty, I had been so obsequious to the waitresses, looking down at their shoes the whole time, that he must have mistaken this for a foot fetish. "There are plenty of parts to admire on a woman," he'd said, as if we were talking about nothing more than his hot rods. We'd never gone back.

"He finally quit though," Wild Thing said. "Sometimes there's just no curing people."

Months later, in a gesture that would shock our church, my father would receive permission from the jail to marry two of the inmates who had known each other before incarceration, proving that he could still reach the women in some capacity, that this sacred ceremony might lead some of them to the straight path. He would stand with his back to a large maple tree, recite 1 Corinthians—*Love is patient, love is kind*—allow the other inmates to throw a short reception in the big cell, and arrange for a conjugal visit that night. *Marriage knows no boundaries*, the gesture seemed to suggest, *so long as it is sanctified in God's eyes.* The ceremony would earn him even more respect than he already had, inspiring many female inmates to kneel on their concrete cell floors and ask Jesus into their hearts.

Wild Thing dug his hand into the back pocket of his jeans. When he pulled it out again, he was holding several multicolored tracts. He held out a stack for me.

"Now we just hand the women a stack of these and hope they learn something from Christ's message."

I tucked the bag of M&M's under one arm, took the stack, and thumbed through the thick pages, the bright red and gold Comic Sans typeface glinting up at me in the dim light. I flipped through to the end of a booklet, to a watercolor illustration of a heavenly mansion with one large street of glittering gold stretching out in a straight path in front of it. THERE IS ONLY ONE WAY TO ENTER THE KINGDOM OF HEAVEN, the booklet read. J-E-S-U-S.

I had seen these tracts lying around our house each time I

came home, more and more of them littering our counters, our tables, the seats of our chairs. When I would leave again for college, my father would urge me to take a few just in case I found the chance to minister to a lost college student. The most I had ever done was leave a few of these tracts on top of a toilet-paper dispenser in the library bathroom. Exiting the stall, however, I'd imagined strangers flipping through these pages, their fingerprints melding with mine; it had given me a thrill to know that this would occur at their most vulnerable moments, jeans bunched around their ankles. Like my father, I knew something about temptation. It seemed the best option, in those cases, was to toss the tracts and keep walking. Given enough time, a solution might present itself.

"You know what?" Wild Thing said, running a hand through his phantom hair, forgetting, like always, that a tangled greasy mess no longer covered his head. "We should hand out some of these tracts while we're waiting for your dad."

"That sounds good," I said, pocketing the tracts. The words felt hollow, but I was committed.

"Good," Wild Thing echoed. "We can head in opposite directions, talk to a few men, and meet back here."

"Good," I said.

He turned away. His faith in me was instant: I was my father's son. The path had been rolled out right before my feet, unfurling all the way to the edge of God's gilded throne. Wild Thing must have believed that *I* was the lucky one, skipping so many steps.

I watched him walk down the hallway in the direction of the entrance. He headed down an adjoining hallway, and I was left alone.

I flipped back to the beginning of the tract. *Are you lost?* it read. There was a drawing of a small brown-haired boy standing in the middle of a poorly lit street. Leaning on a lamppost in the distance was a dark-cloaked figure, Satan himself, cartoonishly evil, with a crooked cane and a sharp red tail sliding out from the back of his cloak. Despite his menace, Satan looked lonely, standing there by himself in his isolated patch of darkness.

THERE HAD BEEN only one year when I hadn't felt alone. I was twelve years old, a time when Missionary Baptists would say I was born again, the moment in every true believer's life when you accept Jesus Christ as your personal savior and vow to be a Christian for the rest of your life. Though the feeling had waned since I was a young child, I could still feel God's all-encompassing love emanating from some deep shelf behind my solar plexus. The feeling mounted itself there on a night when I was lying in my bottom bunk and feeling as though I didn't deserve to live. This was after our preacher gave a fiery sermon about how Christians must humble themselves before the Lord, how we must realize how wicked and small we are the minute we leave our mother's womb. That night, within the empty echo chamber of my mind, a place usually reserved for the petty

considerations of the day, I asked, "Am I loved?" The answer
came in the form of a physical burning that traveled through my
whole body, sent my limbs trembling. In that instant, I loved the
feel of the sheets on my back. I loved the way the bedroom carpet felt cool beneath my toes when I stood up. I loved every face
I had ever seen, every blemish and worry line. I covered my face
in my hands and wept for joy. In asking for love, I had given it
to myself and others. And at the time, I believed that God had
lent me this capacity. As I grew older, however, and as love came
to me less easily, I began to wonder if that feeling wasn't all just
a hallucination. After all, this had been an untested love. Love,
over time, could either blossom or wither, become a source of
wonder or a remembered ache.

I LOOKED UP to see the inmate across from me sitting upright
in his bunk. He was watching me. He must have been listening
to us the whole time. He was older, with gray hair cuffing his
ears. Half-moon worry lines etched the skin around his eyes,
and his long arms fell between his knees like limp vines.

"Hello," I said. "What's your name?"

The man nodded, his eyes still watching me. I tried not to
follow the length of his arms, tried not to look at the slight slope
of a bulge between his legs. It was all too familiar, with him sitting on the bunk that way. I felt something overturn inside my
chest, some hidden pocket of rage I'd previously forgotten.

"Where are you from?" I said. It was a stupid question. The inmates were all locals. Most of them had been born and raised in this town.

The man coughed, blinking. "What do you have there?" he said, his voice a dry rattle. "Candy?"

"Yes," I said, holding the bag of M&M's in front of me. The tiny marbles shifted to one side. "But I have these, too." I reached inside my pants pocket and pulled out a wrinkled batch of tracts, stepping closer, holding them out for the man to examine. I didn't touch the bars, afraid they might crumble at the slightest pressure.

He looked from my hands to my face, from one to the other, as if trying to decide which was more dangerous. A look of fear passed between us. As his eyes watched me, I thought of all the doors that kept this man from seeing the view of the Ozarks outside, from seeing the way the fog lifted over the peaks each morning in pink ribbons. It was no wonder my father's tracts worked so well, their bright streets a stylized dream of the world outside.

"I know what those are," the man finally said. "Your dad's been trying to hand me one for ages."

"Oh," I said. I looked away, my gaze circling once again to the bunk. I couldn't help it.

"Your dad's funny about those things," he said. There was a slight pause. "If I took one, would you give me those M&M's?"

My eyes adjusted to the dim; I could just begin to make out the man's weak attempt at decorating his cell: a few magenta crayon drawings on the wall from what looked like the hand of a child, a faded calendar open to the wrong month, a stack of letters on the corner of his desk. Unlike the large men's cell where my father and I would be handing out candy, there was no television here to distract him. Perhaps he had done something violent. Perhaps he had killed a man, assaulted a woman.

"If you can recite two Bible verses," I said. "I'll give you a handful."

The worry lines of the man's face grew more pronounced, his eyes receding deep behind his furrowed brow. "I don't have a Bible," he said.

"My dad probably has one in the next room," I said. "I can get you one real quick, and then you can find two short verses. It'll be easy."

"What if I told you I couldn't read?"

I looked at the stack of letters on his desk. Did he have someone to read to him or was he simply telling a lie he couldn't be bothered to conceal?

"Maybe I could read them to you," I said, "and you could repeat them."

"What if I told you I have a bad memory?"

My throat tightened. I closed my eyes. *Left palm facing out. Breathe. Turn the left hand in.* The man continuing to watch me from his bunk. *Breathe.* All I had to do was hand this man a tract and walk away. It was the least I could do. *Do not say to yourself, "Turn the left hand." Awareness is all.*

"Why don't you just take one of these tracts," I said, "and we can talk again next week?"

"No," the man said. The word was harder than the steel between us. I didn't press him further.

That was the best I could do. When my father returned a few minutes later, I would hide my failure behind a smile.

THERE WERE DETAILS I would sometimes forget about the night of my father's ultimatum. The memory would dissolve, and then it would return at unexpected moments. Waiting in the jail hallway for my father to come back, tracts glued to my sweaty hand as I stared at a patch of bare concrete above the exit, I remembered the worst moment from that night.

It had been sometime after midnight. I was on my way to the kitchen for a glass of water. I had paused before the sliver of lamplight between the door frame and door of my father's bedroom.

"What about the doctor?" my mother had whispered, her hand cupping the cordless phone receiver. My father sat next to her on the edge of the bed, watching the carpet. I had no idea who might be on the other end of the line, whom they might be talking to about me.

"Do you think it could be hormones?" my mother said.

"It can't be hormones," my father said. "The boy doesn't need a doctor. All he needs is to read the Bible more."

"How do you know?" my mother asked, covering the receiver. "How do you know what he needs? Maybe he needs a doctor."

My mother looked up at that moment. I couldn't tell if she saw me, but she scooted over on the bed out of my line of sight.

I walked into the kitchen, stared up at the half-moon just outside the window, at its reflection gliding along the softly rippling lake, unprepared for whatever lay ahead.

AFTER THE JAIL, after walking away from the unbeliever and wandering the hallways with my unopened bag of M&M's, I began to look forward to the mysterious doctor I'd overheard my parents talking about. Though I had no idea what this doctor might do for me, and though I didn't ask my parents if they had scheduled an appointment, I hoped this exam might be easier than the ones that had come before. I began to look forward to the idea of a needle pricking my skin, to blood funneling into labeled vials, to anything concrete that might tell me what was wrong with me or why I couldn't perform what seemed to me then the simplest of tasks: a humble exchange from one hand to another, the passage of Jesus's Word between two people. Maybe my mother had been right. Maybe something was off about my hormones. Maybe my hormones made me less of a man. I had failed my father's test at the jail, though he hadn't even questioned me about the tracts, though I wasn't certain either of us even knew what a passing grade might resemble. Perhaps it would look something like Wild Thing's smiling face when he came back empty-handed yet armed with stories of the men who courteously took his tracts into their hands, said they'd read the words before his next visit. I didn't know anything more now than I had before my visit to the jail.

A WEEK PASSED. My parents visited with Brother Stevens while I was away at college, discussing whether or not there might be a cure for my condition. He knew surprisingly little about how Love in Action operated but seemed to think that this was the best organization of its kind. An ex-gay umbrella group, Exodus International, had recommended it to him, and with a strong endorsement from the fundamentalist Christian group Focus on the Family, my parents were sold. LIA was the oldest and largest residential ex-gay therapy facility in the country. If they couldn't turn me straight, no one could.

In order to prepare me for ex-gay therapy, LIA wanted me to attend some intro sessions with a staff-approved therapist. My mother drove me to Memphis at the beginning of Thanksgiving break to attend one of these sessions. The therapist's office was adjacent to LIA, but we weren't allowed to go inside LIA's facility until I had completed an application process that would take months for final approval. Inside the counselor's office, I confessed what I would later learn was my first Moral Inventory, detailing my same-sex attractions in a vague, desexualized language, leaving out all the stuff about David but including as many sexual fantasies as I could recall. When the counselor asked me if I'd had any relationships, I told him about Chloe, about how guilty I'd felt lying to her through omission.

"She might have helped you through your struggle," the counselor said. "If you'd told her the truth and both of you had confessed before God, you might have had a future together."

I couldn't say anything in response. I wanted to tell him about the pressure I'd felt, about how Chloe and I had almost had sex in order to cure my condition, but I was afraid he'd just tell me more about what I'd done wrong. I grew quiet, and the counselor used this as an opportunity to preach about the need for true repentance. When our hour was up, my mother asked if she could speak to him alone, and when she came out of the office, her eyes were watery and red. I knew he had told her something, and this something had finally convinced her.

Once we were inside the car, she said, "We're going to take it one step at a time. We're going to try every option."

We were silent the rest of the way home.

THE SUNDAY before Thanksgiving break ended, my father was in a rare mood. It was late in the morning, but he was still sitting in his leather recliner, wearing camouflage boxers and a white V-necked T-shirt, one pale leg propped on the glass coffee table. His eyes were trained on the television, where a young

Clint Eastwood narrowed his crow's-feet eyes at a desert landscape and prepared to set off into the unknown. Always the sharpshooter, Clint never missed his mark. You could see it in his eyes.

I brushed past my father to grab my car keys on the table. Even though I no longer had to work the projector, I often left early to clear my head before the service.

"He's not afraid of anything," my father said.

"What?"

"Clint," he said. "He walks right into the line of fire."

At the jail two weeks earlier, my father had preached about the importance of courage. Real men, he said, weren't afraid to show emotion. Real men followed Jesus. As I sat beside him, passing out the M&M's through the bars, I had thought, *Jesus wept.* The one verse he told them not to memorize even though it would have fit in so nicely with his sermon. Such a simple, compact verse at first glance, but one every bit as difficult to interpret as any other.

"We should know something about the doctor this week," he said. "Don't worry."

I headed into the kitchen to find my mother sweeping a patch of tile near the door. "Hi, honey," she said. "You go on ahead."

I couldn't leave without asking her what my father had meant about the doctor. "What will we know," I said, "at the end of this week?"

She looked up from her sweeping. "Dr. Julie's going to give you some tests over Christmas break," she said. "Something to

do with testosterone levels. And then we'll move from there."
Dr. Julie, our family doctor, was a woman I'd visited for the
past five years. She always knew how to make me feel comfortable when she read over my charts, casually reciting her litany
of cause and effect. I felt better knowing that this "something"
would at least be performed by her.

I left the house that morning in a stupor. I hardly noticed
when my parents entered the church. I hardly heard a word of
Brother Stevens's message.

And when I drove back to college that afternoon, my stomach full of roast and mashed potatoes and gravy from the
church potluck, the Ozarks sinking into flatland on either side,
I almost didn't notice the auburn-colored blur that edged its
way to the line of pines, slipping past my periphery like a spot
of dark light. I didn't brace myself, but the impact never came.
Only a second before, the doe would have sent me spinning into
the sharp granite wall flanking the road. Still, the afterimage
remained: the hesitant doe, one foot hovering above the unkind
asphalt—a stray drifting from her natural habitat, afraid of
where her steps had taken her.

II

Outside the context of a political war between faith
and reason, more nuanced arrangements may be safely
undertaken.

—JENNIFER MICHAEL HECHT, *Doubt*

Rules are empty in themselves, violent and unfinalized;
they are impersonal and can be bent to any purpose.
The successes of history belong to those who are capable
of seizing these rules, to replace those who have used
them, to disguise themselves so as to perfect them, in-
vert their meaning, and redirect them against those who
had initially imposed them.

—MICHEL FOUCAULT, *Language,*
Counter-Memory, Practice

THE SMALLEST DETAILS

Thanksgiving break had ended, I had gone back to college, and my mother had been washing dishes all afternoon. The mail had just arrived, but she was too afraid to sort through the stack. Thanks to a phone call Brother Stevens had made on my parents' behalf, she and my father had been expecting a reply from Love in Action any day now. They had also scheduled an appointment for me with Dr. Julie over Christmas break to test my testosterone levels. They were taking all possible steps to cure me, but my mother felt that everything was moving too quickly. Only a few months ago she hadn't even known anything was wrong. Half a year ago it had seemed her only son had found the girl of his dreams. If only she could slow things down, get a chance to breathe, to think a little more clearly. Brother Stevens had set things into motion too quickly, telling my parents that they needed to act fast or else I might fall into even greater sin while away at college.

My mother was letting her hands air dry. She took a deep breath and walked over to the stack of envelopes, sifting through them until she found LIA's. She tore it open and pulled out a glossy brochure, one wet thumb against the freshly shaven jawline of a familiar-looking boy. When she moved her thumb away, the boy's face appeared newly distorted. His colors bled. His neck rippled out, bulging. His nose grew twice in size. But his eyes, they were the same haunting green.

"The first thing I noticed was his eyes," she will later tell me, nine years after my time in LIA. It will take all of those nine years before either of us will feel confident enough to sift through our memories in search of all that we have chosen to put behind us. It will take all of those nine years before we can talk about what happened without entering into spirals of blame and self-doubt. She will stare into the surface of the shiny black voice recorder between us and ask to be understood, for her words to be recorded, and I will sit at the other end of the table, hands in my lap, thinking, *This is the most uncomfortable it will ever get.* I will force myself to hear her side of the story, listen for her voice amid the buzzing of harmful memories I thought I'd buried for good.

"His eyes were so sad," she'll say. "They were calling out to me."

"Take your time," I'll say.

"I wanted to save the boy in that picture. I wanted to save you. But I didn't know how."

All those years ago, standing in her kitchen on what should have been a normal afternoon, she had imagined this boy's trapped eyes might be his real eyes, capable of looking outside the red border that framed his portrait. The eyes of his soul, a reverse Dorian Gray, the eyes growing kinder rather than more sinister the longer she looked at them. During the months leading up to LIA, she read *The Picture of Dorian Gray* at my request, after I had first experienced in Wilde's seductive language a justification for the sensitive side I was discovering during my freshman year of college, years before I learned that this book carried weight in the history of LGBT literature. Standing there in her kitchen, she imagined this boy, this reverse Dorian, looking past the whorls of her fingertips, past her standing figure, into a kitchen she had filled with what he might recognize as the familiar relics of a healthy childhood home: a stack of dishes in a white ceramic sink, the open mouth of a Frigidaire dishwasher, the freshly swept expanse of tile abutted by oak molding, the cream-colored carpet of an adjacent family room. She imagined a boy like this one in the brochure—trimmed sideburns falling just above his earlobes, button-down shirt stanchioned by a white crewneck, sensitive curled lashes protecting his eyes from seeing too much of the world at once—would find in this house a sense of peace. There was order here, and cleanliness. There was the scrubbed surface of her hands, the hot water she had left running on her thin fingers until the blood rose to her skin. *And what else*, she thought, *could this boy need?* Coming from a home like this one, how had he later come to be trapped inside this red-bordered brochure, surrounded by the portraits of the sin sick, the spiritually crippled, the chronically addicted?

She walked to the kitchen table in the corner of the room. As she passed the sink, a soap bubble erupted on the surface of the topmost plate, one that a second before must have held the trembling reflection of her standing figure in a floral night-gown.

"I remember the soap," she will later tell me, eyeing the recorder between us. "A strange thing. But then all of it was strange."

"Take your time," I'll say again.

"I remember the smallest details."

Like a drop of water trickling down her bare freckled arm. Like the afternoon sunlight hitting it at just the right angle, a golden glinting streak. She had brushed away the spot of cool wet light from her arm that afternoon. She had smoothed out the pages of the brochure on the surface of the table and sat. Yes, the features were nearly identical, this boy's and mine. She felt dizzy. She could see, as in the endless snaking reflections of two facing mirrors, a different mother peering down at this portrait of a familiar-looking boy, this mother in turn imagining someone like my mother doing the same, all of these mothers asking, in polyphony, *What else could this boy have needed?*

She waited for the dizziness to pass. She had felt this before, at moments when someone in church would speak of eternal life, of living forever in Heaven without end, when she had felt tired just at the thought of eternity, had waved a hand in the air in front of her face, and had said, "My mind can't handle this. It's too much."

The smallest details. The late-morning sun falling across one half of the table. The dust motes spiraling into what looked like columns of sand. Outside the double-hung windows, algae-striped water lapped at the steep shore that divided our property from Lake Thunderbird. During the tourist-heavy summers, my mother would sit on our balcony to watch the speedboats cut Vs through the water, daring the waves to come closer. On winter weekdays like this one, however, the lake sat still and quiet, and she kept indoors most of the day.

She glanced at the other portraits that staggered—left, right, left, right—down the page. One girl resembled her childhood friend Debbie, a skinny brunette who always bunched up her curly hair with a clip when they visited the public pool together to cool their feet in the shallow end and stare at boys. Another, an older man, resembled our previous family doctor, Dr. Keaton, who always made sure to warm the metal diaphragm of his stethoscope before pressing it to my mother's bare back. *What are they doing here*, she thought. *What went wrong?*

But, of course, these weren't the people she knew. The difference resided in their smiles. These trapped faces were smiling in an altogether different way, the corners of their lips stretched beyond the limits of normalcy. Even in her happiest moments, even in her sixteenth year—when friends and family had turned in their pews to watch her lace-veiled figure float up the aisle to meet my father—she had never seen such smiles before. It was the kind she would come to know as the ex-gay smile. Once she saw it for what it was, this smile would trail her through the next nine years. She would imagine seeing it almost everywhere, even on the faces of townspeople she met every week, as if the whole world had been carrying these secret ex-gay lives all this time without her knowledge. Turning down a grocery aisle, the wobbly shopping cart steering away from her grip, she would seize up—freezing, hands clenching the plastic handle—the moment she felt this smile sweep over her, as if a gunman had just waved a pistol in her direction. Such was the power this smile would hold over her, over us.

She read the words that floated beside these faces.

Since coming here, God has shown me a great deal about my selfishness and fear, which I had used to keep myself trapped in a cycle of homosexuality.

In my time here, I've learned that I am loved and accepted even though I have been involved in sexual addiction.

Being at Love in Action has given me a second chance with my family.

All of these faces saying what sounded at once foreign and familiar to her. Foreign, because she was unaccustomed to the way Love in Action's institutional jargon could rearrange perception until even the most complex human emotions could be boxed and labeled as "selfishness," "fear," or "addiction"; familiar, because the church was designed to be God's extended family, His lost tribe on earth, His chosen number to survive the Rapture, with words like "love" and "acceptance" digested alongside every yearly dose of unleavened bread, every plastic thimble of grape juice.

She slid the brochure away from her. The remainder of the kitchen table was covered with the loose sheets of the Love in Action application form that had been included in the same envelope as the brochure. The top sheet featured Love in Action's logo, an inverted red triangle with a heart-shaped cutout in its center.

"Even then I knew that logo was strange," she will later tell me. "The heart was cut away, like that was all it took."

I've felt this, I'll think, pressing pause on the recorder, playing back a few seconds to see if I've captured all of my mother's sentences. You cut out what was once dear to you, ignore the ache in the back of your throat, erase the details you want to forget. Toss the first half of the story in the trash, as my counselors had. I've lost so many friends in the years after LIA, gone without talking to old boyfriends for years just because it came so easy for me to ignore something I'd once felt. I've been so heartless without even trying. The truth is, being heartless came so easy for post-LIA me that I didn't even have to think about it. The trick was to believe that cutting people out of your life was a necessary step in your development. It was like those fields that used to burn for hours in the late fall outside the living-room window of my childhood home, the orange wall of fire leaping right up to the edge of the property: slash and burn to make room for next year's crop.

And so I had. Chloe, Brandon, David, my college friends Charles and Dominique—and Caleb, the senior art student who so fascinated me during my freshman year, the first boy I kissed.

"Let's stop for now," my mother will say, standing up from the table, sliding the recorder in my direction. She will stand in the middle of that field if that is what it takes for me to notice her pain, refuse to budge even as the fire draws closer. She will wait for my father to join her.

SATURDAY, JUNE 12, 2004

It was the gummy bears. Red and yellow and green, coated in plastic, the plastic coated with a film of dust. No one had touched this package in months. I stood frozen in the Conoco aisle, trying to decide between gummy bears and gummy worms, the need sudden and unexpected. My mother was outside waiting in the car, but we weren't in any hurry, we still had two hours to go before the ordination ceremony, and it seemed as if we had planned this stop without saying a word to each other, as a sort of way station between the two worlds we now inhabited. Only now that I stared at the candy, it seemed that the simplest decisions had taken on an endless complexity, as if this were a death-row meal or some red-pill, blue-pill moment after which we would never be the same. I wanted to return to the car with the right bag of candy in hand, some surprising choice that would delight my mother, an intuitive leap that would send her voice into upper registers—"I haven't thought of those in *years*!"—only I was no longer so sure I knew my mother well enough to surprise her.

I left the gummy bears hanging on their metal rod and walked up the aisle, the refrigerated glass to my right so cold it was almost hot, bright labels flashing in my periphery, metal cans lit up with pearl-white phosphorescence. The cashier, an older woman with a frizzled white ponytail, acted as sentry, eyeing me from the moment I first walked into the station. I must have looked out of place that morning: dark blue blazer and white button-down, cuffs barely visible; matching pants; black penny loafers—a college kid headed to Sunday school on a Saturday morning when he should have been vegging out on his couch watching television, maybe even recovering from a hangover.

A camera was perched above the woman's head. For a brief confused moment, I wondered what this footage could later be used to prove. If I died sometime in the near future, or if I was an accessory to some terrible crime, would a police officer later comb through this footage in search of my brief appearance, analyze the look of hesitation on my face for traces of fear or malice? It was silly, not to mention overdramatic, to think such things, but I couldn't help it. I'd just come from five mornings in group therapy with suicide cases, with lives that had been wrecked in an instant and never fully recovered, and I had begun to expect the unexpected. A moment of grace or terror— arguably the same thing—could descend without any warning, and now seemed about as good a time as any for God to resume

His communication with me. Lying about my sexuality in front of hundreds of people while standing beside my father as he took his holy vow—this felt like the lightning rod, the pillar-of-salt moment, the thing I couldn't turn back from.

I headed to the bathroom and locked myself inside the last stall. According to the rules in my handbook, I wasn't even allowed to be in this bathroom by myself: "During any trip to public restrooms you must be accompanied by two other clients, one of whom has been a Source client for at least two months." At once I knew why the counselors had made this rule. I recognized the usual bathroom graffiti, the casual seductive tone etched into the lacquered stall door. There was a number beside the offer, and a name, Mark. Without really knowing why, I took out my RAZR and keyed in the number, saved the contact under Mark Bathroom. I exited the stall without peeing and straightened my jacket in the mirror. I twisted the dirt-caked faucet knob and cupped my palm under the hot water, used the water to smooth the cowlick at the back of my head. I wanted to make sure nothing looked out of place. At the very least, I could look the part of the Good Son.

I turned off the faucet and listened to the quiet in its wake. In my pocket was a kind of charm against whatever might happen today: A number I could dial, and even if I didn't plan on doing anything with this mysterious Mark, the act of dialing would be my secret, something no one else would know. It felt good to have a secret again, to be free of the blond-haired boy and his palpating hands, almost as good as it would have felt getting my Moleskine back and entering the secret world of stories that belonged only to me. Mark's number filled me up, squared my shoulders, and puffed up my chest. Why hadn't I noticed this before? It was telling people the truth that got you in trouble.

THE PREVIOUS AFTERNOON at LIA, while working in our Addiction Workbooks after the mask activity, our group had been offered two scenarios to test the intensity of our addiction to gay sex. I had very little personal experience, but I was still expected to repent. The first scenario had been remarkably similar to the one I later found on the gas station's bathroom wall.

The two scenarios Cosby presented us were almost comically opposed, and I had to keep from laughing as I read them that afternoon, even as I felt the familiar longing throbbing beneath my open handbook, the blood taking its familiar course to my lap.

1. It is Saturday, you do not have to go to work, but have the whole day free. You know from reading the graffiti on the walls of a local men's room that there will be a man there at three o'clock who will sexually service any who comes along. In less than five minutes you can achieve orgasm. You have thought about it all week. Will you choose to be there at three o'clock?

2. Again, the same circumstances, it is Saturday and you
   are free. A friend you love is coming to town this day,
   and has asked you to go to the beach with him. He is
   your very close friend and you have much to talk over.
   Will you choose to go to the beach with your friend?

"You need to be honest with yourself," Cosby said, standing
at the front of the classroom with the fingers of both his rough
mechanic's hands barely touching, channeling a less Zen *Zen
and the Art of Motorcycle Maintenance*. I stared into the gaps
between the pads of his fingers, thinking about how people
were never really touching even when they thought they were
touching, how it was really our electrons doing the touching, a
fact that made me feel slightly less guilty about the one major
transgression I'd written about in that morning's MI—kissing
an art student named Caleb—but also a little sadder about living in a world where one illusion could so stubbornly dictate
the way I saw every interaction with the people around me. It
was a concept I'd encountered in one of my all-night reading
marathons, its word sharp and satisfying as I'd silently mouthed
it. "Osculation": two curves touching but not intersecting,
never intersecting. From the Latin *osculationem*: a kiss. Intimacy as a parlor trick, an illusion. But what was one more illusion when it seemed the whole world operated on so many of
them? With each passing day at the facility, it seemed as though
becoming straight was simply a matter of good lighting, of ignoring what you didn't want to see.

"Think about what you'd really do in this situation," Cosby continued. "Write down the scenario you'd choose. Take your time. Really think about it."

A choose your own adventure story, I'd thought. Only in this situation, the wrong choice could send you, invariably, to Hell. Sitting next to J that day, staring through the window his legs made to the carpet, it seemed that either choice would send me directly into the fiery pit. What if this best friend whom "you love" and with whom you wanted to experience a beautiful day at the beach takes off his shirt to reveal the body you've thought about all those years you've spent away from him? What if an innocent day at the beach becomes the beginning of a complicated love story, one you repeat to friends decades later? I could imagine all of this happening with someone like J. The two of us sitting in a snug beach cottage on opposite couches with thick Russian novels propped in our laps to hide our erections, shooting suggestive looks at each other, searching for seashells just before sunrise, collecting them in pouches formed from our T-shirts, the dampness cold against our stomachs, the sand scratching our feet.

The Addiction Workbook made it clear which choice was the right one: "The person who choose [*sic*] to go the beach may look at his watch around three o'clock and fantasize about the sexual encounter, but he knows he has made the right choice." Whereas the person who chose to go to the bathroom may regret his decision "especially if when he arrives at the men's room, the police are there."

Exiting the gas station bathroom with the mysterious Mark saved in my phone, I half expected the cold slap of handcuffs against my wrists. I half wanted it. At least a trip to the police station would have saved me from lying to so many people—from lying, once again, to myself.

I RETURNED to the car empty-handed. If my mother was disappointed, she didn't show it. Her heavily mascaraed eyes were already trained on the pine-studded Ozarks we'd soon be entering. I sank into the seat as my mother started the car.

There was a loud ding from the dashboard.

"Oh," she said. "We're almost out of gas." We'd meant to stop only for a bathroom break and a snack. Somehow we'd ignored the gas indicator the whole way. "Think we can make it?" There was a dare in her voice: *Could we really make it or might we find in our breakdown the best possible excuse* not *to make it?* I ignored the dare. Too obvious: the preacher's son and wife stalled on the side of the road, some congregants' car passing us on the way to the church, pulling over to save the day. *That was a close call*, people would say. *Satan trying to block your path.* And my mother and I sitting with the knowledge that we were the Satan in my father's story, that perhaps this was what we'd always been.

"The gas is pretty low," I said, already opening the door. "I'll get it."

My mother pressed the button for the tank. "You *are* your

father's son." Meaning my father and I didn't take these kinds of risks with cars, having worked at the dealership for so long. Meaning these weren't the risks that mattered to us. But the truth was, I wasn't really like my father in this respect. I had yet to take the kinds of risks he'd taken at my age. At nineteen, he'd already married my mother and taken over the family cotton gin, changed the entire trajectory his life was to take. Now in his midfifties, he was about to change everything again. Time was running out for me to turn out like my father. I had yet to make the jump into hetero life, work miracles with my hands, create something stable.

I slid the nozzle into the tank, pressed the trigger. I'd always enjoyed the rush of gasoline beneath my palm, the knowledge that such a simple act could propel us such great distances. The myth of progress, of unending supply: I, like my counselors, still clung to it. I read enough articles each day to know that President Bush was continually telling the country how important it was to tap into our own oil reserves, reduce foreign dependency. And why couldn't faith operate the same way? Couldn't God's love come back to me in all its abundance if I just searched in the right places? Couldn't I still be cured if I dug deep enough—went far enough behind the mask—to the source of my true hetero self? Or had I already dirtied myself too much by pressing Mark's number into my phone, harboring the enemy in my pocket? *Make me pure*, I prayed, gallons of unleaded gasoline rushing through my fingertips, soon to be

converted into something useful. *Please-help-me-to-be-pure.*
Pleasehelpmetobepure.

HIS SON. HIS WIFE. For a while, it seemed my mother and I
had lost ourselves in the abundance of all that my father had
come to represent for the people around us. We couldn't blame
him for it, but still, he hadn't done anything to stop it from happening. Perhaps he hadn't even known it was happening. For
him it was natural, and I suppose it was natural for us, too,
since the Bible continually advised the lesser members of a family to get behind the head of the household, support the father's
belief system.

But hadn't there also been times when my father had urged
me to become my own person? Hadn't he, of all people, learned
the importance of individual character? His father, the drunk,
had brought him to God, taught him the importance of the
church, all the while beating him and his siblings whenever he
got into one of his foul moods. Statistically, my father should
have turned out to be the same violent drunk as my grandfather
was; instead, he had rebelled against this childhood trauma
and taken on the more radical faith of the fundamentalist. By
Love in Action standards, it should have been my father who
turned out gay, not me, since he'd suffered all of the trauma
while my own childhood had been relatively peaceful. By Love
in Action standards, my father's life made no sense.

. . .

I SLID BACK in the seat, kicked off my loafers, and propped my black-socked feet on the cold vent, my toes instantly submerged in what felt like icy water. A sliver of sun burned the side of my face.

"How do you feel?" my mother said. Her hands were firmly fixed at ten and two on the wheel. This vigilance, this never taking a risk when you didn't have to.

"I'm fine." *We're all faking it.*

"We can stop again if you need."

"That's okay." *It's just that some of us are more aware of it.*

Silence. My big toe toggling the vent open and closed. With Mark's number in my pocket, I suddenly knew that what I was thinking was true. Keeping a secret, telling a lie by omission, made it much easier to see all of the other lies around me. An expert liar wasn't merely an expert on his own lies, but those of others as well. Was this why LIA's counselors were so good at challenging their patients, at calling them out? Was this why Smid and the blond-haired boy didn't fully trust me?

"Are you hungry?"

"No." *I can tell all of this to you later, after the ceremony. I just have to wait for the right moment.*

"Are you sure?"

"Are *you* hungry?" *But I'm afraid you'd be disgusted with me. I'm afraid you'd vomit again, right here in the car.*

"A little." The car turned a sharp curve, a stray pen tumbling out of the cup holder and rolling across the floorboard, a ping as it hit the metal bar beneath my feet. I could have picked it up, uncapped its top, and written my confession right then and there, had LIA's rules permitted it.

"Let's stop, then." *I realize this now, that all of it might come down to me being afraid. That all of this supposed change is just to please him, to please you.*

"I'll pull into Sonic. What do you want?"

"Just some fries." *But I'm afraid of losing you. I'm afraid of what I'll become if I lose you. I'm afraid because I think I've already lost God. God's stopped speaking to me, and what am I supposed to do without Him? After nineteen years with God's voice buzzing around in my head twenty-four hours a day, how am I supposed to walk around without His constant assurance?*

"An order of fries, please, and a Coke." Beneath the speaker's static, the clanging of metal in an invisible sink. "And a Sonic burger."

"Can I get tater tots instead?" *I don't even know what it would look like to be gay. I can't even imagine a life where my friends and family would want to talk to me if I was openly gay.*

"Make that tater tots instead of fries."

"I'm not really that hungry." *I can do this. I just have to fake my way through until I can take my big risk, whatever that will be.*

"You're going to be hungry later," my mother said, pressing the button for the automatic windows, the glass sliding behind her and thudding into rubber insulation. "The ceremony's going to take a while and you're going to be hungry. Let's pray to God we don't have to stay for the reception."

THE CHURCH was just as I remembered it. The sanctuary's walls were bright and eggshell white, with handsome wooden rows spaced evenly to the stage. A white projector screen took up stage center, and behind it stood the bottom of a large wooden dove backlit with shattered light that Brother Stevens had created, perhaps unconsciously, to mimic the great Roman Catholic artist Gian Lorenzo Bernini's golden flutes of light. This setup was a flaw in the sanctuary's design, covering up the most beautiful object in the room, but Brother Stevens made up for it by requesting that whoever ran the projector flip the button to retract the screen at the end of his sermon, at the exact moment when he began calling for people to walk down the aisle and accept Jesus Christ as their personal savior—"Would you do the right thing this morning? Would you follow Jesus where He leads you?"—the screen buzzing in the quiet auditorium, the dove revealed midflight, its wings flame-tipped, its light glistening on the blue baptismal waters below it, where on a good day Brother Stevens would baptize a new congregant "in the name of the Father, and of the Son, and of the Holy Spirit." The slow reveal was breathtaking, and it had often worked, inspiring many people to take the first step out of their pews and approach this holy dove, this one extravagant object in an otherwise bare sanctuary.

It would later occur to me that much of the success of the Baptist Church in this part of the country could be attributed to its elegant use of contrast. Unlike the heavily adorned Catholic Church, the Baptist Church sought to dazzle with just one or two displays of beauty—sensing, perhaps, that most of the congregants, who came from humble backgrounds, would feel overwhelmed by too much ostentation. People like Brother Stevens and my father were proud of the church's austere, Spartan embrace of utility. This plainness lent weight to my father's life story, rising as he had out of a modest family. You could see this sensibility reflected in the way congregants spoke of worldly possessions, quoting passages on the corruptive influence of money—"It is easier for a camel to go through the eye of a needle than for a rich man to enter the kingdom of God"—the way they constantly joked about how poor they were, how abject their circumstances had become. It was a badge of honor to stand before the pulpit and reveal a testimonial that featured at least one fall from a great coffer-filled height. These, they believed, were the humble beginnings of Christ's church, barely modernized for today's audiences. These were the circumstances necessary and sufficient for grace, the ramshackle stable planted, as this church was, in the middle of an empty field.

A hand on my shoulder, pinching the back of my neck. "You must be so excited for your dad."

Fingers gripping my elbow, spinning me in the direction of an elderly woman's worry-creased face, large glasses perched on the end of her nose. "Do you remember me?"

A middle-aged man at my side, poking me in the ribs. "Read *The Da Vinci Code* yet? Pretty blasphemous, but it really pokes fun at all those Catholics. All that ugly Mary worshipping."

These people gathered here to celebrate my father's life, to usher this new family into the pastorate. These were the same good people I'd loved and trusted all of my life. *Still, we're all lying to ourselves,* I thought, my hand glued to the phone in my pocket, one quick press of a button and all of this would end. *Why are we all still lying to ourselves?* It was confusing to slip back into this crowd of people who cared for me and wanted only the best for me—all the while I knew that, had they known what I held in my hand, they would have run straight to Brother Stevens and demanded my father's immediate resignation. Everywhere I turned, another smile behind which I sensed a thousand swirling repressions. Hadn't we all heard the stories, the church rumors? The man who cheated on his wife with a dozen other women. The couple who videotaped a youth group sleepover at their house, the camera discovered by a young girl who spotted the blinking red light between stacks of church literature? Of course, I knew the whole world was filled with such things. The only difference here, in this sanctuary, was that people were trying to become something greater than the sum of their parts. Or, really, it was their parts that they were trying to erase, and this new Christ-filled body—this baptized, cleansed, noncorporeal body—had no room, could spare no tolerance, for the old ways of living.

A trembling hand at the small of my back, Brother Nielson's wrinkled face staring up at me. Brother Hank at his side, holding the old man's thin elbow to steady him. "Finally back from your fancy college? Did you learn anything there you couldn't learn here?"

"Not too much," I said. *I've learned that your nuke-'em-all philosophy isn't worth a damn. I went in with everything I had, and here I am, still as lost and confused as ever.* I gripped Brother Nielson's weak hand. He'd grown so fragile in the year since I'd last seen him at the dealership that I didn't want to tell him what I really thought. How it must have been so easy for him, a straight man, to live such an outstanding life and then sit back and watch the fruits of his labor flower before him in the form of younger deacons, younger preachers like my father whom he'd inspired with his unwavering devotion, his unerring connection to God. How he didn't have any idea what it felt like to be cut off without warning. *Pleasehelpmetobepure.*

"Leave the boy alone," Brother Hank said, smiling, his teeth blindingly white. I'd once heard him brag that he used Crest White Strips every night since he'd become a car salesman. "Keeping myself pure, boys," he'd said. "The customer can't resist."

"It's fine," I said. *It's not.*

A few more people crowded in, shook my hand. I spotted an empty aisle and made my way through it, hoping to move to a less crowded part of the sanctuary. The space was narrow, my knees knocking against the polished wood, and I found myself in the awkward position of turning my back to most of the congregants just to get by. I could feel their eyes on my back, and I wondered, once again, when the lightning strike would come. Would God wait for the moment when I stood on stage and blatantly lied, or would He do it in this quiet moment, in this lull before the storm? The space around me was contracting, the lights brighter, blinding.

"Where have you been?" A familiar voice. I turned to face a smiling Wild Thing, his hand already waiting for mine.

"College, mostly." I shook his hand. I wondered if he somehow knew where I'd been this past week.

"Always knew you were smarter than I was," he said. He seemed even more clean-cut than when I'd last seen him at the county jail, his sideburns perfectly trimmed and his white shirt starched. "Got your Ph.D. yet?"

"Not yet." *It's easy for you, too. Living out your life the way you want until someone like my father comes along and cleans you up. Now you do the same for others. But I've never really lived out my sinful life. I never knew what it was like, so I don't know the first thing about conversion.*

"I'll be right back."

Once I got out on the other side, a whole new crowd had formed, waiting and eager to greet me. I could feel the self-pity building behind my fake smile, but I couldn't stop it. My palm felt hot against the RAZR. I was beginning to draw short of breath.

"It's been such a long time," another voice said. "Where have you been?"

There was that question again, posed by another familiar stranger. I could never remember people's names, a shortcoming that sent a ripple of panic through my chest as the sanctuary began to fill up. My father simply knew too many people, had done too many favors for too many families, and so people knew my name by heart, prayed for me along with the rest of my family, worried over my future success because I was His Son. How many times had my father sat beside someone's hospital bed and prayed for God's healing power? How many times had he attended the funeral of one of his friend's distant relatives, usually a person he hadn't even seen, just to offer some extra emotional support? To most people in the church, the number seemed infinite.

I made a beeline to my old perch at the back of the sanctuary. I needed space. I thought my lungs were going to collapse. The air had disappeared from the room. I walked up the narrow steps leading to the empty booth and sat before the monitor. The projector had already been set up for the ceremony. Happy photos of our family standing next to the foyer's fake plastic plants, all of us beaming for the camera. My father with his hand on the hood of his award-winning 1934 Ford, the one he built himself. My father standing in front of our blue cotton gin, ribbons of cotton plastered to his shirt. BROTHER CONLEY'S ORDINATION, the screen read. I highlighted the text and changed it to small caps instead of all caps, a small tweak that always made slides look better. Having something to do calmed me a bit, slowed my breathing. Later, I would come to recognize these symptoms as the first signs of a panic attack. At the time, they felt like the first symptoms of dying.

"Thanks for that."

I turned to face my father for the first time since coming to LIA. He was looking up from the bottommost step, his hand on the booth railing. His smile was genuine, his eyes sparkling.

"Wish me luck."

Three steps between us, but a thousand syllables between what I wanted to say and what I actually said. "Good luck."

WHEN I WAS BORN, after my mother and father held me and just before the nurse took me away to the nursery, my father had used the sharp point of his hunting knife to gently etch a small zigzag in the bottom of my left foot, a tiny scar that would prove I was his, a symbol to ensure that the nurses hadn't mixed me up with some other baby. He was paranoid. He had just witnessed a miracle. He didn't want to lose his son the way he'd lost the other one.

After my parents told me this, when I was eight or nine, I'd scanned my foot for this zigzag, tried to read the faint wrinkles for a sign of his penmanship, though, of course, it had faded within a few days of my father's etching. It had filled me with pleasure, thinking about this special mark, and though I couldn't read it in the bottom of my foot, I felt it there, the way one feels love in a certain room without necessarily identifying its source. When I first read the Harry Potter books and learned about the lightning bolt scar on Harry's forehead, I thought, *Of course.* Of course love worked that way. Of course it left its mark on the beloved. This secret mark protected you, kept you safe from harm, reminded you of who you were. All it took was the smallest symbol and you were safe. As I grew older and discovered my love for literature, I externalized the markings, wrote them down in my Moleskine, kept my notebook close—so much so that when the LIA counselors took away my notebook years later, they took away much of this protection. But they didn't take all of it. The empty pages still carried ghosts.

As I made my way to the sanctuary stage to join my mother and father and all of the Baptist Missionary Association members, I thought of this secret mark etched into my foot, imagined it was leading me forward, keeping me protected as I mounted the stage. God's lightning bolt wasn't about to strike; it was already etched into my skin. It seemed one talisman had activated the other: Mark's number taught me that there were secret loves crouched and waiting in the last place you would likely go searching for them. What was Jesus's compassion anyway but some well-crafted graffiti on the corridors of history, an invitation to follow Him into the most unlikely places? Love could come to you even in a room that seemed drained of it.

The projector screen rose, the white dove revealed its fractured Bernini light, and it really was as beautiful as I remembered it. The pastor asked a series of questions about my father's life, about his devotion to the Lord, about what led him to this day. Finally, the pastor spoke a simple question into the microphone—"Will you do everything you can to fight against the sin of homosexuality in the church?"—and my father's clear unequivocal answer swept through the congregation. As it happened, I felt something snap inside of me, a warm glow that spread through my limbs—a feeling of love surrounding me, coursing through me, the same feeling I'd experienced when I lay in bed and called on Jesus to enter my body—and I suddenly realized that I never had to take Mark up on his offer. I had already been called. I didn't know if this feeling was from God or my parents or some hidden inner reservoir, but it didn't seem to matter. I knew I still had a long struggle ahead, but I also knew at least one other thing: I wasn't going to erase Mark's number. Let the counselors do what they wished.

"Yes," my father said. "I'll do my best."

My parents never had any reason to worry about the nurses. In the end, it had been them, not the hospital staff, who had switched my identity.

DIAGNOSIS

The movie theater was packed, sold out, as everyone had said it would be. A hush settled over the crowd as the white-haired man made his way up the aisle. The man cleared his throat, stood with his back to the screen, and waited for the hush to settle into silence. For the next two hours, this would be the quietest our audience would get, a relentless succession of choked sobbing, coughing, sniffling, and moaning running like an alternate soundtrack behind the torture sequences that were so vital to the success of 2004's *The Passion of the Christ*.

I sat in the back, between Charles, my new roommate, and Dominique. The twins usually came as a pair, as they had to our college—a singing pair, singing almost everywhere they went—though here, in this room full of evangelicals, they kept it to a minimum. Just one week earlier, the last week of February, I had attended one of their recitals, watched Dominique march up and down the theater aisle in her floral-print muumuu and scarf ensemble and belt out "Summertime" in a tone that struck me as both garish and beautiful. I had delighted in her exaggerated minstrel expressions, her imitation of how white people thought a black person should look, only because she seemed so self-aware, so politically charged, in a way I could hardly imagine for myself. On scholarship for singing, Charles and Dominique were ostracized, if not intentionally, then at least by default, and it was often hard to tell where one of their performances ended and another began, so uncomfortable were they with the whole setup. They were also struggling along with me in my Comp II class, a fact that, given their near-total refusal to open their ranks for anyone else, made it possible for us to become friends, to spend all-nighters in the cramped dorm lounge writing papers, knitting together our growing impressions of the world.

"Do you think it'll snow while we're in here?" Charles said. We'd been arguing about it for the past week, ever since the meteorologist first mentioned the possibility. This was around the time when I'd first suggested that we watch *The Passion* together. "You know," I'd said, my voice a practiced monotone, "just to see what it's all about." Though Charles and Dominique weren't very religious, they had also grown up in a Baptist church and were interested in seeing what all the fuss was about. I knew it would be impossible to ignore this movie, that my parents would soon be calling to ask if I'd seen it, and I thought seeing it with Charles and Dominique might give me some perspective, allow me to mock it in some way, decrease the power

Christ seemed to hold over my life. If all went according to plan and LIA accepted my application, I would be attending ex-gay therapy at the beginning of June, only three months away. My intro therapy sessions at LIA's neighboring office had suggested to my parents that LIA would be the best path forward. I had visited the therapist a few more times over Christmas break, and he'd told my mother that I was making progress, that I would be a good fit for the program, though I couldn't really see what had been so positive about our conversations. Most of the time I'd simply listened to his lectures on sobriety and self-restraint, trying to hide my trembling hands. A few times I had parroted back the therapist's jargon in order to move past any long uncomfortable silences. He must have interpreted this as humbleness, as a form of repentance. Though my parents hardly ever mentioned LIA these days, they certainly weren't making any of our family's usual summer plans to visit Florida, and their silence on the subject only made my enrollment feel more inevitable. Watching *The Passion* with Charles and Dominique would either strengthen my ability to cope with whatever I'd soon face in ex-gay therapy or it would teach me just how much stronger I needed to become in the next few months.

"It might be too warm outside," Dominique said. "But I bet there'll be at least a little snow."

"Of course it'll snow," I said. I wanted to put an end to the debate. I was tired of the argument, and I half believed that the late-season snow had a greater chance of falling if we closed ourselves off to it, as we had in this auditorium, like the times in my childhood when my mother would drive us to the city to watch one of her romantic comedies and, directly after leaving the auditorium, we'd find a thin blanket of snow waiting for us under the streetlamps, the ground newly soft under our soles. The roads snow-chapped and treacherous and unsalted, my mother would drive us back up the hill to our house after our weekend movie, laughing the whole time. "Isn't this *wild*?" she'd say. And it truly had been wild, my father off somewhere in his shop building cars or in the house reading scripture, blissfully unaware that his tiny family was making its journey through snow. We could do it without him, at least for a few miles.

"I think it has to snow," Dominique said, eyeing all of the white-haired people who passed by our aisle. Their heads swooped past like tiny unthawed islands of snowdrift. "Preacher hair," my mother used to say, long before my father had accepted God's calling, before his salt-and-pepper hair began turning to that soft cotton that so reminded us of angels' wings.

"It won't stick any," Charles said. "It's too warm."

"Negative Nancy," Dominique said.

"Don't give me a white girl's name."

"There's no such thing as a white girl's name," Dominique said.

If I closed my eyes, I didn't seem to be in a church crowd at all. I was about to watch a movie with good friends. It was just a normal Friday night. This was exactly what I wanted, what I'd planned for: a secular miracle, my father and his entire mission defrocked before my eyes, openly mocked by these new nonbelieving friends who didn't give a shit, these friends who could sing their way through any tragedy. None of this awful school year had to matter: not the extensive therapy sessions I'd attended over Christmas break, not the slow but steady march into treatment, not the slice of suburbia I'd recently suspected might hold the key to my future as an ex-gay. Here, I didn't have to think about being gay *or* straight. I didn't have to worry about upsetting Christ anymore. Instead, I could laugh alongside Charles and Dominique at the spectacle of His death. A catharsis, I'd recently learned in my Western Lit class. The snow would arrive and blanket everything, and we would step out of the theater as new people, made clean and carefree, just as the transcendent church hymns had also promised long ago, *washed in the blood of the Lamb.*

MY EX-GAY THERAPY SESSIONS at LIA's neighboring office, begun just after my trip to the jail, felt like part of a different life. Since my mother kept putting off scheduling my doctor's appointment, I hadn't yet visited Dr. Julie to check my testosterone levels for deficiencies, but I already knew, after my first session, that I was diseased, possibly incurable. I never told Charles and Dominique any of this, worried they would think the same about me. All they knew about my background was that I had grown up Missionary Baptist and that my father was becoming a preacher. I wanted to keep these two parts of my life separate, a choice that leant a sense of timelessness to my secret life, a sense that I could pretend to be one person—a complex, evolving, educated person—while at the same time I would always remain a hell-bound diseased sinner. This secret life pressed against my student life at all times, always there in the back of my mind, and the moment my student life began to make any progress (better grades, more friends), I would be reminded, once again, that there was a world of sinfulness awaiting me, that perhaps it would always be there.

In my secret life, I was always at Love in Action. There, the air grew colder, and holly wreaths decked every front door of every suburban house I passed on my way to the facility. In my secret life, I found myself thinking of snow as I sat before the thick-browed counselor and watched his lips move with no clear sound attached. Then, gradually, his phonemes merged into real words until there was no way to keep from hearing them.

I looked away, searched the window for the tiniest flake, the smallest fraction of hope. My parents and I had opened ourselves up to this hope just when I seemed most lost, accustomed as we were to the habits of faith, and this hope shot us through the tight circuitry of the ex-gay industry to the heart of things, to this place.

"Do you think you're masking a deeper problem here?" the counselor asked, leaning forward in his chair. He was sitting across from me, staring, waiting. "Do you think all of this gay business is really connected to your relationship with your parents? Wouldn't you say you and your mother are extremely close?"

Oh, I thought, looking into his dark eyes, *so all along love has been on loan. This man has come to collect.* So I sat straight up in the padded chair, trembling, nodding, smiling, and I said something like "Yes, my mother and I *were* too close, so I craved that close bond in every one of my friendships." And with that first ex-gay utterance, with that strange tongue still vibrating in the air around me, my mother became something less to me. The bond between us grew less magical, less mysterious, bound to the assigned descriptors, to the role she must have been playing in my narrow little production of sin.

In my secret life, when I left the office for the second time, glossy brochure in hand and a next appointment already scheduled a week before Christmas, there was no snow waiting outside to soften my steps. Over the next few months, the snow still didn't arrive. I was told that these things took time. I was told that I needed to be patient. Sitting with my friends in a movie theater several months later, spring well on its way, I felt as though it was long past due.

"It *has* to snow," I said. Charles and Dominique turned to me and smiled. In that moment, I thought of saying something like "Yes, you *are* the family I've never had. Yes, you *are* surrogates." But this was not my secret life. The counselor wasn't here, not in this place, though he had already patterned his thoughts into the white mass my mind had become.

. . .

"Where have you taken me?" Charles said, digging into the popcorn bag between us. It was a good question. Here sat white-haired, pale-faced elderly people. Here sat intermittent sprinklings of local church youth groups huddled together in brightly colored bunches, their matching T-shirts lit up beneath the canned lighting like unstrung Christmas lights. A few more white-haired men, most likely deacons, stood with their backs to the burgundy-curtained walls, their pale hands crossed before their flies, the curtains behind them trembling with their slight stirrings.

The white-haired man at the front of the theater cleared his throat again, and the crowd grew quiet. "Some of you will have questions after watching this powerful film," he said. "Some of you will feel moved by its message."

Charles tossed a piece of popcorn at Dominique. It traveled in an arc in front of my chest, landed on her shoulder. Dominique picked it off as if it were a cockroach, raised one finger to her lips, and shushed us. *This is serious*, her eyes said, though the glimmer in them suggested the opposite.

In only a few months, *The Passion* had become one of the most popular movies of all time, largely thanks to evangelicals. I hadn't told Charles and Dominique that my father was just like these white-haired men, standing in front of audiences in my hometown and asking people to be saved, that my mother had called to tell me of the large number of people my father was leading to the Lord at every screening. "You wouldn't believe it," my mother had said breathlessly, as she sometimes was, in awe that my father could inspire others, believing, perhaps for the next few weeks, that there might be something truly miraculous about his ministry. "It's a sight. All those people crying, down on their knees."

When I left each weekend for home, I didn't tell Charles and Dominique where I was going. We didn't discuss my rapid weight loss or my sudden dip in GPA. The thing that passed between us for concern—the "You're too damn skinny"—said all we needed to say. The world outside our tiny circle was a scary place, and it always would be, but the arrogance of youth made these problems seem like a skin you could shed. We were here now, with one another, and everything else was just so much white noise.

As winter settled on our campus, frosting the triangular patches of grass between our academic buildings, the three of us spent most of our time together, watching movies in the dorm, one lazy pile of warmth held up against the cold that whistled through our poorly insulated windows. Our limbs splayed everywhere; we became inseparable. Mutual friends used the word "creepy" to describe the way we folded around one another, finished each other's sentences, walked to the cafeteria only when all three of us were hungry, our appetites surprisingly in sync. We hardly ever spoke of our families, who nevertheless would have been suspicious of one another, my parents never having set foot anywhere even remotely similar to their side of town. But we didn't feel the need for such things in order to be close. We were here, together, sheltering under the slats of the bunk, the glow of the screen.

"We'll be available for counseling after the showing," the white-haired man continued, pointing to the men along either aisle, his fingers tracing invisible lines, a kind of flight attendant preparing for our ascension. "Jesus can wash away all of your sins, make your garments spotless. He'll help you walk away tonight with a clean heart." I lowered my gaze to where my feet plugged into a darkness I wanted to slink down inside until the movie was over.

I kept my head down. Charles, Dominique, and I could ignore almost anything. Once, after walking into a J. C. Penney to buy Charles a new pair of jeans, we were all but asked to leave, the white staff shooting us angry looks, staring us down, trailing us through circular blossoms of brightly colored dress shirts. *Why are you here with them?* their eyes seemed to say. We left in a hurry, hardly talking on the drive back to campus, and when we got back to the room, we drank half a bottle of whiskey and watched one of the three idiot fraternities on campus recite its idiot creed on the idiot quad. You're too damn skinny. Drink up.

IN MY SECRET LIFE, the counselor turned to me and said, "Can you tell me a little about your first sexual experience? The very first one?"

The question wasn't as shocking as it could have been, given the circumstances. Still, I couldn't help but feel as though this man was overstepping his boundaries. *Bullshit*, I thought at first. *This is therapy. I'm not a person who needs therapy. I'm not a person who needs to tell my sexual fantasies to other people in order to feel better.* Besides, this man was a marriage counselor, someone whose job description didn't seem to provide the ex-gay cure I needed. But as the man began to ask more questions about my fantasies, as he continued to nod and suggest that I reveal more about my interests, my dreams, my porn habits, I began to settle in for the long haul. He didn't want to know all of this for personal reasons. He was a professional, a disinterested professional. I could see this in the way he nodded his head so casually. I could see this in the way his brows knitted with concern. Real concern.

"I guess my first time was with Brad," I said.

"And who is Brad?"

"He was on all the sports teams in junior high."

"Were you on any teams?"

I waited a moment. There seemed to be an implication in this. "No. But I did take tae kwon do for several years."

"Tell me what happened with Brad," the counselor said. "In nonexplicit detail."

"In nonexplicit detail? Well, Brad was a close friend before it happened. I was staying over at his house, as I usually did on the weekends, and I remember Brad's house was being remodeled. It was already a beautiful house, a really big house with two stories—"

"What happened in the house?"

"Well, there was a part of the house that wasn't finished, and we went in there to get an idea of how it would look. His parents weren't home at the time, I think. We climbed the wooden stairs up to this loft, and Brad got this look in his eyes, and we pushed past the plastic sheet and headed into the loft and we both sort of—well, we both knew—"

"Mutual masturbation?"

I couldn't believe he'd said the word. It felt like a cold slap. The way he said it was clinical, but there seemed to be a slight hint of disgust somewhere behind the words.

"Yes."

I looked out the window to the empty plot of land opposite the facility, and though there was no snow and there was probably never going to be any snow this season (I could see that now), I remembered how my grandmother used to dance with me down the length of her long shag-carpet hallway, reciting faux Native American chants, her wrinkled hand covering and uncovering her mouth; how the week after all that chanting it wouldn't stop snowing; how, in fact, this had been the biggest snow either of us had ever seen—so that now I could see how there might be some truth to that absurd magic of faith. The power of the mustard seed, the smallest snowflake: This is how therapy continued.

"Try not to think of this as therapy," the counselor said. "We're just having a chat." And with the addition of only a few words—"dependence," "self-loathing," "masking," "selfish-

ness"—the story of my childhood and my developing sexuality took on new colors, new associations. Beneath my shame,
the counselor suggested, a hidden ecosystem had been growing. It was my responsibility to put an end to it. Peer just
beneath the surface, and I'd find the whole writhing, unconscious mess. *Earthworms*, I thought. *Basking on the surface of
the wet soil. They weren't there before the rain, and now they
suddenly are.*

"Have you filled out your application?" he asked.

"Not yet," I said.

"Let's get on that. I don't think there's any time to waste."
He leaned back in his chair, plastic casters creaking.

My gaze dropped to the wooden arm of the chair, to the
swirl of its grain. It was a slice of some dead tree's years, all
those wet and dry seasons stacked side by side. The tree had
had no idea, when the ax fell against its bark, that I would
make use of those years.

THE CAT-O'-NINE-TAILS was striking Jim Caviezel's exposed
and bloodied back. Again and again, leather met skin.

"This is some bullshit," Charles whispered.

"Don't say that," Dominique said, her tone full of mock concern. "That's Jesus."

"*That* is not Jesus."

"How do you know?" Dominique said. "Do you have holy
visions? Does He visit you in your sleep?"

"I study history. Anthropology. Whatever. Jesus was blacker than that."

"You study *music*."

"Among other things."

I looked around to see if people were listening. A woman to my right was clutching her purse to her chest, jumping with each on-screen laceration, her eyes wet. People farther down the row were already on the edges of their seats, as if they had no idea what was about to happen next. This was the magic of Mel Gibson's directing, drawing so much suspense from such a familiar story like the Gospel. Each time the cat-o'-nine tails landed, I half expected Jesus to just die already, though I knew that that wouldn't be the case, that there was so much more to come. There was a drawing out of the violent act, a close-up on the details of violence, that made the violence itself fascinating, its universe of punishments populated with infinite gradations, infinite shades of red and pink that I had never before been taught to notice. During the first few frames of sudden violence, I had read no subtlety into it, the blood no more nuanced than the garish red droplets sometimes accompanying the Catholic stations of the cross or the ones splattered all over the painting of the bloodred gnarled Jesus hand my father had had commissioned for his jail ministry and pasted to the back of his truck, the words CHRIST DIED FOR SIN SINS SINNERS bolded in red. *Bullshit*. Then, slowly, the blood became something else. Art. I wanted to find other names for it. I wanted to watch the movie again just to see how the Jackson Pollock blood fell.

Charles and Dominique had already stopped their bickering and were now watching, incredulous, as each one of Jesus's features was systematically reduced to bloody shreds. The message of this film was clear: Violence had replaced all other considerations. It no longer seemed to matter whether the man on screen was black or white. Here was a horror that seemed to belong to people of all races and creeds.

"I can't watch this," Charles said, shielding his eyes with his palms. "This is too much."

"It's almost over," Dominique said, tossing back another handful of popcorn. "The good part's coming up."

"Father, forgive them," Jesus said, his voice muffled by blood, his teeth chattering, his eyes fixed on a future no one else around him could possibly see. "Forgive them, for they know not what they do."

A tear-tracked Mary dug her hands into the ground and gripped two fistfuls of dirt, her features distorted by grief, by disbelief. Critics were saying the movie was supposed to be more accurate than the Bible, that Gibson had spent a great deal of time and money making the crucifixion seem real, but as I watched Jesus's flayed torso struggle with gravity, I couldn't believe that the human body was capable of sustaining such violence. There had to be some limit, some point at which the Roman authorities checked for a pulse. Or perhaps we all had different limits. Charles and Dominique had sometimes spoken of their ancestors, born into slavery, who would receive extensive whippings for no reason at all, and yet many of these same

ancestors had lived long lives of servitude, their wounds healing over, their skin becoming tougher, the nightmare proceed-
ing on as planned.

Compared to the on-screen pain, my pain felt pointless, a
thing of no significance. I hadn't been whipped or beaten. I
hadn't suffered for my goodness. It was certainly true that since
the moment David had outed me some part of me had still been
lying in the backseat of my mother's car, watching the milky ribbon of stars and waiting for the blows to come—but even as I
knew more of them would surely come, I also knew they would
never add up to what I was seeing in the theater. I didn't have
the right to complain. I would go through with the therapy. I
would complete my application.

THIS WASN'T the first time I'd made a decision based solely on
guilt. My first fantasies of martyrdom arrived the day I turned
sixteen. Chloe had gifted me her copy of *Jesus Freaks: Martyrs*
for my birthday, suggesting that it would draw us closer
together if I read it. "It changed my life," she'd said. "I'm not
afraid to follow Christ now, no matter what happens. I don't
care if someone holds a gun to my head."

I had felt special, reading those stories, a series of grue-
some deaths at the hands of unbelievers serving as examples
of the kind of extreme devotion required in these End Times.
I would read the book for hours in my bedroom, the door
locked, and imagine armed SWAT teams bursting through

every lock and hinge to interrogate me. I would imagine how proud Chloe and my parents would be if they heard me speaking into the barrel of a machine gun, biting down hard on the muzzle, mumbling: "I will not renounce Jesus Christ as my personal savior."

But in truth, I worried about what I would really say when the Apocalypse finally arrived. I worried mostly because I felt I was evil somewhere deep inside, in the same place I had stored my fantasies of older men—some of them men from the dealership, some from the church, though their features hardly mattered. Pressed tightly beneath my fear and shame, their faces and bodies swirled into one ominous mass that threatened to rear up and expose me.

Focusing on the violence, even taking pleasure in the fantasy of it, actually did manage to draw Chloe and me closer together. It made it easier for me to ignore my temptations, focus on doing the right thing, imagine a future as a husband to a kind and beautiful Christian wife. And for a few years, we were united in our love of Christ, in our love of martyrdom.

I felt this strong undertow once again while watching *The Passion*. I had come to this theater to mock what I should have known could never properly be mocked by someone with my background. I wanted to run away, hide my face in the cleft of the rock, as Moses famously did in God's presence. As the canned theater lights brightened, I turned away from the white-haired deacons kneeling at the front of the theater, but only after a tentative look back.

. . .

THE AIR OUTSIDE was cold, and a low, lonely wind accompanied us to the Explorer my father had bought for me just before college. Only a few scattered cars dotted the parking lot, some of them no doubt belonging to the kneeling moviegoers. It was strange to see them there, to see my car alone at the other end of the lot, to see all of the buildings and factories that had brought us to this point in history, two millennia removed from the world we'd seen on screen. A canopy of fog had lowered in the distance and seemed to be spreading over the length of our small city. It was going to cover everything, put a blanket between us and the stars. *What's the point of all of this*, I thought, *once everything goes?*

"Where are you going?" Charles said. Charles and Dominique were already standing in front of the Explorer, waiting for me to unlock its doors. I had walked past them without realizing, headed some place I didn't know.

A few minutes later we were sitting in McDonald's, the only well-lit building for miles around. I wasn't certain how we'd gotten there, oblivious as my mind had been since we'd left the theater. It was a wonder I hadn't wrecked us. Driving under these conditions was just another stupid thing about that evening.

"You look like you've seen a ghost," Dominique said, dipping a greasy fry into a paper cup she'd filled to the brim with ketchup. The clock above her head was drawing close to midnight, but I had no place to go, tomorrow was Saturday, and we all seemed a little restless.

"I can't get over it," I said, unwrapping my Big Mac. These burgers never looked how you wanted them to look. I tried pushing the second patty back beneath the bun, but the sandwich began to fall apart, so I took a bite as quickly as I could.

"It's just a movie," Dominique said. "None of it was real."

Charles snorted into his Coke. "I've seen worse."

"Maybe it was worse than what we saw," I said, feeling the burger glide slowly to my stomach. The bite was too much, I realized. "Maybe we'd lose our minds if we saw how the crucifixion really looked."

"Maybe," Charles said, standing up. "Maybe we'd lose our minds if we saw a lot of things."

Dominique slapped the table. "Try watching someone get shot in your own neighborhood."

"Have you seen that?" I said. The burger was stuck in the middle of my esophagus. I was going to be sick.

"No," Dominique said, "but I'm sure I will if I move back home. It's bound to happen."

"It happens to everyone in our neighborhood," Charles said, heading to the counter to fill several more paper cups with ketchup. There were never enough paper cups. It seemed as though someone had designed the cups so you'd have to get up for more ketchup every few minutes. It made the condiments seem precious, lined up in a row across our table, a string of rubies glistening beneath the fluorescents.

All of this is so fake, I suddenly thought. I imagined walking into Charles and Dominique's neighborhood, watching a pedestrian get shot, blood sweeping across the face of a white T-shirt. Would everything seem less fake if I saw through to the heart of this violence?

"Doesn't it feel wrong," I said, tossing the sandwich back on the table, the marbled sauce dripping on all sides, "eating after what we saw?"

"It seems natural to me," Charles said, returning with the cups. "We have to eat."

"Listen," Dominique said, dipping another fry in the ketchup. "We only came because you wanted us to, and now you're acting like we did something wrong. So the movie was a little more intense than we thought it'd be. So what? We're here, we're alive, and we've got good grades. God would want us to be thankful for that."

"God wants us to make good grades?" Charles said. "Oh, Lord."

"And God would want you to eat that Big Mac," Dominique added. "Speaking of which, are you going to eat that? Because if not . . ."

I pushed my Big Mac over to Dominique. "You don't get it," I said.

This wasn't their fault, of course. I'd told them almost nothing of what I was going through with my family, and it must have seemed unfair to them that only a minute before I had been so nonchalant about my Christianity, whereas now I must have looked like a zealot, like my father. I knew I would never be able to tell them what was going on, that no matter how many days we spent together I would continue walking through life with one foot in a world they'd never seen, just as they had lived with one foot in a neighborhood I'd never visited.

"You know what you need?" Dominique said, tapping her foot on the tile. "You need a song."

I could feel the burger churning in my stomach now. It took all of my energy to keep from making a face.

"Please, no," Charles said, rolling his eyes. "It's all we do." A spot of ketchup clung to his bottom lip, garishly red. I thought of the article I'd read, the one about the new blood they'd developed for *The Passion*, a sickeningly sweet one—red dye, fatty gums, all suspended in glycerin—in order to make it appear more viscous.

Dominique stood up, wiped her salt-covered hands on her navy blue blouse, and cleared her throat. She looked around for a few seconds. There were only about three or four people in the restaurant. Outside the windows a hazy orange fog roiled over everything, obscuring the road. A few snowflakes clung to the window, melted, and traced lines down the glass. For a moment it seemed we were part of some extravagant snow globe, that someone had shaken us up and turned the key for the music box. Dominique grabbed Charles under his arms and forced him to his feet, nearly toppling over the line of ketchup cups.

"Summertime," she sang, incredibly in tune, incredibly out of season.

Some of the people turned their heads. *What are you doing with them?*

Charles joined her. I kept quiet.

"There's a'nothin can harm you," they sang in harmony, "with your daddy and mammy standing by."

I rushed to the bathroom and closed the door on their singing. I stared into the placid water and waited, but nothing came. It was just the reflection of a skinny face I could barely recognize.

IN MY SECRET LIFE, ex-gay therapy grows inside me, takes up residence under my excess skin, grips the lining of my stomach. My stomach churns with the tide of coffee and the Egg McMuffin my mother forced me to eat on the way to the session, the yellow wrapper crinkling and the car's tires thumping over the Mississippi-Arkansas Bridge. My mother has been doing this a lot lately, forcing me to eat calorie-rich food, sneaking real mayonnaise into my sandwiches when I'm not looking, and it's as though the work I've been doing to make myself invisible is all for nothing.

"Your thoughts are harmful to God," the ex-gay counselor says, his eyes fixed on the glass-topped desk between us. From this angle, his eyebrows look like two large black commas. He is here to interrupt me. "They're disgusting, unnatural. An abomination." I keep thinking about how he'd said the word "masturbation." The word sits somewhere in the room, refusing to leave.

"I know," I say. "I'm trying."

"Your mother and I think you should attend the Source," he says, holding out a sheet of paper. "It's a two-week program. Very brief, but effective." The Source. The stories I write almost daily now also have the ability to hide the source of my pain, to obscure me from my sinful nature. When I'm not sitting in front of this counselor, when I'm instead sitting with Charles and Dominique in my dorm room and scribbling in my Moleskine, I forget about my affliction, feeling only the joy and frustration of the written word, how it refuses to wrap around what my mind is seeing. The writing is both bigger—and so much smaller—than what I'd imagined. But I can't run from my pain, as this counselor has told me many times. I can't run from my disgusting nature, no matter how skinny I get. Eventually, I must return to the source.

THE CAMPUS was quiet that night, with only the muffled thumping of fraternity subwoofers giving life to the evening air, a peaceful vibration that made it seem as though the unlit corners of the academic buildings might hold some promise of excitement, some other world just outside this one. The top floor of the humanities building shone in the distance, and on the terrace just outside the faculty lounge stood a lonely figure, a late-night studier on a Friday night, a skinny student who seemed to live inside the building at all hours. He never failed to arouse some feelings of guilt in me, some fear that I hadn't read the assigned section of *The Faerie Queene* as well as I might have. He could have been me, really—a far more focused me, someone with both feet planted solidly in one place, eyes trained on a future full of books and wood-paneled rooms and late-night coffee sessions. Years later, I would be jealous of people like him, people whose brains never seemed to turn against them, even though I really had no idea what he thought on all those lonely nights.

I slipped past a few more buildings, dead grass crunching under my shoes, the air cold since I sported only a light black sweater. "Why are you going out like that?" Charles had said. And I hadn't provided him a real answer, just that I was restless and wanted to feel the cold air on my skin.

I reached a small garden, kicked up gravel in my path, and made my way to a cold stone bench. A tall hedge kept me hidden from the quad, but just above its bare branches I could make out the campus chapel's steeple lit up on all sides by three generous floodlights. One night during the beginning of the school year, I'd climbed to this steeple with a group of friends, Charles and Dominique among them, David among them. We'd leaped over the struts of the chapel ceiling, big brass organ pipes gleaming in the refracted moonlight below, and made our way up a rusty ladder, trying to stifle our laughter the whole way. Just before we reached the very top, as we stood before a dark stairwell that would open onto a narrow terrace bounding the steeple, a senior pressed a finger to his lips and told us that we needed to know the truth about this place. He told us that the college used to be a Masonic home for orphans that had burned to the ground in the early 1900s, killing several children. Three of those burned children were rumored to stand each night at the base of the steeple and hold hands. Three children with no names, their features erased by flames.

The story added a bit more adrenaline to what we already felt while climbing all those rungs in the dark, brushing past thick cobwebs and holding hands with people we barely knew but were already calling friends, already trusting those friends to hoist us across the gaps, the thought of all that scarred flesh, all those lonely children trapped inside with no one to mourn them, mixed with a kind of superstition that only complete darkness could still inspire in a student body as skeptical as ours. When we finally reached the top and the warm late-summer air met our skin, we were shocked to find only scuffed concrete and dust, and all of us held hands around the steeple in memory of those children, feeling, as we all must have felt, as I remember feeling with David's warm palm gripped in mine, that the bonds we formed that night would hold forever.

Outside the garden, fog was falling over the academic buildings, over the humanities boy who never stopped studying, and the bench I was sitting on began to feel like a tiny island adrift in a sea of white. *The Garden of Gethsemane*, I thought, remembering *The Passion*. The night before His crucifixion, Jesus had tried to comfort the disciples, to let them know that all of the pain they would soon endure would be worth it, that the violence would fulfill His promises. I wondered if it had been the same for the orphans. Had there been someone around to comfort them before the fire began to lick their arms?

I hugged myself, wrapped my arms as tightly as I could around my chest, the feel of my skinny ribs good to me, the cold good to me. All of it was good, I realized, if you only trusted that everything would make sense in the end. The snow had yet to arrive—only the hint of it—but it would come, eventually, even if it was this late in the season. It would cover everything, build its strange gardens over secreted objects, sculpt the world into something new.

IN MY SECRET LIFE, therapy engulfs me, swells over me until I am breathing only it, until my air is it. It's been only a week since my last visit to the counselor's office, and for perhaps the first time in many weeks, I'm not thinking about my next visit. I'm with my family. It's late evening. It's Christmas. Fire crackling in one corner, giant fir in another, overdecked hall stretched out between me and a view of the half-frozen lake that's polished and gleaming with a distant neighbor's twinkling Christmas lights.

The dark hallway yawns at my feet. My mother emerges from the kitchen to stand beside me. I can feel the warmth of the oven radiating from her self-tanned skin, a faint whiff of gingerbread trailing her. She's wearing a cashmere sweater whose central feature is a large snowman's face. The snowman's plastic carrot nose grazes my shoulder as she turns to speak to me.

"What about next week? Is next week okay?" she says. She can't help herself. The doctor's visit has been on her mind, and only hers, for the past few weeks. No one else wants to talk about it, especially my father. But someone has to keep everything together.

I look down at her shoes. Shiny and black, with clear plastic heels trapping two identical miniature Santa Clauses, a small heap of snow gathered around their own miniature black boots. Each time she walks, the Santa Clauses walk with her through twin blizzards, trapped in their isolated cells. When my mother used to pick me up from elementary school, my classmates would place bets on the outlandishness of her outfits. Would there be a red ribbon this time? Would there be a matching polka-dotted bag? It made me feel proud, those bets, but it also made me feel shameful, as though some part of me was reflected in her physical garishness.

"Dr. Julie's planning on checking your testosterone."

"Oh," I say. There's nothing else to say.

"It'll be quick. We'll have some answers."

"Good," I say. The twin Clauses stare up at me, snow settling at their feet.

"Make sure you tell your professors you'll be gone Tuesday."

"Okay."

"What's wrong, honey?" One of the Clauses edges closer.

"Nothing," I say. "It's just weird."

"I know," she says. "It'll be over soon." The Clauses turn their backs to me, lost again in their private blizzards. As my mother walks back to the kitchen, her pale cashmere becomes a flicker of white flame in the dim.

I turn back to the hallway, to the glittering lake framed by the window. It is a dark gift waiting to be opened. It is precious, delicate, wrapped in all those twinkling lights. Perhaps this is just my low testosterone talking. Perhaps I will lose this precious image the minute Dr. Julie manages to spike my hormones. Perhaps I will lose all of my most treasured memories, those moments of transcendent beauty, when I finally visit Dr. Julie. Perhaps this is a small price to pay for a normal life. I stand in the hallway and try to will my testosterone levels to increase. If I can just make myself stop thinking. *Left hand, palm down. Do not say to yourself, "Turn the left hand."* I clench my hand into a fist and dig my nails into the soft lake of my palm until my breathing draws short. I want to punch the wall, rip my knuckles on the splintering wood, draw blood—but I can't. I can't make myself feel something that isn't there. I can only feel what I wish wasn't there. I wonder what I'll do when I can no longer fake it. I wonder if people will notice. Perhaps the testosterone really will solve all of these problems, hijack my brain in a way meditation and prayer never could. Perhaps all of it really does come down to the body.

I remember the taste of unleavened bread on my tongue, the words *This is the Body of Christ* echoing through the sanctuary. *This is my body given for you. Do this in remembrance of me.* I remember the shock of grape juice, the Blood of Christ, the fear that this juice might actually turn to blood in my stomach, though the Baptists never believed such a thing was possible. I remember the one time I felt guilty about eyeing the Brewer twins in the front aisle as I sipped my juice and listened to all that unleavened bread being ground to grist by hundreds of molars, the Brewer backs so straight and perfectly sculpted I couldn't help but look, and so I rushed to the bathroom after communion and forced myself to vomit up the Body and Blood of Christ, fearing I would be punished for my blasphemy if I kept Him inside of me, the sight of Christ's floating remains similar to the curdled flesh I'd later see on the movie screen. This should have been a sign, I realize now. I can now see how the body controls the spirit.

It was Christ's body that finally turned His ideas into reality, the proof of its absence the very fact that finally convinced so many nonbelievers to convert to Christianity. It was David's body that first brought me to therapy. It was my lack of contact with Chloe's body that began all of this. If I can just learn to whittle my body down to a sharp blade, I might be able to harness this power of the body, this same power I will feel all over again while watching *The Passion*, this same one that my father knows how to wield so well in his sermons. All I need is a little help from Dr. Julie. I begin to hope. I feel the warmth from the kitchen on my skin, lending me strength, propelling me forward.

I'm still standing in the hallway, watching the Christmas

lights dance on the frozen lake outside. Someone is playing Nat King Cole. I remember Dominique telling me that she hates Nat King Cole. "That voice is so lifeless," she'd said, though I don't agree. I think of Charles and Dominique singing their way through the holidays in a neighborhood so unlike my own. Charles once told me of a stray bullet that bored a hole into the side of his house, nearly making its way through to where he was sitting on the couch. An inch more, and Charles might not have been alive to tell me that story. I think of his pain, of what he's been through and where he's come from and where he is now, singing so beautifully in the college's cloistered theater. And before I can stop myself, I feel lucky to be alive in this moment—warm and happy—with this family who, despite the awkwardness with which they've treated me since they found out about my affliction, despite the fact that they've handled me as they would an unwanted piece of family china, are still a part of me, still share the same warm blood that's pulsing through my veins as I walk barefooted down the hall, the swell of their voices behind me now, a nice dull rhythm with indistinguishable words, not the words of anger or disgust or pity or love I imagine they've got poised in the backs of their throats, and so I step slowly, one foot in front of the other, out of the gold light toward the glittering lake, and I swear it's all too beautiful for one life, that I should be able to split into multiple versions of myself to savor the many flavors of this moment, knowing that these kinds of feelings might leave me once I visit the doctor's office, thinking, *How can I ever repay this gift?*

How can I ever repay these people and the god these people worship and the god I still seem to worship?

The dog, Daisy, brushes past my leg, panting. She looks up at me, her eyes watery. Her naked trust is too much. I look away, grateful for the feel of her beside me in the dark with all that light behind both of us, as though the light is ready to buoy the two of us up directly into the window, hoist us out into the night sky above the lake. *How can I say no to all of this?* I think. *So many people have brought me to this moment, and I've trusted them. Couldn't there be even greater moments ahead if I only trust them again?*

Tuesday comes and I don't visit Dr. Julie. "Something's come up," my mother says. Nothing else. I'm as confused as ever. I wonder if my parents have lost hope, if maybe all of this might fizzle out. My mother and I go a week without talking. The silence worries me.

And it's only months later that I realize how strong the pact is that I made with myself that Christmas night with my family. It's only months later, after sitting for hours on a cold stone bench in a garden outside the humanities building, after walking in a daze down the path to the lake and staring into my dark silhouette in the placid water with all that moonlight at my back, my academic life packed squarely behind me, that I begin to realize just how far I will go. I will take this skinny frame and baptize it in the icy water, and I will walk back in my wet clothes, nearly frozen but more alive than ever, and with my exhausted body warming beneath the scalding shower stream, eyes trained on a drop of water tracing the showerhead, between my chattering teeth I will mutter the simplest of prayers to that Great Physician: *Lord, make me pure.*

Exiting the shower, I will find my cell phone and text my mother, waking her from a dream. "I'm ready," I'll write. "Dr. Julie."

LESS THAN A WEEK after watching *The Passion* with Charles and Dominique, my mother and I were sitting in Dr. Julie's examination room.

"That painting's in almost every doctor's office," my mother said. "It's a pretty good painting." She couldn't seem to stop talking.

"Yeah?"

The painting was a print of a famous photorealistic Rockwell piece: the little boy pulling down his pants for the anonymous white-coated doctor, light streaming in from closed blinds behind him. The boy's gesture seemed so simple, part of the rosy-colored past Rockwell was so talented at capturing: A moment of fear just before the relief, all the more sentimental because the pain was such a minor thing, nothing to worry about, really, and the child would soon learn this after a few more visits to the doctor's office. The boy's fear was a fear most people got over early in their childhoods, and it was humorous, in the way adults often found childhood humorous, to see this boy's fear as trivial, as a phase he simply needed to grow out of: A prick of the needle, and it would all go away.

"I wonder how long Dr. Julie will be?" my mother said.

"She'll be here soon," I said stupidly. "She's always busy." There was nothing else to say.

Dr. Julie did always seem to be a busy woman—flipping through charts and consulting medical records and prescribing medications on square white sheets and ripping them from their glued spine with a dignified flourish—but she always made it seem as though she didn't enjoy that part of her work nearly as much as she enjoyed the company of her patients.

"Let's get down to business, shall we?" she said once she finally arrived, as if by entering the examination room, she was fending off the technical part of her life—antiseptic, full of jargon—clicking the door shut on the tail of all that necessary nonsense so that she might finally crack her scrubbed knuckles, roll up her sleeves, and sit down on the creaking stool to hunch forward and stare into the eyes of the people who made her job worth it, becoming, in that instant, not a doctor per se but also the little girl from just outside Salem, Arkansas, who used to wake up early mornings before school to feed the chickens. There were moments when the little girl and the doctor shared the same features, though they were rare occasions. She had attended my college, a fact that felt particularly salient on the morning I finally decided to connect my college life with my family one.

"What brings you two here today?" As though she didn't

know, that farm-sunrise face of hers placid, loosed from the worries of the day, my mother sitting in all of her lace at the other end of the room, barely able to conceal the tremors that had seized her from the moment she'd first found out about my sexuality.

"I don't know where to begin," my mother said, clutching her purse to her chest, though there was no other starting point than the ugly truth of it: the secret stain that had fallen on our family. I knew she had already talked to Dr. Julie about my sexuality, that the two of them were close, that Dr. Julie wanted to protect my mother from the stark reality of having a gay son in the South in a strictly religious community. I knew all of this just by the way they spoke to each other, sympathy running like a current through the room, my eyes now focused on the mottled tile beneath my dangling feet. I had the feeling that merely looking up at them would instantly sweep me into that current, so I kept my head down.

"Why don't we start with the obvious?" Dr. Julie said. "You're worried about your son."

Shifting. The rustle of lace on lace. Despite everything, my mother had walked to my bedroom that morning to ask if I thought she looked cute, standing in my doorway like some kind of ice-draped queen, her purposefully yellowed Point de Gaze stacked in stitched layers across her chest and repeated as a skirt below a high-waisted black belt. *No*, I'd thought, *more like the snowdrop flower*, the *Galanthus*, in all of its wilted beauty. Even in her gloom and fear, my mother knew how to be fashionable. It was the thing that took her out of the situation, this love of texture, of fine cloth and fine detail. She had wrapped herself in as much of its exaggerated beauty as she could, calling up the spirits of postantebellum anguish to defend her against what she now had to face in the light of a doctor's office. She was no Dolly Parton, as many Northerners errone-ously assumed, with the heavily produced, heavily mascaraed optimism of a South no one would recognize in daily living; instead, she was fierce and determined, like many Southerners, if only you looked beneath the smile and the lace, a woman whose situation had changed for the worse in the past decade— first after losing her parents, then after becoming a preacher's wife, and now after finding this stain on the family that must have been there all along, right under the small nose she'd inher-ited from her mother's side. Nevertheless, she'd been taught to persevere, to wait it out within all of the glory she could muster. And what could she say now, sitting across from Dr. Julie, when she hadn't even admitted to herself that the words "gay" or "homosexual" might actually have currency in her life.

"I don't think he's eating enough," she finally said. "He's lost at least ten pounds in the past month."

I shifted my left leg so the blood could get to it, my toes already numb. Paper rustled under my thighs. No matter how I sat, I always managed to tear the paper. It was embarrassing, that quiet ripping sound in the middle of a quiet examination room, every motion amplified—and just beneath the paper, the squeaking plastic—as though part of the examination was designed to measure your ability to sit perfectly still, to remain calm in the face of whatever diagnosis you might receive. I couldn't help but feel that each of my mannerisms was being recorded, graphed into a chart that could be used to determine the extent of my homosexuality.

"You do look a little skinnier," Dr. Julie said, squeaking on her stool to face me.

"I'm eating the same," I lied. "Just running more."

The campus trees slipping past me in the dark, yellow lamp-post after yellow lamppost guiding me into their narrow circles of light, the lake glistening moon white and wind whipped in the distance: That part was true. I hadn't stopped running since my parents told me we needed to consider therapy. The lie about the food, however, was pointless, though we all knew I needed to say something to account for my sudden weight loss, for the way my clothes no longer clung to me, my cotton sweater now meeting my skin only where it fell against my collarbone, my shoulders, the lengths of my skinny arms. I wasn't eating, and it was apparent to everyone in the room, as easily measured by the naked eye as a good tap on the knee measures the reflexes, though Dr. Julie tended to shy away from such formal introductions, skipping ahead to the heart of the ailment.

"I'm worried," my mother said. "Nothing fits him any-more."

Often, it felt like a small victory to realize that another point of contact had lost its hold on me. I was in control of how quickly I lost the weight, and it felt good not only to feel the past leaving my body—all that fat like rings of a trunk now narrowing, disappearing—but also to see the shock on people's faces, the lack of recognition at first glance, the double take. I was a different boy.

"I think he's trying to torture himself," my mother said, turning to face me, her high heels tapping against the tile. I remembered the cat-o'-nine tails falling across Christ's blood-ribboned back. No, this wasn't torture. This was control. Once Dr. Julie helped me increase my testosterone levels, I would gain even more control.

"Honey, I think you're trying to torture yourself."

"I have some ideas about what's going on, Garrard," Dr. Julie was saying, pronouncing my name as though it were a delicate thing caught in the grip of her slight cowgirl drawl. And it was truly delicate. Part of a family history that took pride in the men who inherited the name, passed down from great-great-grandfather to great-grandfather to grandfather and finally to me. My mother and Dr. Julie and I were aware that, should I fail the test of manhood, I might never add another namesake to our family line. Instead, my name might come to be associated with the moment our family fell apart, a big empty space beneath my entry on the family tree.

"Did you hear us?" Dr. Julie said. "We think it's best if I speak to you one-on-one."

My mother was rustling out of the room. The door was closing. The lights were blurring on the tile, reemerging as bright orbs.

"Now," Dr. Julie said, the room suddenly too quiet for her loud voice. This whole thing must have been new for her as well. Talking openly about the subject of sexuality wasn't an option in most Arkansan towns like this one, even, I suspected—no, *especially*—in a medical setting. The idea of a sin having a biological basis would have shocked most people in my congregation, but this was just what many churches were beginning to suspect as they began stocking their foyers with brochures from Love in Action. Most people simply didn't read the brochures, passing by the plastic sleeves without so much as a single glance.

I looked up from the tile to see Dr. Julie just inches from me, her face carrying a look of genuine concern.

"Listen," Dr. Julie began, "I know what it's like to torture yourself. I've done it myself."

"That's not what I'm doing," I lied.

"Yes, you are," she continued, crossing her arms over her chest. "And that's fine, as long as it's just a phase. I've always had a weight problem, and until I had gastric bypass surgery, I used to binge. If I thought this was purely a weight thing, I'd be all right with checking your weight every now and then, doing some checkups. But this isn't just a weight thing, is it?"

I didn't feel like answering her rhetorical question, so I kept quiet.

"No, this is a sexuality thing. And what your mom is worried about is how this is going to affect your future. You're already wasting away. Imagine what you'll be like when more people find out. Now, my question for you is, Do you want to change? Because I know plenty of people who've accepted this part of themselves, and they've managed to make a good life of it. It's difficult, but they've managed. There are plenty of rumors, people who talk about them the minute their backs are turned, job opportunities lost because of personal vendettas, but they've managed. Is that what you want?"

"I want to change," I said. "I'm tired of feeling this way."

"It gets easier," she said. "You can move somewhere else, to a bigger city."

"I don't want to run away. I love my family." It felt ridiculous to say these words. They were so simple, so childish. But I couldn't help myself. They were true.

"Listen," Dr. Julie continued, turning toward the door, her stool squeaking, "I'm going to have someone draw blood to test for testosterone levels, white blood cell count, things like that. I don't expect to find anything irregular. I don't expect this to do anything but satisfy your mother. She just wants to know she's done everything she can." She let this sink in for a few seconds. It was the equivalent of *Let's say we did and not*, though we would actually go through with the blood test out of formality and, weeks later, find everything to be perfectly normal. There would be no clear diagnosis. "If you ever need to talk to someone, you know I'm here, right?"

"I know," I said.

"You wait here while I go get the nurse," she said, leaving the room.

I fished out my vibrating phone from my jeans, the paper

tearing under my thighs. It was Charles. We hadn't talked in more than a week. I'd been in and out of the room to get my things but mostly kept to the library every night until midnight. "When are you coming back? Are you alright?" his text read. "You disappeared."

I sent him a quick response so he wouldn't worry before I could think too much about my answer. "I'm a ghost," I wrote. "Never better."

Later that morning, when I walked outside with my mother, a patch of cotton taped to the crook of my elbow, I agreed to stay home for a few days just for her sake, knowing that these next few weeks would be harder for her than they would be for me.

"Let's go to the movies," she said. "My treat."

And after we finished watching some romantic comedy, the snow still hadn't fallen. I would wish for snow for the rest of the season, all of two weeks. I would imagine the two of us falling back into a pile of snow and sculpting wings as wide as our arms could go without breaking.

MONDAY, JUNE 14, 2004

The Hampton Inn suite where my mother and I stayed during my time at LIA was large, but it felt too small. Though we shared separate rooms, the only privacy we had was a small plywood door that separated the living-room area from the bedroom where my mother slept. After my first week of therapy, details about the room we never would have noticed under other circumstances began to take on menacing qualities. At night, a single lamp glinted at us from the corner of the room, its defunct twin dark in the opposite corner. The overhead light connected to a fan and couldn't be switched on without the blades whipping the air above our heads into rapid, unpleasant currents. Our sturdy metal door's sliding-chain lock seemed suddenly inadequate in the dim light; it was easy to imagine a pair of pliers gripping the taut chain in its teeth. At any other time in our lives, this would have been a perfectly fine, safe room—and yet each night I pushed the coffee table flush against the door, hoping I might at least hear scratching on the small patch of linoleum before an intruder could manage to fully enter the room. Standing in front of the bathroom mirror, I would imagine hidden cameras aimed at my naked body. Taking a shower, I would think of Hitchcock and his gleaming *Psycho* knife. I would think of Janet Leigh hightailing it out of town with a stash of stolen cash in her passenger seat, pulling into the one nondescript motel where she might find temporary asylum.

It was telling that my mother and I never asked anyone to fix these minor problems. Though I didn't realize it at the time, these problems comforted me, the space they occupied in my mind a bulwark against the more threatening intruders who crouched and waited somewhere beyond my limited perspective. Every inch of the room palpable in the dark, learned by heart: *the* room. One article out of place, one minor change, would have had the power to alert me to the more drastic changes occurring just outside of it. If the improvements started here, in *this* room, then they would have the power to continue ad infinitum outside of it. What then would stop me from immediately acting on my current plan?

SUNDAY NIGHT, I snuck out of the hotel again sometime after midnight to run through the suburban streets. I ran so long and hard that I began to lose track of time, and in that timelessness I watched the moon slide down the night sky. I imagined how small I must have looked from above. God was a bully, I decided, messing with such small people. Why had He done this to us, to our family?

"Fuck God," I said to the moon, once again half expecting to be struck by inexplicable lightning. When nothing happened, I repeated the curse, louder each time, the words echoing through the empty neighborhoods. "Fuck God fuck God fuck God."

I returned to the hotel room and doubled over near my cot, nearly vomiting from exhaustion and fear. Who was I? Who was this man who cursed God? Better yet, who was God? Had He abandoned me or had He never existed in the first place?

As I sat there trying to slow my breathing, I decided I would fake my way through this second week, grit my teeth and pretend that everything was fine. Therapy was turning me into someone I didn't recognize, and I needed to leave this place with my heart still relatively intact. LIA's logo, the heart-shaped cutout, glared up at me from my handbook each day, threatening excision, and I worried that what lay on the other side, post-op, was T and his many cardigans.

One thing was certain: I didn't want to act too quickly, alert the LIA staff to my intentions. I knew they would immediately inform my parents, and my parents would then be forced to suggest that I stay longer, do the three-month residency, then the one year, then the two years—until I wound up in the position of my counselors, trapped in a cycle of progression and regression, never knowing who I really was. In his own way, the blond-haired boy had already warned me of this. Thumbing through my phone's contact list the next morning, he'd glanced up briefly, and said, "I hope you're serious about your time here. People are thinking you might not be serious." I couldn't tell if he'd noticed Mark Bathroom's number, if he might use this information later as evidence against me, but it didn't seem to matter. The message was clear: The important thing was to keep things looking exactly as they had the week before.

And as Smid had walked us through our prelunch Authority and Trust session, as he began to speak of the evils and delusions of self-sufficiency, the sun haloing his graying blond hair, I'd nodded my head along with the others, smiled, plastered on a face of concern, the face of someone contemplating the words of a great leader. When asked, I turned to page thirty-three of my Addiction Workbook and read the words as Smid read aloud: "We strongly conclude that self-sufficiency will provide us with the security and comfort we're aching for. We start looking for a way to avoid or numb our pain." I pretended that self-sufficiency would only lead to a dead end, that I had given up my life to the authority of the counselors and, by extension, to a God who had refused to answer my prayers since I'd come to the facility. I pretended that I didn't trust myself, all the while thinking *Fuck God*, repeating the curse in my head during those moments when Smid's words felt as though they might drag me back into the self-loathing I'd narrowly escaped at the ordination ceremony. I acted the devotee, but with a pinch of struggle. For inspiration, I consulted my childhood memories, but I never mistook the self-loathing I unearthed there for the real thing. I couldn't forget the love that I'd felt emanating from some deep place inside my chest as I stood on the sanctuary stage with my family.

"We learn to manipulate," Smid added. "We learn to be seductive, purposely unclear about our motivations in relationships as self-protection." I looked up from the workbook. The words didn't seem so naked, so vapid, when he said them.

It was easier to lie when you believed the lie.

"IT's STUFFY IN THERE," my mother said that evening, closing the plywood door behind her. She entered the part of the suite where I slept each night on the foldout couch. Before the gap closed, I caught sight of her rumpled bed. It was rare for my mother to leave a bed unmade, and from where I was sitting, I could see that she had made no attempt to even tuck the ballooning edges of the white sheets into the corners.

I was sitting in the corner of the hotel room, trying to come up with another sinful transgression for my Moral Inventory. It was getting late, but I wanted to finish my homework before we ordered dinner, and though it was still painful to look directly at each of my sins, I was beginning to find enjoyment in the simple act of writing, in putting everything down in longhand. My cursive looped in arabesques, nearly diving off the edges of the pages. I practiced making each line perfect. Looking down at my yellow tablet notebook, I could squint until the words blurred into a single lead-colored tapestry. LIA's standard phrases—*We are affected by a sinful world system, our sinful flesh, and the manipulative attacks of Satan*—became an exercise in wrapping each of my sloping *f*'s beneath the letters preceding it in the word.

My mother sat on the couch and folded her hands in her lap, nodding her head to some inaudible and internal monologue. The kohl-like eyeliner circling her eyes had diminished to a thin band, and her hair was no longer in vibrant curls. The strands were slack, hanging limp on her shoulders. She'd stopped visiting the tanning salon during the long afternoons before she picked me up from the facility, but her skin was still darker than usual, as though she'd fallen asleep in a field somewhere and wandered back to civilization without ever bothering to check her reflection. She looked at least ten years older than when we'd first arrived in Memphis.

"Your dad asked how we're doing," she said. I could see now that she clutched a pink cell phone in one hand, that she must have been talking to my father in the other room. "I told him we're okay."

"Yeah."

"We have a few more days," she said, checking the cell phone for the time, the white screen lighting up in her palm. Though she hadn't said it, I knew how to complete the sentence: *for you to be cured.*

I tapped the mechanical pencil against the yellow tablet. I was halfway through the assignment, but nothing new was coming. I tried searching my memory for a longer sexual fantasy, one to fill up a whole page, but I'd already exhausted most of them, and what was left seemed almost too minor to note. The many times in high school when my eyes had followed the sloping curve of a boy's leg until the shadowy interior of his gym shorts swallowed up the mystery. The underwear ads I would walk by in the clothing section of Walmart, pretending to be only casually interested in the cut and fit of the boxer briefs, squeezing the material behind the posing model's abs as though I were testing the strength of the material. It was a problem I was glad to face—being relatively free of sin—but it was still a problem. I had confessed this to J just that morning, looking to his extra months at LIA for guidance, and J had admitted that he now made up most of his stories.

"I ran out the first week I was here," he'd said. We were alone on the patio, with no one around to hear us. "So I thought I'd try to imagine new ones." The rest of the patients were huddled near the kitchen, secure in the air-conditioning. I could already feel the sweat beading at the top of my forehead, the sun burning my hair.

"Really?" It was almost always one-syllable answers with J. I felt stupid standing next to his intelligence, his pain. There were things I wanted him to know about myself that I couldn't say. How, under different circumstances, I could be really smart. How I read good literature. How I was going to be a writer one day. But I never knew how to work them into the conversation without sounding awkward and egotistical.

"If I repent for sins I haven't even committed," J said,

tucking a long strand of hair behind his ear, "I figure God might even bump me up to Step Five." According to J, Step Five took an infinitely long time. And Step Five was still seven rungs below the finish. In the distance between his current step, Step Four—*making a searching and fearless moral inventory of ourselves*—and Step Five—*admitting to our Heavenly Father, to ourselves, and to another human being the exact nature of our wrongs*—stood the vastness of the abyss, stood hellfire. It was one thing to admit the approximate nature of our wrongs, but the *exact* nature? We could barely understand our own sinful urges. Even had I been fully committed to discovering a cure at this point, from where I was standing at Step One, explaining these urges to another person in great detail seemed nearly impossible. Even Smid never claimed to have made it through all the steps without stumbling every now and then.

"Most of us learn to forgive ourselves for backsliding," J said, brushing my shoulder as he turned to look back at our group, his touch a sudden jolt that left a metallic aftertaste under my tongue. "It's all part of the process. We acknowledge it, forget it, and move on to the next step."

I could already imagine the disgusted looks in the staff members' eyes as I said, "I experienced a fantasy," and as one of them said, "Without describing too many sinful details, could you explain the situation?" It would be even worse during my one-on-one therapy session with Cosby. I would be asked to describe the contours of my fantasy, the ways in which this fantasy had held me in Satan's vise grip, how it now disgusted me, Cosby's face twisting into a look of revulsion that I would need to mimic if I wanted to convince him of my progress.

I reread the sample MI in the handbook beside me, searching for inspiration.

I do not need sex or anything else to medicate with, even though I still desire to do so at times. I have a lot to say and I choose to share it appropriately. I have worth. I am intelligent, funny, caring and strong. I am masculine.

My mother and I kept silent for several minutes, my pencil poised over the page. "Masculine." The word looked so greedy, sitting there at the end of the line, summing up everything that had come before it. But wasn't that the end goal? Masculine meant strong. Masculine meant straight. If we could only learn the essence of what it meant to be masculine, then we could learn the rest. I ripped out the page of cursive, wadded it into a ball, and threw it in the trash can. Too feminine. The best I could do at this point was copy everything down, write it in sloppy print, make myself appear as masculine as possible on paper and in person. I began a new sheet. My sentences grew shorter, my verbs blunter. Before the counselors took away my notebook, I had been producing poor imitations of Faulkner;

now, I tried imitating Chekhov, Hemingway, Carver. I wrote about my fantasies with a coldness I hadn't even known was possible.

When I first met him, I had impure thoughts. He was attractive to me. He was a vision of masculinity that I craved because I had been denied it at a young age. I was angry with myself for liking him. I knew I was wrong. I knew I needed to ask God for help.

I didn't even know who this fantasy person was. It could have been any boy I'd ever had a crush on. It could have been J. I added a few more stock details to make sure no one in our group thought it was J: "He was much older. He drove a pickup truck. He smoked Marlboro cigarettes."

I'd been extra careful that morning, distancing myself from J to make sure no one noticed my growing attraction to him. Standing on the patio during break, just the two of us with the sun hot on our arms, I'd made sure to keep a generous patch of concrete between us. And when J said, "We aren't really supposed to be alone back here," I agreed with him, walked up to the door without hesitation and slid it back and put a pane of glass between us. Rule number two: WHEN IN DOUBT—DON'T.

I LOOKED UP, the afterimage of the handbook's words floating like red banner across the dark room, my mother's face half hidden in shadow. After a few seconds, I finally broke the silence. I wanted to let her in on the therapy lingo, test it out on her and see what her reaction might be.

"Was Dad ever an alcoholic?" I said.

We watched each other's reflections through the shadow world of the empty television set, where the distance between us was even greater.

"Why would you ask me that?" she said.

"It's for a project," I said. "Genograms. The sins of the fathers. I want to make sure I got everything right."

The moment slid once again into silence. I thought we might drift into that dark shadow world, never speak again.

"What about the sins of the mothers?" she finally asked.

We must have sat like that, staring at each other in the empty television for a long time. "That, too, I guess."

"Your dad had some experiences with alcohol, but your grandfather was the real alcoholic. Anyway, it was a long time ago."

I thought of my grandfather, my father's father, the drunk. On the rare occasions when I'd visited him, he'd barely recognized me, and even in moments when he had recognized me, he'd called me by my middle name—Clayton, Clay—as if the name I'd inherited from my maternal grandfather was part of an identity he didn't want to recognize. He was a small man with small arms and a small desiccated face—the face of someone who'd already traded all of his good smiles for that last drop of alcohol. It was hard to imagine how he'd ever had enough power to whip anyone, how he'd ever managed to inspire fear with those small muscles of his. Standing beside my father, my grandfather had seemed a tiny man, the opposite of masculine—and yet, somehow, my father had managed to take those raw materials and form his own version of the ideal Southern man. What was *I* missing, then? Where was the defect? The more I thought about these things, the more LIA's logic began to break down, and I wanted my mother to be there when it happened.

"I can't understand why you'd need to ask me this," my mother said. She was standing up now. The lamplight met her at a sharp angle, the freckles on her face and arms a painter's absentminded, expert flicking of wetted brush.

"Well," I said, drawing out my words. "They need to know where all of my sexual feelings come from."

"I don't understand any of this," she said. "Why do they need to know so much about our family? What does our family have to do with sexual feelings?"

"They say a lot of it's caused by childhood trauma."

"What step is this in?"

"I'm still on Step One."

"How long does each step take?"

"I have no idea. Months. Years."

"Years?"

"Some of the new counselors have been there for more than two years. The older ones have been there for a decade."

My mother was straightening her wrinkled blouse. She

looked to the mirror hanging on the opposite wall, teased up her hair. After a few seconds, she grabbed the car keys from the coffee table. I wondered if we were going to leave right then. I wondered if she might march into the office and demand an explanation.

Before the silence fell on us again, she said, "Let's go out tonight. Forget the rules. Get some real food."

LIA was very clear about its "safe zone" rules. There was a map on one of the facility's walls that listed the few areas in the city without any malls, restaurants, movie theaters, secular bookstores, or porn shops. Every part of the city was forbidden except for places with the word "Christ" in it, really. Our hotel was situated directly in the center of LIA's map, as far from sinful influences as possible. The idea of leaving, if only for a moment, was tempting. Something other than stale KFC biscuits, cold gravy, a pile of picked bones tucked away in a paper box. Something other than half-empty parking lots and homogenous strip malls. I closed the handbook, the plastic sleeve cracking along the spine. I pictured the crack of my grandfather's belt, my father in a corner with one forearm raised to protect his face.

"Did he ever fight back?" I said. "Dad? Did he ever try to leave home?"

My mother walked past me to the door. She slid the chain through its gutter and unbolted the deadlock: a hollow slicing sound. "There are some questions I don't ask."

· · ·

Outside, the air was even hotter and more humid than I remembered, but a slight breeze followed us to the car, daring us forward. After I had sat in the facility's antiseptic light for hours, the promise of an elegant dinner in a good restaurant was like the promise of manna in the desert. I half expected LIA staff members to flag us down as we exited the hotel parking lot, their arms waving wildly about our car, but the parking lot remained empty as we made our way to the interstate. My mother's face soon relaxed into a sweetness I had known when we used to go shopping in the city together. And as we traveled farther from the hotel, we managed to wrestle free of the present, to slip into an alternate future that only a few moments ago had seemed impossible.

It wasn't that she had given up on the therapy. In the hour that followed, my mother would ask me at least half a dozen times if I thought I was going to be cured. We just decided to ignore the details for the moment.

"Where are we going?" I said, watching the soot-stained lines of the interstate sound barrier skip past the window.

My mother switched on her blinker. "It's a surprise."

As we exited the interstate and turned the curve, the mirror façade of the Adam's Mark Hotel towered over us, a rare glinting diamond in the center of the city, and my mother said the same thing she always said as we passed it: "Your dad and I used to go there every New Year's Eve. It used to be so beautiful inside. Everything was so beautiful." But we weren't going there. We were going someplace else to make our own memories.

I OFTEN THOUGHT of the life my parents had shared before me, how inevitable it all seemed. My father the quarterback. My mother the cheerleader. Everyone in town cheering for their success. Champagne glasses held up each year on New Year's Eve, the only night they allowed themselves to drink alcohol: a toast to the next year, and the next, and the next, until, finally, it must have been my mother without a glass in hand standing before their friends on the top floor of the Adam's Mark Hotel, toasting to a new birth that would never arrive that first time. And then there was me, the boy in whom they placed their dreams. It was hard to imagine the degree of their love for me, the easy faith they must have placed in God at the moment of my uncomplicated birth. It was hard to imagine how disappointing it must have been for them to figure out I wasn't quite all that they had hoped for, a stain on their otherwise perfect union.

Just that morning, I had read Smid's testimony at the back of the handbook, one that had suggested we could all one day follow the path many of our parents had followed. In "Journey Out of Homosexuality," Smid wrote that he had met his second wife, Vileen, while doing yard work. "How romantic!" he wrote. I imagined her in a floppy sunhat, long sundress catching on her knees, thong sandals on her pedicured feet. She must have caught sight of Smid's dimples as he approached his next weed or stray branch with the simple smile of a child, the smile that had wooed so many men to the ex-gay lifestyle. A hiss and spray of automatic sprinklers pivoting rainbows. "She is aware that my attractions haven't changed in general toward men but that I love her deeply and make choices daily to remain faithful to our marriage and have not regretted that decision."

Like my father, Smid was excellent at conversion, at justifying whatever sudden mood overtook him. He had skipped over most of his former life in his testimony, never explicitly mentioning it in our sessions. It was hard to imagine that he had ever been married, the way he talked about how many men he'd been with. Until I read his testimony, I had no idea just how vast his journey had been. "I had developed an addictive habit of masturbation that carried into my marriage," Smid wrote. In the same way that my father had condemned everything before his calling as rubble, as fodder for God's greater purpose in his life, Smid had consigned every failed act in his first marriage to the sin of addiction. Rising out of this sin, Smid now believed a higher power had elected him to lead other gays out of their addiction into successful marriages. He believed he could do this because he knew a thing or two about the familial circumstances that had contributed to the formation of homosexual addiction. My father's story carried an obvious parallel: Working with criminals—"thugs," as he called them—had compelled him to begin the jail ministry in our small Arkansan town. Why did good men turn out to be thugs? Because they came from circumstances like his, families in which the alcoholic father had done something brutal.

But what had held their lives together before the conversion, before the A-to-Z logic of sin reduced human complexity to a syllogism? What form had their faith taken, however limited, in their long lives as preconverts? Christianity is, among other things, replete with converts. Peter renounces his atheism to become a fisher of men. Saul becomes Paul on the road to Damascus, wiped clean of a past in which the execution of good Christian believers was his life's work. But the Bible never shows us the beating heart of a preconvert. Crumple the first half of the story and toss it in the trash; all else is distraction.

And who was I before Love in Action? A nineteen-year-old whose second skin was his writing, whose third was his sense of humor, and whose fourth, fifth, and sixth were the various forms of sarcasm and flippancy he had managed to pilfer from his limited contact with English professors during freshman year at a small liberal arts college two hours away from home. Remove the skin, and I would be no safer from the threat of suicide than T. Remove the skin, and there was nothing but an ache to fit squarely into my father's lineage, into my family. According to LIA logic, the only option was to convert, smother one's former self in the branches of the family tree, and emerge, blinking, into a Damascene sunrise.

.   .   .

My mother and I stood in the lobby of the Peabody Hotel, where the big tourist draw was a flock of mallard ducks that lived in the lobby fountain. The ducks spent half of their days waddling in formation to the rooftop, and that must have been where they were now, the fountain empty save for hundreds of pennies flashing gold in the dim. My mother and I watched the water ripple over them until they became indistinguishable.

"Want to make a wish?" my mother said.

I imagined grabbing a handful of pennies and tossing these strangers' wishes over my head. "Not really," I said, noticing how, in the low lobby light, all of these pennies looked exactly the same. Most of us weren't going to get what we wanted.

The lobby was quiet, but this was a quiet my mother and I could handle: the murmuring of cheerful voices amid the low light of chandeliers, the plashing of the fountain, the echo of expensive shoes against polished marble. We added our own less expensive shoes to the echo as we made our way to a small candlelit Italian restaurant at the back of the lobby.

"This is nice," my mother said. She was rushing ahead, and I was trying to keep up.

The restaurant was mostly empty, with a few middle-aged couples sitting in booths along the walls. My mother and I chose a booth in the back, hoping to get a good view of the room and the people in it. The waiter handed us two menus, smiled, and disappeared behind the kitchen door before I could get a good look at him.

"What do you think their story is?" my mother said, darting her eyes to a couple directly across from us. Arms tangled in wineglass stems, candles lighting up the man's cuff links, plates half full: Food seemed to be the last thing on their minds. Every few seconds, the woman would tilt her head back and smile.

"Do you think they're having an affair?"

"I don't know." I glanced back at my mother. She now held herself upright and stately, the mirror image of the way she had looked in the newspaper clipping we kept on our refrigerator at home, the one where she'd been photographed in her sequined ball gown at the Peabody Hotel premiere of Sydney Pollack's *The Firm*, the whole evening a twenty-fifth anniversary present from my father. In the caption below the article, my mother had been mistakenly labeled an extra in the movie, a modifier that always managed to thrill her. The word seemed mysterious to me: someone standing on the outside, but also a little extraordinary. I'd often wondered if these people whose lives we constructed might be doing the same for us, if we might be the extras in their dramas. It was comforting to think that what we were going through might be a minor part of someone else's production.

"The woman's at least twenty years younger," my mother said.

"Twenty-five," I said.

"Thirty."

We opened our menus, and my mother propped hers on the edge of the table and leaned in to shield part of our conversation from view. "Want to hear my big idea?"

"What?"

"We're going to make a lot of money with this one."

"What is it?" It was fun, once again, to add a flare for the dramatic to our conversation, to tint the scene with a few choice words, to feel like a character in a movie. After listening to the naked liturgy of our therapy group's various suicide attempts, HIV prognoses, and tailor-made Bible hermeneutics, I was ready for something fun.

"Well?" I said. She was stretching it out. My gaze wandered over the bar. Men in suits, a few of them with leather briefcases resting near polished shoes. I thought of *The Firm*. Some of the cotton used in Tom Cruise's escape scenes was from our family's cotton gin, and even though we hadn't seen our names listed in the credits, we'd still felt important, involved, watching Cruise land in a soft white bed of our making. I felt a familiar wave of family pride wash over me.

"My brilliant idea," she said, draping the words between us for a few dramatic beats: "*Preachers' Wives Gone Wild*."

"Like *Girls Gone Wild*?" I pictured dozens of middle-aged women slipping blouses over their heads, perms tangled in fabric, their pale breasts shaking for the camera.

"Wouldn't it be great?" she said. "Your dad would completely lose it."

"That's crazy."

"I don't see why I can't make a little money out of God's work."

This was my mother, the woman who was supposed to support my father in everything he did. What was she thinking? "But that's blasphemy."

"Is it? Sometimes I can't tell the difference between blasphemy and fun."

"Oh my God."

"I guess you can be a little blasphemous, too."

The waiter came to take our order, and we picked the first items we saw, not even bothering to listen to the evening specials, happy with anything they might bring us. For a moment, my mother's eyes lost their playfulness as she examined my face for the amount of interest I paid to our handsome waiter. I tried not to look at him, even as I felt his warm smile beside me. I knew she would be watching for signs.

After the waiter left, we both leaned in closer to the middle of the table.

"Your dad and I have been married too long for him to think I'll just turn into one of those old preachers' wives," she said. "The kind that wears ugly denim skirts and smiles at everyone and bats her eyelashes at all the other ladies." Lit by imitation Old World lighting, my mother was beautiful again. Her blond hair took on a gold sheen, and the red veins threading her blue eyes receded behind a warmer exterior glow.

I hadn't seen her this passionate in a long time. She looked more like herself, and I was beginning to feel more like myself. I wanted to hold on to this moment: the secular glamour, the gleam in our eyes. LIA was telling me on a daily basis that a loss of self meant a gain in virtue, and a gain in virtue meant I was drawing closer to God and therefore closer to my true heavenly self. But the means to that end—self-loathing, suicidal ideation, years of false starts—could make you feel lonelier, and less like yourself, than you'd ever felt in your life. In the process of purification, you risked erasing every minor detail you'd ever cared about. You became all telling with no showing: not the extraordinary extra, but the stock player in a harp-and-halo bit. I came to therapy thinking that my sexuality didn't matter, but it turned out that every part of my personality was intimately connected. Cutting one piece damaged the rest. I had prayed for purification, but the minute I felt its icy baptismal waters burning away everything I'd ever loved, I'd begun to open myself up, instead, to a former possibility: unconditional love, the original flame that had drawn me closer to God and my family and the rest of the world. I counted, and I didn't count; I was part of a much larger mystery—and my mother had given me all of this the minute I was born.

"Oh, look!" my mother said. She slapped the table with one hand and pointed to the lobby with the other.

Someone dimmed the restaurant lights, and the Peabody

mallards began their waddle from the hotel lobby to the roof, leaving behind puddles of chlorinated fountain water in their wake. Their quacking reverberated along the marble hallway through the quiet restaurant to our booth.

"They've been doing that ever since I was a little girl," she said, her voice thick with the past.

Those ducks, part of a family line with origins somewhere in the forests of Arkansas. Someone had converted them. Somewhere over the years, those ducks had forgotten the feel of unchlorinated water.

SELF-PORTRAIT

I t's almost like having a death in the family," Barbara Johnson writes in her book *Where Does a Mother Go to Resign?* "But, when someone dies, you can bury that person and move on with your life. With homosexuality, the pain seems neverending."

My mother and I had both started reading Johnson's book just after Thanksgiving break, around the time when we'd also started reading *The Picture of Dorian Gray* together, and we hadn't finished either book. It was March now, only two months before I would attend LIA, and it seemed as though nothing in our lives would ever be complete again until we knew for sure if ex-gay therapy would truly change me. We were putting the world on hold, leaving things half-finished, until the summer.

Johnson's book was being passed around ex-gay circles, mainly to fundamentalist Christian families who had just discovered that they had a gay child, and it was touted as a healing story. Johnson had heroically met her son's affliction head-on, refused to back down until he admitted it was a sin. No mother should ever have to go through this, her book suggested. No mother should have to feel the pain she'd felt.

"I couldn't get very far," my mother admitted over the phone. I walked to the couch in the corner of the empty dorm lounge and sat, stared up at the flaking white wall. I was talking on the dorm's landline, the yellow phone tucked between my knees. As usual, I was ignoring homework. What was the use in studying if I couldn't even imagine how my life would turn out? It was possible I wouldn't even have a career if I couldn't change who I was. My parents certainly wouldn't pay for my education and, for all I knew, employers didn't hire gay people.

"Yeah," I said. "Me neither."

There was a long pause. A static-filled breeze passed through the line. As often happened, I imagined the virtual space between us as a desert landscape, a single black wire curling in a long S through the glittering sand. It was a mental tick of mine, one of dozens I resorted to in moments when I wanted a situation to seem less frightening. Sometimes, in order to calm my mind at night, I would imagine my mattress falling rapidly down an endless elevator shaft, protected even as I fell.

"We have to answer a few more questions," my mother finally said. Since I was supposed to submit my supplemental essays electronically, she had decided to complete the primary LIA application for me rather than mail it to me. I had stopped going home as often in the past few months, claiming that I had way too much homework, though the real reason had to do with the fact that, with LIA approaching, there was very little our family could talk about that didn't feel awkward. The whole process would be quicker if my mother helped me fill out the forms. She'd received some extra questions in the mail, so we were now on the last leg of the application. The process seemed endless; we were now required to attach a recent photo of me to the application, along with an eighty-dollar fee.

I tucked the yellow receiver into my neck. My mother inhaled sharply. "It's asking if you've ever had any physical involvement with other people."

"No," I said quickly. There was Brad, of course, the boy on all the sports teams who I'd fooled around with in junior high, but I wasn't about to utter the words "mutual masturbation" to my mother, and the therapist I'd spoken to over Thanksgiving and Christmas breaks had hardly ever taken notes during my sessions, so I thought there was a good chance LIA wouldn't know about Brad. I thought of Chloe. We'd barely kissed, and even when we had, there'd been too much awkwardness to sustain contact for very long. I remembered the overly sweet taste of her mouth, the Doublemint sugar pocketed away in the folds of her tongue, the shudder of fear that passed through my chest each time my tongue met the band of her braces. Why wasn't it considered a sin to treat a nice girl like her so horribly?

I was glad my mother hadn't asked about *wanting* to have physical involvement with other people. I'd recently attended an art exhibition for a senior art student named Caleb, a tall, broody type in paint-splattered jeans that sculpted his ass so perfectly I couldn't help but pay attention. I'd watched him circle the gallery, illegal glass of champagne in my hand, thinking of the things I wanted to do with him. I'd stepped close to one of his paintings and imagined the brush moving with his deft fingers, those fingers wiping excess paint off with a palette knife and smearing it into ripped jeans, those jeans lying in a pile next to his bed as he slipped into paint-stained sheets. When he circled around to me, I'd said something stupid about all the lush colors he'd used.

"Thanks," he said, smiling. "You need another glass of champagne."

"I'm fine." We were standing in front of a painting entitled *Oedipal Jesus*. Like all of his paintings, this one was a dramatic self-portrait, with Caleb as a crucified Jesus and Mary as a Tori Amos look-alike who held a knife up to Jesus's already bleeding side. I had no idea what any of his paintings were really about, but they all felt highly blasphemous, as if just looking at them might set you on fire.

"I have a private bottle of champagne in my room," Caleb said. "We can go get it if you want."

I hadn't answered him, had simply walked over to his next painting and pretended to be overly interested, but I'd thought about what he'd really meant by the offer.

"About how often do you or did you engage in sexual sin with another person?" my mother said.

When I didn't answer immediately, she added, "It has these little boxes I'm supposed to tick. Daily, weekly, monthly, less often. If less often, please explain."

"Less often," I said. I tried to find a pattern in the flaking dorm wall, but all I could see were random flakes with no meaning. "As in never."

"Okay," my mother said, the tension in her voice leaving for a moment.

Why couldn't they at least paint the walls? It seemed like a huge oversight, leaving the walls so ugly. It made you think ugly thoughts, and those ugly thoughts would inevitably seep into whatever you might do in this lounge.

"It says, 'I have been involved in the following activities,'" she continued, "and then it has more of these little boxes. Do you want me to read them all?"

"Go ahead." The receiver felt hot against my ear. I held it away from me as she recited the list, but I could hear the words, tinny as they were, words I had never heard my mother say before and have never heard her say since: "Pornography, compulsive masturbation, voyeurism, mutual masturbation, heterosexual sex, homosexual sex"—each syllable declaring itself in that small room, so that after a few words I began to cup the speaker with my palm, afraid Charles or Dominique, both currently in my dorm room, might hear—"exhibitionism, sadomasochism, bestiality, prostitution, pedophilia, mannish or boyish attire, drag or cross-dressing, telephone sex, anonymous sex, or other."

So there it was, proof that I was just as bad as David, that I might as well molest a child or start having sex with animals. To hear my mother say these words all together and all at once, to hear the fear and expectation in her voice as she said them, her anticipation of some horrible revelation—it was too much. And though some part of us must have known that this list was bullshit, that there was something terribly wrong with grouping all of these acts under one common denominator, we couldn't battle against it. We didn't know the first thing about untangling this mess of sin.

APRIL PASSED, I'd had a quiet nineteenth birthday party at a Mexican restaurant with Charles and Dominique and a few other friends, and now it was May, the school year was ending, and we had less than a month to go before I was scheduled to attend Love in Action.

"Why did Dorian treat Sibyl that way?" my mother said one night over the phone, her voice distant. "I don't understand."

I held the yellow phone in one hand and stood at the dorm lounge window, watching for Caleb's light, the cord draped across the room. My copy of *The Picture of Dorian Gray* lay on the couch behind me. My mother and I had already given up trying to read the rest of Barbara Johnson's *Where Does a Mother Go to Resign?* The preliminary application had been filed, I had been accepted, and all that was left were a few more surveys. My mother and I did everything we could to avoid talking about it.

"Dorian cared only about her art," I said. "She wasn't interesting to him as a person."

"But she was so nice."

"Yeah, I guess so. I can see how she might have been a little boring though."

"That doesn't matter. Being a good person is all that matters."

For the moment, it seemed like the two of us could go on this way forever, living only for literature and each other. For a moment, it seemed like being a good person was all it took. But love was always moving, always pushing us forward—always in action—and we often had no choice but to submit to where it lead us.

I SPENT several weeks as far away from Caleb as possible, taking the long way around the quad to and from classes, though I occasionally passed him in the hallways, and every time this happened, he would send a flirty wink my way. Then, one night in early May, for reasons I can't remember, something drew me to his dorm. It could have been the crushing loneliness I often felt during that period of my life. It could have been the accumulation of all those late nights walking aimlessly up and down Walmart aisles simply because the store was the only place open twenty-four hours and nobody in there asked too many questions. Feeling too restless to return to my dorm and sleep, I had tried collecting my thoughts out of the hundreds of products shining around me, tried to make sense out of what my life had become. Whatever finally sent me to him, the fact remained: I was now standing in Caleb's room, looking at God.

"This is just a sketch," Caleb said. "I plan on doing a whole series."

God was a string of red and pink dots on white canvas. Caleb planned to glue six large canvases together to form a God cube.

"The all-seeing Eye of Providence," I said.

"What?"

"Every step that you take this great Eye is awake," I said, reciting the lines to a church hymn I used to sing in our family church. "Every day mind the course you pursue."

"That's some creepy shit." Caleb headed toward a cot in the corner of the room. He picked up a small marbled glass pipe and scattered some ashes on the floor. *Drugs*, I realized, a thrill shooting down my spine. This was just what my Sunday school teachers warned me about. But as Caleb placed the pipe on a nearby table, the whole thing felt so much smaller than I'd imagined: a little pipe laid gingerly on a pile of wrinkled papers, set aside for what must be the greater sin I would soon be tempted to commit on the cot. Caleb patted a space beside him on the mattress, and I joined him. I reminded myself that all sins were equal in the eyes of God.

"They really fucked you up, didn't they?" Caleb said. He could see I was shaking. My skin was going to split open. *So here it is*, I thought. Here was the skin I so wanted to shed, vibrating with anticipation. One swift movement from Caleb, and the surface might break, reveal a version of me that had lain dormant beneath my church self so many years. Nothing could have prepared me for this. Not Chloe, not David, not any of the books I'd read.

"Did they tell you this is wrong?" Caleb said, leaning in. I couldn't respond. How could I even begin to explain just how wrong my friends and family back home thought this truly was. His eyes were close now, a flickering blue. The small dorm room contracted to the space between us, and I was watching him through a narrow tunnel, and outside also, watching us lean closer to each other. God was watching, too, and for once I didn't care.

CALEB AND I kissed that night, but we didn't make out. We didn't travel any farther than the surface of our lips. Instead, we lay on his cot in the darkness of his room and listened to hours of Björk's "Pagan Poetry" on repeat, our fingers interlocked. The quad lights filtered through his metal blinds, igniting our cheeks, our lips, and then an orange sunrise worked its way through, sliding up the wall opposite the cot, tracing a series of ladders that led nowhere more interesting than where we lay. We had already climbed as far as we wanted to go. By the morning, I knew every inch of that room, every wadded sheet of drawing paper, every stray piece of charcoal, every wavering brushstroke on the canvas of God. The whole room seemed to have waited for me to join it, to see it for what it truly was: a work of art.

"I've never paid that much attention," Caleb said, after I'd closed my eyes and recited a list of the objects in the room from memory. "You should be a poet."

"I don't want to be a poet," I said. I wanted to be a short-story writer. I wanted stories that sprawled, took on lives of their own. Still, I had chosen to enroll in the only creative writing class of the semester, a poetry workshop. The weekly assignments had proved difficult, usually with me sitting in front of my computer monitor for hours, staring at the blank screen until a rush of frustration produced the thirteen lines my professor required.

"Seriously," Caleb said. He turned on his side to face me. At some point in the night he had kicked off his paint-splattered jeans, and the white sheet fell from his hip to reveal a smooth patch of skin, the tight V of his pelvis leading to a darkness untouched by the morning sun. I was going to be late for class if I didn't turn away.

"You've got a poetic mind," he said. It felt like his words were entering me, taking up residence on little hooks I hadn't known were hidden somewhere in my head. My skull was throbbing with the weight of them. It seemed no one had ever said anything so kind, so true. We were inventing a language for each other, and it was better than any I'd ever tried to use in my Moleskine stories. For a brief moment, I remembered the frustration I'd experienced so many times in my dorm room, moments when words had failed to capture the essence of an idea. I wondered if Caleb had felt the same, mixing his oils night after night, adding circle after circle to his portrait of God. You reached after a perfection that couldn't exist beyond the moment, and when you failed at it—as you inevitably would—you moved on to the next piece of art, the next phase.

"I'm actually not very good with words," I said, tossing the sheets back. I really had to get to class, and I was still in my pajamas from the night before. "I get frustrated. I can't capture what I want to capture."

"Just keep doing it," Caleb said, standing. "You've got to be insane. Never take no for an answer." He walked to the corner of the room, lifted the marbled glass pipe from his desk, and began to pick at something that lay scattered at his fingertips. The orange light filtered through the blinds and played on his thighs, igniting blond hairs. He lifted his left heel and his calf contracted, a sharp wedge. How could I capture a fraction of what I felt in this moment? I could never be a poet.

I watched him pick at what I assumed were pieces of dried marijuana. I had no idea how drugs worked, and the whole business terrified me. I looked away. Something else was bothering me. I crossed my legs and leaned forward with my elbows on my thighs. "Don't you think it's sort of hypocritical?" I said. "Trying to paint God at the same time you seduce freshmen boys?"

"What do you mean?" He began to pack something into the pipe with the wooden end of a stray paintbrush.

There was a long silence. I was trying to get at something I couldn't really explain. Wasn't Caleb trying to do the same thing as my father, reaching after a God he couldn't ever fully know? Yet his process seemed entirely different. For Caleb, it was inspiration, not sacrifice, that conjured his God. It didn't seem fair that someone with such a vastly different way of seeing the world could even refer to the angry God I knew. What about all of the sacrifices my father and I had made just to seem pure in God's eyes? What about the many nights I'd spent curled up in bed with the sharp scissors tucked into my fist, trying to bargain with God? Yet here was Caleb doing whatever he wanted with God, painting pair after pair of God's eyes just so he could declare them good and move on to the next project. No, it didn't seem fair to consider Caleb's God equal to our own. For the first time in months, I felt the need to defend my father's God.

"Don't you think you'd have to be perfect in God's eyes in order to paint God?" I said. "I mean, what about being gay?"

Caleb struck his lighter, the bowl igniting in a quick puff, smoke curling up into a slice of the sun. "What have they taught you? That God wants us all to just sit around and praise Him all day? Fuck God, if that's the case. I'd rather be in Hell with all the interesting people."

"How do you know you're not just making Him in your own image?"

"I don't." He inhaled deeply, held it. A long pause, and then he released the smoke with a low groan. The smell was sharp and pungent; it was like some dark part of the forest I'd explored so many hours behind my house, some musk at the center of its heart. "But I know being gay has nothing to do with it."

What Caleb stood for was dangerous, just as dangerous as what Dr. Julie had told me, just as dangerous as the smoke that now filled the room and curled around me. My head was already dizzy from a lack of sleep, and now the smoke seemed to be entering the crevices of my brain, curling up beside Caleb's words. I needed to guard myself against all of this. I still believed, like my father, that Hell was real. I still believed that I would feel its fire licking my skin for all eternity if I continued on this path. I thought of the Masonic orphans who had once lived on this campus, of the fire that overtook them when they'd least expected it. If it had come for them, then it could surely come for me. I grew terrified of the pot smoke, of the Hell it signified, and within that delirious second I considered trying to convert Caleb. I could still turn my mistake into an opportunity for ministering. It wasn't too late for me. My mother wouldn't have to tick off any more boxes.

"Are you sure you've really searched your heart for the answer?" I said. "What if you're wrong?"

"Oh God," Caleb said. "The good ones are always crazy."

"I'm just asking."

"My heart isn't separate from the rest of me." He took another hit. "This is just me. All of me. See?" I was admiring all of him then, the way all of him, with his back bent over the table, formed a question mark against the orange sun. "Why would God give me so many feelings if he didn't want me to feel them? Why would God be such a jerk?"

"I have to go," I said, standing up. Caleb's words were buzzing in my ears. I wanted so badly to believe him, but I was afraid of what would happen if I did.

"So? Be late."

Despite my daring from the previous night, I was still a straitlaced student. I hated the idea of being late for class, of the professor asking my classmates where I was. My poetry course consisted of only ten students, and my absence would certainly be felt during workshop that day.

"Stay," Caleb said. "They won't teach you anything. You can write a poem right here."

I thought I might never leave if I didn't leave the room right then. The smoke was reaching its crooked fingers down my throat, hooking me.

"What?" Caleb said, releasing another puff of smoke, shaking his head at the sight of me squirming in my skin.

I wasn't the one to convert him. I was already lost.

WEDNESDAY, JUNE 16, 2004

There are no photographs from this day. There are no photographs from any of these days. A year of my life is missing, undocumented. My mother and I joke that this was the year we were abducted by aliens. This was the year of the body snatchers. But the truth: Even as all of this was happening, we knew we would never want to look back.

It would be easier with a photo. With a photo, I might read between the gaps in my memory, see in this boy's ex-gay smile an indication of the pain he was feeling. As it stands, there are only before and after photos: a chubby kid in a tight Tommy Hilfiger polo and husky jeans, followed by an emaciated Underground Man in a *Legend of Zelda* T-shirt. I don't even know if I'd recognize the boy between the two photos.

.   .   .

SMID'S INSTRUCTIONS on my eighth morning at Love in
Action, on how to recapture repressed memories: "If you're at a
loss, begin with a small piece of your life. Try connecting this
piece of your life to your father's life. Find the moment when
everything changed for the two of you. Sometimes a second is
all it takes."

Our group was sitting in our usual semicircle in the main
room. There was the smell of burned coffee and pencil shav-
ings, the nervous tapping of erasers against the pages of our
handbooks. There was the ticking of some distant clock I'd
never noticed before.

"I want you to focus," Smid said. "Think back to an important moment."

I sat opposite J, who wouldn't look at me. This was a tactic
it seemed we'd both adopted without consulting each other: to
keep a distance between us at least half the day every day during our time at LIA. The counselors were growing more and
more suspicious of me. When I had arrived that morning, Cosby
had drawn me into his office to ask if I needed to tell him anything. He'd motioned to a chair beside his desk, but I'd stayed
standing, shaking my head, trying to be as casual as possible.

"No," I said. "Being here is a process. Some days are better
than others."

"Are you still praying?" His crow's-feet winked from the
corners of his eyes.

"All the time," I lied. The truth was, I hadn't tried praying for two days, not since my mother and I visited the Peabody, when I had felt, for a moment, what it might be like to live another life. "I wish we could stay here tonight," I'd said, watching the dim candlelight play on my mother's self-tanned face, the odd auburn color converted to gold in this large elegant room: an alchemist's trick of light. I'd wanted to stay there and never leave. "Me, too," my mother had said.

"Good," Cosby said, walking me back to his office door, his hand briefly touching the space between my shoulder blades. "You're going to have to be more vigilant than ever. God's letting me see something in you right now. Something rebellious. I'm not sure you can even see it."

My gaze fell to the carpet, to Cosby's gleaming black loafers, laces bound in tight Xs. It was the first time I'd noticed his small feet. This detail—his smallness—lent me a temporary strength.

"I'm working harder than ever," I said. It wasn't a lie.

SMID WAS standing in front of me. He was clasping his hands tightly together. "Close your eyes if you have to," he said. "The devil wants to keep those memories repressed. The devil wants you to get confused. But we're not going to let Satan win here today."

I kept my eyes open, watching Smid watch the other patients. He was wearing his white wrinkle-free button-down, one button unfastened, a little patch of thin white T-shirt underneath, and beneath that, the pale peach of his chest. There were these cracks in the foundation everywhere you looked if you knew how to look for them.

S slid to her knees beside me, her hands gripping the edges of the padded seat. Her long hair kept her face hidden from view. I wondered if she was remembering the moment she'd told us about, the day her parents had found her with the dog. But, of course, this moment couldn't explain everything about her sexually deviant nature. One of LIA's many assumptions was that we were all here because of some kind of abuse, some kind of neglect. "The influence is clear," our handbooks said. We were all here because sinful cycles of abuse continued in our families. "Logically, you'd think someone who'd suffered because of such sins would never follow the same course, yet we find just the opposite, strains of addictions running through many generations of a family."

I tried remembering the moment when everything changed between my parents and me.

"Would anyone like to share?" Smid continued. "Has anyone here come to a realization today?"

DURING MY EARLY TEENS when I worked for my father at the cotton gin, I used to walk to the edge of our property, to the place where we kept rows of dusty white modules, those large rectangular stacks of cotton the farmers gathered from the field with large combines, and I would hide from the world. I would find a long module in the middle of the field, one at least ten feet tall, and I would gut the packed cotton from its sides, dig my fingers into the dirt and grime and the sharp pieces of boll until I hollowed out a space for myself in the middle. As I climbed inside, the cotton still warm from the fields, the smell of pesticide and dank earth flooding my nostrils and the bitter taste of the country on my tongue, I would think of my father's warning that the cotton could collapse at any second, that it could smother me without warning—and I would feel strangely safe. Here I was, curled up in the middle of this packed cotton, and the walls still hadn't collapsed. Hidden away from everyone, in a place where no one could find me, and the cotton hadn't swallowed me whole. The cotton soft on my back, I would close my eyes and drift into sleep and occasionally awaken to watch the fading blue patch of sky until it got to be too dark and I knew my parents would start to worry.

My father was predictably angry when he found out about the hollowed-out modules. "You'll kill yourself doing that," he'd said. But what he was really thinking, what he must have been thinking, was *why*. Why would I want to hide? Why would I want to risk my life for something that didn't seem worth risking?

His response was to explain the whole process of cotton manufacturing in careful, plain language.

"One day this will be yours," he'd said. "One day you will inherit this."

He led me through the ginning process step by step, quizzing me to see if I'd remembered what he said. I never did, never cared enough about cotton manufacturing to remember, but I would pretend to search my memory for the answers just to make him feel better. I was more interested in the way things looked than how they functioned, in the way the cotton pressed against the metal teeth, cottonseeds falling in a white waterfall to a receptacle that collected them for further use. The fuzzy streams that fell so beautifully and softly in the midst of all that din. As we walked through the steps, my father would shout over the sound of the machines, guiding me with his rough hand on my shoulder through the various stations, asking his employees to add some nuanced detail to the explanation. I would nod my head and pretend to listen, watching the dust and fuzz fly through the shafts of light around us, sniffing the air for the odd, intoxicating scent of a mechanized field.

The final product, the end of the ginning process, was a pure white bale of cotton wrapped in a burlap covering and held together by several metal bands. I thought it was a beautiful thing. I ran my hands along the surface of the warm, tightly packed cotton and closed my eyes, blocking out everything else around me—the loud machines, the scurrying employees, even my father. When I lay in bed at night, I imagined my pillow and sheets were from our very own gin, a sensation I would carry with me to every bed I've ever slept in, one that never fails to comfort me when I suffer from a bout of insomnia.

This is what my father gave me: a deeper appreciation for my isolation, an understanding of the work and sacrifice others often make for my own personal comfort. The process of accommodation takes time. I never expected my father to accept every shifting detail of my life overnight, nor I his. Our moments of misunderstanding, though often damaging, were still far from abusive. This was something LIA could never understand.

"Do you have anything you want to say?" Smid said, looking down at me.

I looked away.

THAT AFTERNOON, our group was asked to sit in two rings of semicircles in LIA's auditorium. Sunlight filtered through the white slatted blinds, each of us cloaked in a separate silence. J sat beside me. I allowed myself this one afternoon of sitting next to him. I could feel his gaze at the edge of my own.

"This week has been tough," Smid said, carrying a metal folding chair to the center of the auditorium stage. "Emotions are high. But it's important that we push ourselves as far as we can. We need to get to the bottom of our addiction."

The rest of the morning session had been difficult, with T admitting, once again, to suicidal ideations he'd had the night before. As T stood before our group and confessed, we all repeated, "We love you, T." But my heart hadn't been in it. I did feel sorry for T, and I would have told him so if I'd had the chance. But I didn't love him. How could I love someone who acted so broken all the time, who demanded my sympathy with each scar, each confession, who I didn't really know? It seemed pathetic, and a little selfish, to mark oneself out for love. To think that God and the people around you would suddenly recognize your worth if you were seen as damaged and admitted it. This was LIA's currency, the trading of literal and proverbial scars, and I hated it. Everyone was trying to one-up everyone else, to render the most painful account. After all, Jesus was most identifiable by his scars, and we were being asked to take up His cross and follow Him. Some deeper cynicism was threatening to take control of my thoughts.

Smid flipped open the folding chair with a quick flourish, the hinges creaking like a startled crow. "You're going to face your fears today. You have the chance to show how courageous you really are."

J pressed his leg against mine. "*This* is new," he whispered. I slid my eyes down his chest to his legs, presently hidden from Smid's view by the chair in front of him, watching the way he pressed them together and pulled them apart. I thought of Bathsheba, King David's temptress, bathing at the edge of the palace. David a perched voyeur on his roof. Over the past few days, I'd begun to see something beautiful in J. Here was someone who could understand me. Unlike Chloe or Caleb or any of the counselors, J didn't demand anything of me other than what I was: that same confused, swirling mess I'd glued to the surface of my mask. One minute I wanted to walk out of the facility and put an end to my ex-gay therapy, and the next I wanted J to pull me under, hold me down here with him, force me to read the clobber passages again and again until I finally understood them. His beauty made me think there might still be some truth to the ex-gay experiment.

Smid placed another folding chair opposite the first one. He dusted his hands, turned to us, and smiled until his Jeff Goldblum dimples showed.

"Who wants to go first?" he said.

The semicircle tensed, our collective breathing quieting. We didn't yet know what this activity was all about, but we knew it had something to do with the childhood abuse we'd explored in the morning session. Lie Chair, our schedules called it. I imagined a syringe filled with truth serum, or maybe a polygraph test, wires glued to my chest. I felt a spasm run through J's thigh as it swung back and pressed against mine. I pushed his leg away, too hard, and he nearly slid off his seat, the legs of the chair moving audibly against the tile.

"J," Smid said, turning to face the sound. "You seem eager."

"Yes, sir," J said, pushing past me to the front of the auditorium. I moved my legs to one side, his thigh grazing my knee. He shot me a dark look as he passed.

"I want you to sit here," Smid said, motioning to the chair. "I want you to sit here and imagine your father sitting across from you. I want you to sit here and imagine your father sitting across from you and you saying everything you've always wanted to tell him but couldn't."

J did his best with a smile, settling into the chair and crossing his arms over his chest. He cleared his throat and stared into the spot where his father was supposed to be sitting. I

looked behind me to see if the others were buying it. S was biting her nails, and T was sitting beside her with his hands in the
pockets of his black cardigan. The blond-haired greeter stood
in the back of the auditorium with his hands crossed before the
front of his navy slacks, his face at polite attention. He caught
me looking at him and shot me a pay-close-attention-or-else
look. I turned back. Cosby was nowhere to be seen, and I was
happy for it, the room a little more relaxed without his military
stare.

"Confession must come before healing can take place," Smid
said, quoting from the handbook. That it had to be a public confession was assumed, everything at LIA operating on a bare-all-
and-be-saved basis. The Lie Chair was simple, Smid explained:
Pretend to see a father you don't and confess everything negative
you have ever felt toward him in front of a full room. "Don't
worry about how it sounds. Just try to be honest."

I watched a spell overtake J. The long sweep of his hair fell
across his forehead, and he kept pushing it back, as though the
act would deliver his real, breathing father before him. He
leaned forward, elbows on knees, palms cupping his chin: a
sloucher, the posture of a much younger boy. I could imagine
him sitting like this on his living-room sofa reading a fantasy
novel.

"Do you want to say something to him?" Smid said.

J pushed back his bangs again and sat up. He seemed to
glimpse the promise of the next step, his eyes growing soft and
wet. This could be his moment. Smid stood beside him with his

eyes focused on the Lie Chair. In an instant, they both seemed to glimpse the same nightmarish tyrant.

"Dad," J began, "I've memorized each of the eight clobber passages. I've worked hard to be a good Christian man. I've accounted for my past sins, tortured myself to accomplish each of these steps."

Smid circled the two chairs, nodding in either direction, as if he were addressing both father and son. The most important thing here was to believe the fiction, to make the father a receptacle of pain and fear rather than the living, breathing, walking complexity he'd always been when you were around him.

"The person I want most of all to kiss," J continued. The room grew quiet. I was barely breathing. The auditorium seemed to grow hotter with each of his words. I didn't dare look at him. "The warm gut feeling I get when I am close to this other person. The constant questioning that comes from a personal reading of scripture. I understand it now. All of this is temptation sent from the Devil, meant to confuse me, meant to snare me in addiction."

"Amen!" T yelled. "Preach it!"

I could hear S shifting in the chair behind me. The blond-haired greeter walked to the right side of the stage, his eyes fixed on the invisible drama.

"Gambling, alcoholism, cohabitation, abuse. These were all gifts from you, Dad. But not any longer. I don't accept your gifts. I throw your gifts at my feet and stomp them."

As J finished, he collapsed into a sobbing heap on the floor.

Smid ran to him and placed one hand on his back, the other in the air, praying for God to heal this young man. After a few seconds, he led J back to the chair beside me. I still wouldn't look at him. I was afraid of what would happen if I looked at him. Here was someone willing to break in front of me while I was using everything in my power just to stay whole. In the next moment, Smid motioned for me to come to the stage.

"I think it's time you showed us what's going on inside," he said, leading me to the metal seat, his hand on my elbow. The seat was still warm from J's heat. I tried to keep from looking at J, who was now kneeling at the foot of his chair, shaking. There was no way to know if he was experiencing something real or simply faking it—and even now, after the fuses have blown and the antiseptic light has faded, I can no more be certain of his conversion than I can of any ex-gay's.

"Do you see your father?" Smid said, standing behind me. Dust clouded the light in the air in front of me, rivulets twisting in the place where my father was supposed to be sitting. I tried fusing the rivulets into his slacks, his navy business suit, his salt-and-pepper hair combed at the part. I tried working myself up into an angry fit.

"Take your time," Smid said.

The silence was unbearable. I sat there for several minutes, waiting for someone to end it. I thought of the numbers game my father and I used to play: Each of us would guess a number from one to one hundred, and then we would say the number aloud at the same time. I thought of how we were usually only ever a digit or two away from each other, a feat that felt like a miracle. I wanted to tell the group that there were things I'd never understand about my father. There were things that could never be translated into words. But I loved him.

When no one ended the silence, I stood up from my seat. "I'm not angry," I said. "I don't understand why I have to be angry."

The blond-haired boy walked up to the stage. His face was red, and his hands were clenched into fists. "You've been hiding what you really feel all week long," he said. "You're angry, but you're not showing it. You're keeping all of it hidden away, but we can see it."

"I'm not angry," I said. I was on display, standing before a jury of my peers. The sun was hot on my back. "It's more complicated than that."

"It's not complicated," the blond-haired boy said. His face was getting redder. "You're making it complicated. What you feel is anger because your father hasn't accepted you. You need to come to terms with that. You need to scream at him, tell him how you really feel."

"I'm not going to scream," I said. I was trying hard not to show how nervous I was.

"You're shaking," the boy said. "That's how angry you are. It's obvious."

I wasn't going to cry. I wasn't going to let them make me cry. I kept my eyes on the doorway of the auditorium, never looking back at J.

"You should let it out," Smid said. His voice was close behind me. I felt sobs coming, but I held them down, swallowed them. I blinked a few times. The room blurred.

"I'm not even sure you want to change," the boy continued. "I'm not even sure you've been telling us the truth *at all*."

"You're crazy," I said. "You're all completely crazy."

I took one step forward then found I had enough strength to take a second one.

"I thought it was more *complicated* than that," the boy said.

If I kept focusing on each step, I thought I might have the strength to reach the door.

"You have to want to make it past Step One," Smid said. "That's the only way."

I didn't look behind me. I didn't look back at the others. I kept my eyes on the red exit sign.

"If you walk out," Smid said, "you won't ever be cured."

Each step gave me more and more strength until somehow I was sprinting through the hallway, until somehow I was standing before the reception desk. "I need my phone back," I said.

"Can't do that," the receptionist said, smiling. "You know the rules."

"It's an emergency," I said.

"What kind of emergency?"

"It doesn't matter."

The auditorium doors were still closed behind me. No one was coming after me yet. The receptionist dug my phone out from a pile of phones and handed it to me. He was no longer smiling.

I dialed my mother's number. She answered on the first ring.

"Mom," I said, "I need your help."

MY MOTHER and I were quiet for most of the ride home. We still hadn't called my father to tell him what had happened, afraid of what he might say. We didn't know how to start explaining things because we hadn't yet explained them to each other. But as the Ozarks folded around us once again, I began to feel the familiar straightjacket cinch across my chest and along my back. I knew I had to do something or we would continue to live the same way we'd always lived: a life full of secrets, full of unsaid words.

"I never want to go back there," I said.

"They said you needed a few more months," my mother said. "Maybe even a year."

I had heard their conversation from the passenger seat, as Cosby leaned in through the cracked car window to warn her of my erratic behavior. "I'm not even sure he *wants* help," he'd said. "He needs at least three more months. He probably needs a break from college."

My mother steered us into the slow lane. I watched the grassy shoulder glide by us, brown from heat and drought.

"Did you know that man's only college degree is in marriage

counseling?" my mother said. "Why is a marriage counselor telling my son how to be straight?"

The grassy shoulder opened up to reveal a bald patch of dry red clay. The red was glaring, a bleeding wound. "Screw it," I said.

"What did you just say?" my mother said.

I grappled for the plastic airbag cover in front of me, digging my fingernails into the cracks, tugging. I wanted the bag to inflate, to knock me back as far as it could. I pictured the cover as my father's chest: his heart billowing out, exploding, deflating. I wanted T's pain, S's shame, J's anger. I wanted the obliteration of every nerve connected to my skin.

My mother pulled onto the highway shoulder, kicking up a trail of dust behind us. Cars flew by, honking, overcorrecting their trajectories, swerving across the thick double yellow lines.

"What's going on?"

I dug my fingers deeper into the cracks. I was blinking tears, but I wasn't going to cry. Outside the window, the red clay was mocking me. The mountains wanted to hurl themselves on the roof of our car. After several minutes of trying, I finally gave up. I sat back in the seat and closed my eyes.

My mother was quiet beside me, her breathing shallow. "Oh my God," she said. "Are you going to kill yourself?"

The question was simple enough, but what came out of my mouth was a sharp animal cry. I tucked my knees into my chest and pressed my side against the passenger door, my cheek hard against the glass.

"Oh my God," she repeated. "We're stopping all of this now."

She took this as a yes, the only evidence she needed to convince herself to end my therapy sessions with Love in Action. She heard yes, but I had already been given a gift that no one could ever take from me. I was alive, and I now had the benefit of knowing it. I was alive, and this was all I needed.

WHEN I THINK about everything that has happened to me, I sometimes wonder if any of it was real. I sometimes wonder if the facility might have managed to turn me crazy in the end, that perhaps I have spiraled off into some abandoned corridor like my great aunt Ellen, talking only to myself. If it weren't for the handbook and the many ex-gay counselors I've contacted since leaving, I might still be second-guessing my sanity about what really happened during those few weeks. And if my father could have had it his way, none of us would have ever spoken about my ex-gay experience again. Though he didn't ask any questions the day I came home from LIA, though our conversations since have been filled with awkward silences, it seems he has quietly accepted the fact that ex-gay therapy was never going to change me. In the years following my enrollment in LIA, he continued to fund my college education, never asking too many questions about what I was learning in my English concentration. "A writer," he said once, after I'd told him what I wanted to be. "Wouldn't that be interesting?"

On some days, it's hard to believe that I ever lived in a world that operated on such extreme notions of self-annihilation. But then I turn on the news, read a few articles, and realize that what I have experienced may have been unique, but in no way was it disconnected from history. Minorities continue to be abused and manipulated by both nefarious and well-intentioned groups of people, and harmful ideas continue to develop new political strains all over the world. What I can't quite understand—and what I may never be capable of understanding—is how we all came to be mixed up in the ex-gay movement, what drew each of us to Love in Action's double doors. There are no pictures to help me search for clues, so I develop them myself.

I picture Smid walking away from his first wife, leaving everything behind. I picture J, forging a new identity in the face of an angry father. I picture my mother, her former life disappearing as she stands beside her new preacher husband on the stage, perhaps remembering the child she once lost in the hospital, perhaps thinking about me.

Again and again, I picture the Lie Chair. I see my father and the chair. I see him as a child, watching his father tie his mother to the dining-room chair and beat her. I see how he must have cowered, crouching, from his own father. Then, decades later, there he is, sitting in a padded hospital chair beside my grandfather's bed after alcoholism has taken everything from this man's body, the only one of his siblings to visit the dying old man.

Always I circle back to my father. I picture him clutching the invalid hand. I picture him crying silently, waiting to say good-bye. There is a mystery in this, a minor apocalypse somewhere between what these two men once knew of themselves—a holding on to something that, in turn, refused to let them go—and I long to know it, like the old prophets.

EPILOGUE

Smid's voice emerges from the darkness, enclosing me in its soft, lilting syllables. I'm lying in my bed in a tiny apartment in Auburn, Alabama, two years into a master's degree in creative writing, winding down from a night of researching Restoration drama by listening to a podcast of *This American Life*, Ira Glass's voice a haven of liberal thinking in a deeply conservative state, when suddenly—as if some cold hand has reached out of the past to clench my throat—Smid's voice draws me back to Love in Action.

"John, you don't have to live like this anymore," the voice says. It's a recording from one of Smid's many appearances on an evangelical television show. In the interview, Smid quotes God, whose voice once told him that he needed to become straight, that this would only be possible if Smid followed God's orders.

I grope in the darkness beside my bed for the lamp and switch it on. The light burns my eyes. This can't be happening. This private shame made public. I feel strangely protective of the information, as if no one but me has the right to hear this kind of talk. The tone of the *This American Life* interview is winking, with knowing phrases that betray a liberal audience accustomed to joking about "one of those Christian places that claims they can cure homosexuality." It's the tone of so many of my professors, people so far removed from the conservative Christian perspective that they can't help but sound flippant, many of their lives padded by families who've supported them since they were toddlers.

I stand up beside the bed, dots swimming in my eyes, orange and yellow streaks swirling across the mostly bare white walls. Nails mark the places where I've just removed photos of me and my last boyfriend: a reminder of the many casualties suffered in a long string of withering intimacies, advances made and accepted but rebuffed once things got too serious. No one is going to get close enough to hurt me.

But now here it is: This voice I've tried hard to forget reaching through the barriers I've erected to declare a truth that arrives a decade too late to make better what at one point in my life felt as though it could never be made better. "The transformation for the vast majority of homosexuals will not include a change of sexual orientation." As if this is all it takes—Smid's admitting to the obvious lie he'd sold me and my family—to repair the damages inflicted on all of us. As if this could make up for the near decade of confusion and self-doubt that followed the collapse of my faith.

This is the first of many public apologies. Over the next few years, ex-gay counselors will continue to admit their wrongs, pose for magazine photos, readily accept opportunities for interviews. Exodus International, the umbrella company Love in Action worked under, will disband, and in its wake only a few ex-gay facilities will continue their operations, none of them ever as big or prevalent as Love in Action, though a few dogged evangelicals will export ex-gay thinking to places like Uganda. The popular story arc will be one of redemption: the tyrant turned reformer. These ex-gay counselors will even write books. Smid will write a memoir, *Ex'd Out*; publish it at a vanity press; and pitch it in many of his interviews. In his biography at the back of the book, he'll include words that, though partially true by the time he writes them, will cause my entire body to shake from anger.

> Whether he is dealing one-on-one with an individual, a family, or speaking in churches or seminars worldwide, John's message of openness and honesty resonates with everyone who longs to be accepted, loved, and understood.

It will take years before I find the strength to finish the pages of my own story, before I can even approach my memories. I will return to my parents' house from time to time, acting like a stranger. In these moments, my mother will drag me down to the hell my parents had been living in all those years since I left them to insecurity and doubt and the fear that they've committed an unforgivable act from which they can never recover.

"You two have to deal with this directly," my mother will say, pointing first to my father then to me. "I refuse to be in the middle anymore."

But I will refuse her request. I will refuse to even look at my father, the man with whom, post-LIA, I've primarily communicated through brief e-mails and one-sentence answers. I will rush out of the room, enter my old bedroom, and slam the door. I will fall against the soft mattress and stare up at the popcorn ceiling and run my hands over the high thread count, bury my face in the coolness of a freshly laundered bed, my parents still talking in hushed voices on the other side of the door, this call and response of blame that must have settled so gradually into their years of talking that they no longer find it as shocking as it is to me. In order to escape the sound, I will stand up and begin rifling through my closet for the Great Books collection I'd bought in my overzealous classics phase.

Touching the gold-fringed pages, it will just begin to dawn on me how close I came to losing my passion, to losing my life. In the years since LIA, I've had to spend so much time catching up with other people, learning how to believe in a world that no longer teems with angels and demons. Every time I've read a book or ingested a new historical fact that my Baptist upbringing taught me to reject, I've had to fight against the sneaking suspicion that I am being lead astray by Satan. In the message boards and hidden ex–ex-gay Facebook groups I will join, I'll see others talking about their own attempted suicides, and I'll glimpse in these confessions elements so remarkably similar to my own that they will seem, for a moment, to issue directly from my mind. I will see people talk about losing their families, about the yearly trials they've faced as winter holidays approached and the loneliness threatened to overwhelm them once again.

"Sometimes I just want to die," one member of the ex–ex-gay group will tell me, "when I think about how difficult it is just to get through a day, trying to act normal."

"I've forgotten how to be myself," another man will write. "How did I even act before ex-gay therapy? When I try to remember, I keep thinking maybe I'm wrong. They did that to me. They made me question my sanity."

"I don't even talk to my family anymore," one woman will write. "They still think I need more therapy. I think they'd rather see me dead."

The chorus of voices will grow each year, revealing decades of pain, decades lost, families torn apart, relationships ruined because people outside the ex-gay world can never understand what we patients went through. On Beyond Ex-Gay, a website dedicated to surveying ex-gay survivors, users will describe in painstaking detail the lasting effects of reparative therapy.

It elevated sexuality from being part of my life to being the central fact of my life; everything revolved around it and my fear of it and being discovered.

Multiple suicide attempts, two psychiatric hospitalizations. Diagnosed severe type-2 bipolar disorder and moderate PTSD by multiple doctors in two different states. Ex-gay therapist told me the symptoms from these illnesses were caused by my "sexual confusion."

Eleven years later, I still sometimes get nauseous when touching another man. It is difficult (possibly impossible?) to maintain a long-term sexual relationship.

I really lost touch with myself all those years, because I was so busy trying to be someone else. I am now confused about nearly everything—God, faith, where I belong, where I should go from here. I have lost friends. I often feel hopeless. I am trying to get my life back on track.

I will open the LIA handbook, read a few sentences, and feel the old shame wash over me until I can no longer focus. Once again, Smid's voice will swallow my own before I have a chance to say anything. I'll face doubt, distrust my memories, spend hours trying to reconstruct scenes so charged with emotion they'll seem impossible to pin down. I'll call my mother to ask for details, sit with her at a table and record her words, and nearly every time one of us will end up in tears. My mother will apologize again and again. I will try to comfort her, but I'll fail, because all of it truly was as horrible as we remember it, and because it will never really go away, we will never be completely okay. Our family will never be what it otherwise might have been.

And God. I will not call on God at any point during this decade-long struggle. Not because I want to keep God out of my life, but because His voice is no longer there. What happened to me has made it impossible to speak with God, to believe in a version of Him that isn't charged with self-loathing. My ex-gay therapists took Him away from me, and no matter how many different churches I attend, I will feel the same dead weight in my chest. I will feel the pang of a deep love now absent from my life. I will continue to experiment with different denominations, different religions. I will continue to search. And even if I no longer believe in Hell, I will continue to struggle with the fear of it. Perhaps one day I will hear His voice again. Perhaps not. It's a sadness I deal with on a daily basis.

One day, when we think most of the pain is over, my mother will phone to inform me that a deacon from our old church refused to invite my father to preach at a revival service because a man stood up in protest during the middle of a church meeting, claiming that my father's "openly homosexual" son signified a spiritual lapse in my father's ministry. My parents will tell me that if I write this book, my father will risk losing his job as a pastor. The sins of the father. Every step in my success will become a reminder of ex-gay ideology. Every step in my success will become an immediate threat to my father's.

Years later, I will call my father one afternoon to let him know that this book is the book I have to write, that I might not be okay if I don't finally write it, that I won't know who I am until I finish it.

"I just want you to be happy," my father will say, his voice tight with everything he refuses. "I really do."

And I will believe him.

ACKNOWLEDGMENTS

I started out wanting to write only fiction, and if it hadn't been for the encouragement of many fellow writers at the University of North Carolina–Wilmington's MFA program, this memoir would not have been possible. A huge thank-you to Ana Alvarez and the entire UNCW Publishing Lab staff, and to all the great writers and teachers who helped me workshop the first two chapters of this book, especially Philip Gerard and Nina de Gramont.

There are so many other fantastic teachers and mentors who have guided me to this point: Chantel Acevedo (my mentor and dear friend), Martha Beck, Karen Bender, Clyde Edgerton, Patricia Foster, Cristina García, Debra Gwartney, Barry Lopez (who first told me to "keep going"), Helen Robbins, Terrell Tebbetts (my first mentor), Judy Troy, Virginia Wray, and many more people whose names I hope will fill up many future books.

The story of this book's inception is as good as any nonfiction piece, only perhaps slightly less believable than most. Thanks to my friend Kathy Flann, I was invited to a dinner where critic and writer Maud Newton (mentor extraordinaire) was a guest. At some point, after a long, uncomfortable silence at my end of the table, Maud turned to me and asked what I was writing. "I write on fundamentalism, too," she said, after I'd given her a very convoluted explanation of "ex-gay" therapy. "Would you like to go to a party? My agent says I can bring one other person." What followed was a slightly drunken night (open bar) in which I ended up pitching my nonfiction (it wasn't even a book yet) to William Boggess at The Book Group. A giant thank-you goes to William Boggess and Julie Barer at The Book Group, who helped me see this story through to publication, and to my brilliant editor, Laura Perciasepe, at Riverhead, whose edits were spot-on and whose enthusiasm has sustained me. Thank you to Megan Lynch, who first took a chance on the book; to the entire Riverhead team; and to Karen Mayer for legal edits that make me feel lucky to have a lawyer on my side.

I want to personally thank Elizabeth Kostova and the Elizabeth Kostova Foundation for supporting my writing at a time when I was unsure of my potential. Thank you to all of the friends who have supported me and provided important feedback during the writing of this book: Hannah Dela Cruz Abrams, Trey Bagwell, John Becker, Emma Bolden, Ashley Campbell (my first reader and closest confidant in all things craft and all things life), Garth Greenwell, Kerry Headley, Amber Hood, Katie Jones, Gabe Moseley, Ben Thielemier, Rusty Thornsburg, Eric Tran, and many more.

Thank you to Ivaylo Vezenkov, for making me coffee in the early writing hours and supporting me during one of the most difficult moments of my life, being there for me when I had to dig deep into memories I wanted to forget. Thank you to Laurel Zmolek-Smith for brainstorming ideas with me during our long runs after work, and for always sticking up for me. Thank you to all of my students at the American College of Sofia, and to friends and family who have continued to support me. Thank you especially to my aunt, Mary Waddell, for supporting me through a difficult time.

Thank you, most of all, to my mother and father, whose love has made all the difference.